D0932334

VISUAL

ENCYCLOPEDIA OF

space

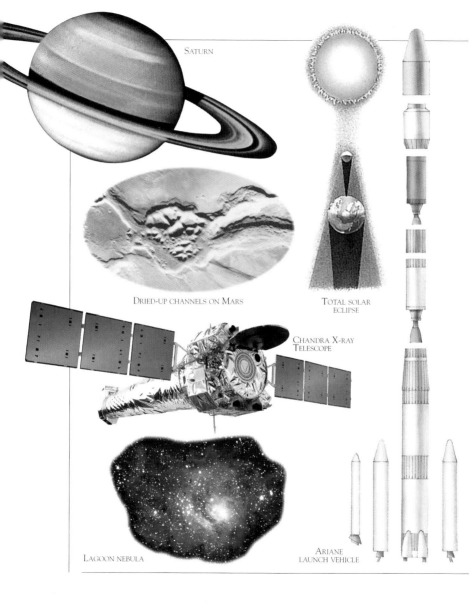

SATURN

DRIED-UP CHANNELS ON MARS

TOTAL SOLAR
ECLIPSE

CHANDRA X-RAY
TELESCOPE

LAGOON NEBULA

ARIANE
LAUNCH VEHICLE

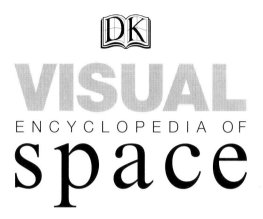

VISUAL
ENCYCLOPEDIA OF
space

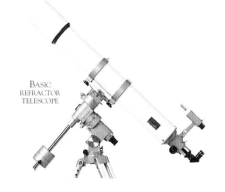

BASIC
REFRACTOR
TELESCOPE

CONSULTANTS
DAVID HUGHES AND
ROBIN KERROD

LONDON, NEW YORK, MELBOURNE, MUNICH & DELHI

DK London
Editor Niki Foreman
Senior Designer Spencer Holbrook
Project Art Editor Philip Letsu
Managing Editor Linda Esposito
Managing Art Editor Diane Thistlethwaite
DTP Designer Siu Chan
Production Controller Luca Bazzoli
Picture Researcher Myriam Megharbi
With thanks to the original teams
DK Delhi
Senior Editor Dipali Singh
Project Editor Aekta Jerath
Editor Larissa Sayers
Designers Romi Chakraborty, Arunesh Talapatra
DTP Designer Balwant Singh
Manager Aparna Sharma

Consultants Professor David W Hughes
and Robin Kerrod
First published in Great Britain
in 2006 by Dorling Kindersley Limited,
80 Strand, London WC2R 0RL

A Penguin Company 2 4 6 8 10 9 7 5 3 1
Copyright © 2006 Dorling Kindersley Limited

Material in this edition has appeared previously in the
following books:
Space Encyclopedia
© 1999 Dorling Kindersley Limited
Visual Encyclopedia of Science
© 1998 Dorling Kindersley Limited
DK Handbook: Stars and Planets
© 1998 Dorling Kindersley Limited
Nature Activities: Stargazer
© 2005 Dorling Kindersley Limited

A CIP catalogue record for this book is
available from the British Library.
ISBN 1-4053-1169-X
Reproduced by Colourscan, Singapore
Printed and bound in Singapore by Star Standard

Discover more at
www.dk.com

CONTENTS

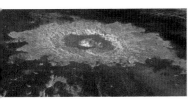

COMETS AND ASTEROIDS 110

STARS 128

HOW TO USE THIS BOOK

These pages show you how to use the *Visual Encyclopedia of Space*. The book is divided into ten sections dealing with every aspect of space, from how the Universe was formed to space travel. A reference section follows, with a comprehensive constellation guide, a timeline, and biographies.

HEADING AND INTRODUCTION
Every spread has a subject heading. This is followed by the introduction, which outlines the subject and gives a clear idea of what each page is about.

At a Glance box

Caption

PLANETS AT A GLANCE
These boxes give information on the individual characteristics of each planet, making it easy to compare features.

Heading

JUPITER
THE FIFTH PLANET FROM the Sun is very different from the terrestrial (Earth-like) planets. Jupiter, the largest planet in the Solar System, is a gas giant. It is all gas and liquid except for a very small rocky core. Its mass is 2.5 times that of all the other planets combined, and 1,300 Earths would fit into its volume.

Introduction

Annotation

Vital Statistics box

CAPTIONS
Each illustration in the book is accompanied by a detailed, explanatory caption that expands on the points in the introduction.

VITAL STATISTICS BOXES
Many spreads have vital statistics boxes, which give important measurements about the feature.

BIOGRAPHIES

The biographies in the reference section of the book provide further information about famous astronomers and scientists.

CONSTELLATIONS

An extensive constellation section includes star maps and sky guides to assist in stargazing.

Detailed maps showing constellations, stars, and other night-sky features

Stunning double-page image

ANDROMEDA

AQUARIUS

FULL-SPREAD IMAGES

Each section is interspersed with full-spread images, showing fantastic aspects of space and the technology we use to explore it.

Picture illustrates features of interest

WHAT IS A STAR?

A STAR is an enormous spinning ball of hot and luminous gas. Most stars contain two main gases – hydrogen and helium. These gases are held together by gravity, and at the core they are very densely packed. Within the core, immense amounts of energy are produced.

ANNOTATION

Pictures often have extra information around them, which picks out features. This text appears in italics and uses leader lines to point to details.

Fact box

DATA BOXES

On some spreads, data boxes give facts, figures, and general data about key topics featured on the page.

FACT BOXES

Many pages have fact boxes. The information in these is related to the main topic on the page.

Data box

INDEX

There is an index at the back of the book that alphabetically lists every subject. By referring to the index, information on particular topics can be found quickly.

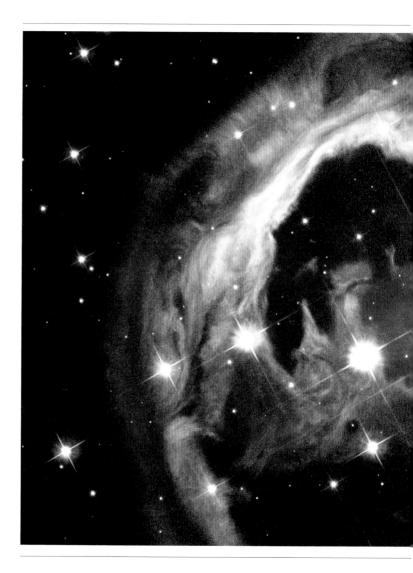

UNIVERSE

WHAT IS THE UNIVERSE?

THE UNIVERSE IS EVERYTHING that exists. From planet Earth beneath our feet to the farthest stars, everything is a part of the Universe. The Universe is so large that it contains countless billions of stars. However, most of it consists of nothing but empty space.

Galaxies

Galaxy containing billions of stars

Quasar – the brilliant centre of a distant galaxy

Supernova – the death of a large star

Comet – a dirty snowball

LOOKING TO THE SKIES

From Earth, we can look into space and study the Universe. In every direction we look, there are stars. There are more stars in the Universe than any other type of object – stars in enormous groups called galaxies, and stars at different stages of their lives, including at least one star that has planets. Despite the huge size of the Universe, we know of only one place where life exists – planet Earth.

UNIVERSE FACTS

• There are at least 100,000 million galaxies in the Universe; large ones contain more than 100,000 million stars.

• The most distant galaxies we can detect are 123,000 million million million km (76,000 million million million miles) away.

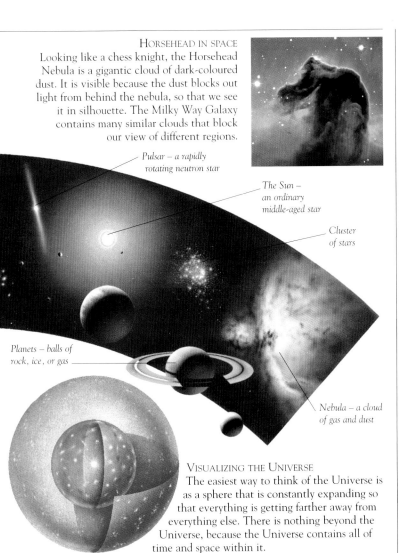

HORSEHEAD IN SPACE
Looking like a chess knight, the Horsehead Nebula is a gigantic cloud of dark-coloured dust. It is visible because the dust blocks out light from behind the nebula, so that we see it in silhouette. The Milky Way Galaxy contains many similar clouds that block our view of different regions.

Pulsar – a rapidly rotating neutron star

The Sun – an ordinary middle-aged star

Cluster of stars

Planets – balls of rock, ice, or gas

Nebula – a cloud of gas and dust

VISUALIZING THE UNIVERSE
The easiest way to think of the Universe is as a sphere that is constantly expanding so that everything is getting farther away from everything else. There is nothing beyond the Universe, because the Universe contains all of time and space within it.

SCALE OF THE UNIVERSE

DISTANCES IN THE UNIVERSE are so great that light is used as a unit of measurement. Light travels at about 300,000 km per second (186,000 mps), and a light year (ly) is the distance light travels in one year. A galaxy can measure thousands of light years across and be millions of light years distant.

GALAXY NGC 4603

STUDYING DISTANT STARS
The Hubble Space Telescope is used to study and photograph the stars in distant galaxies, which can be seen if the galaxies are closer than 100 light years. Studies such as these are essential in determining the age, size, and fate of the Universe.

SCALE OF SIZES
The human world, the world of everyday experience, is dwarfed by the scale of the Universe. Earth is one of nine planets orbiting the Sun, which is one of about 500,000 million stars in the Milky Way Galaxy.

The Sun is one of over 10 million stars in the Milky Way Galaxy

Earth is the third of nine planets orbiting the Sun

More than 6,500 million people live on Earth

The human scale is the familiar one of everyday objects

14

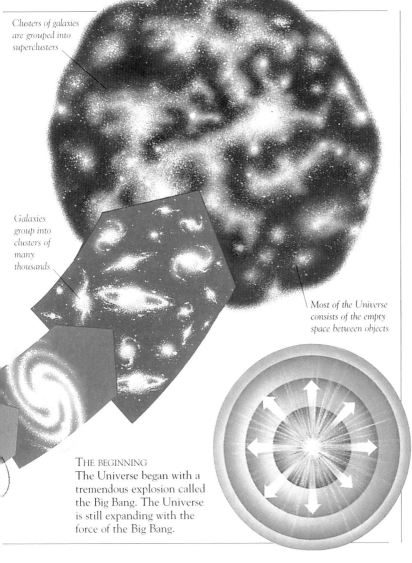

Clusters of galaxies are grouped into superclusters

Galaxies group into clusters of many thousands

Most of the Universe consists of the empty space between objects

THE BEGINNING
The Universe began with a tremendous explosion called the Big Bang. The Universe is still expanding with the force of the Big Bang.

DISTANCES IN THE UNIVERSE

WITHIN THE MILKY WAY, astronomers use radar to measure the distance to planets, and parallax to measure the distances of nearby stars. Beyond the Milky Way, the distance to nearby galaxies can be found by comparing their stars to similar stars in the Milky Way, and then using the distances to these galaxies to find how far away other galaxies lie.

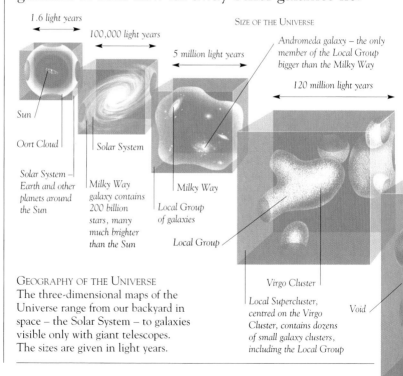

1.6 light years

SIZE OF THE UNIVERSE

100,000 light years

5 million light years

Andromeda galaxy – the only member of the Local Group bigger than the Milky Way

120 million light years

Sun

Oort Cloud

Solar System

Solar System – Earth and other planets around the Sun

Milky Way galaxy contains 200 billion stars, many much brighter than the Sun

Milky Way

Local Group of galaxies

Local Group

Virgo Cluster

GEOGRAPHY OF THE UNIVERSE
The three-dimensional maps of the Universe range from our backyard in space – the Solar System – to galaxies visible only with giant telescopes. The sizes are given in light years.

Local Supercluster, centred on the Virgo Cluster, contains dozens of small galaxy clusters, including the Local Group

Void

CEPHEID STANDARD CANDLES

Cepheid variables are a type of star that appears to brighten and dim with great regularity. This cycle, or variation in luminosity, is longer if the star is more luminous. If two stars generate the same amount of light but one is dimmer, it must lie further away. Astronomers use Cepheid variables to measure distance. They find the luminosity (the energy emitted in unit time) of a Cepheid from the length of its cycle, and then compare this with its apparent brightness to measure the distance to the galaxy in which it lies – once the luminosity is known, the Cepheid can be used as a standard candle.

Nearby Universe contains superclusters of galaxies, which are strung together in vast filaments that can stretch across hundreds of millions of light years. They are separated by huge voids containing very few galaxies

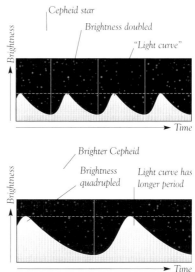

Cepheid star

Brightness doubled

"Light curve"

Brightness

Time

Brighter Cepheid

Brightness quadrupled

Light curve has longer period

Brightness

Time

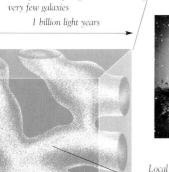

1 billion light years

Local Supercluster

Galaxy filament

DISTANCES FROM SUPERNOVAS

Supernovas are exploding stars so brilliant that astronomers can spot them in galaxies billions of light years away. Astronomers identify different kinds of supernova from the way their light brightens, then fades. Type 1a supernovas always reach the same maximum luminosity, so they form ideal standard candles – though they appear only once or twice a century in an average galaxy.

EXPANDING UNIVERSE

In every direction, distant clusters of galaxies are rushing away from us – the farther a cluster lies, the quicker it is speeding away. Clusters are moving away from each other just as raisins in a cake move apart when it is baked. This expansion is very useful to astronomers – once they have measured the rate of expansion for nearby galaxies, they can use a galaxy's speed to find its distance.

EXPANSION OF SPACE
Although the Universe is expanding, it is not expanding *into* anything. Instead, space itself is stretching, and carrying clusters of galaxies with it.

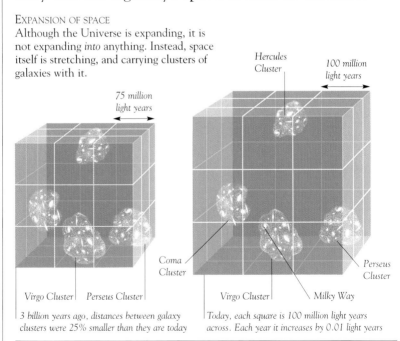

Hercules Cluster

100 million light years

75 million light years

Coma Cluster

Virgo Cluster

Perseus Cluster

Virgo Cluster

Milky Way

Perseus Cluster

3 billion years ago, distances between galaxy clusters were 25% smaller than they are today

Today, each square is 100 million light years across. Each year it increases by 0.01 light years

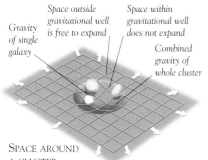

Gravity of single galaxy

Space outside gravitational well is free to expand

Space within gravitational well does not expand

Combined gravity of whole cluster

SPACE AROUND A CLUSTER

In a two-dimensional view of space, massive objects can be thought of as making dents, called gravitational wells.

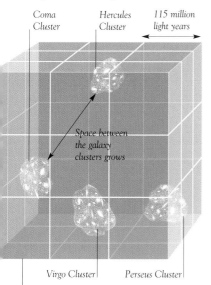

Coma Cluster

Hercules Cluster

115 million light years

Space between the galaxy clusters grows

Virgo Cluster

Perseus Cluster

2 billion years in the future, galaxy clusters will be 15% farther apart than they are today

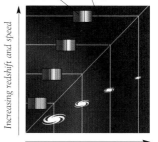

Dark lines formed by elements in galaxy absorbing light

Hubble's law states that a galaxy's speed depends on its distance

Increasing redshift and speed

Increasing distance

REDSHIFTING GALAXIES

If a galaxy is moving away, the dark lines in its spectrum are shifted towards the red (an effect called redshift). The more the lines are redshifted, the higher the galaxy's speed.

2dF spectrometer on the Anglo-Australian telescope can take spectra of up to 400 distant galaxies at one time

MEASURING REDSHIFTS

Huge telescopes have been built to collect light from distant galaxies, which can be used to reveal their redshifts and their distances. Sensitive electronic spectrometers, which measure the redshifts of many galaxies simultaneously, have also been developed.

Distant galaxies
Faint galaxies at the dawn of the Universe, imaged by NASA's Hubble Space Telescope

LIFE STORY OF THE UNIVERSE

All matter, energy, space, and time were created in
the Big Bang around 14 billion years ago. At first
the Universe was minute and blisteringly hot, but
as it expanded and cooled, atomic particles joined
to form hydrogen and helium. Over billions of
years these gases have produced galaxies, stars,
planets, and us.

*The Big Bang creates
the Universe*

*The Universe
keeps expanding*

WHAT HAPPENS NEXT?
The Universe has been expanding since
the Big Bang, and will probably go on
expanding forever. Recent observations
indicate that the expansion is speeding
up as the Universe gets older and bigger.

*The Universe will slowly
cool as it gets ever larger
and less dense*

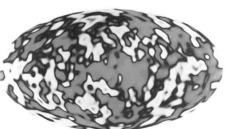

BIG BANG RIPPLES
This map of the whole sky is
based on tiny variations in the
temperature of space. Red is
warmer than average and blue
is colder. These tiny variations
are faint traces of the Big Bang
explosion. The information for
the map was obtained by the
Cosmic Background Explorer
Satellite (COBE).

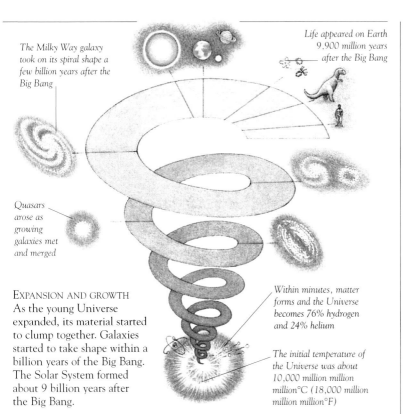

The Milky Way galaxy took on its spiral shape a few billion years after the Big Bang

Life appeared on Earth 9,900 million years after the Big Bang

Quasars arose as growing galaxies met and merged

EXPANSION AND GROWTH
As the young Universe expanded, its material started to clump together. Galaxies started to take shape within a billion years of the Big Bang. The Solar System formed about 9 billion years after the Big Bang.

Within minutes, matter forms and the Universe becomes 76% hydrogen and 24% helium

The initial temperature of the Universe was about 10,000 million million million°C (18,000 million million million°F)

UNIVERSE: COOLING DATA	
Time after Big Bang	**Temperature**
10^{-6} secs	10^{13}°C (1.8×10^{13}°F)
3 minutes	10^{8}°C (1.8×10^{9}°F)
300,000 years	10,000°C (18,000°F)
1 million years	3,000°C (5,400°F)
1,000 million years	−170°C (−275°F
14,000 million years	−270°C (−454°F)

UNIVERSE FACTS
• Scientists can trace the life story of the Universe back to what is called the Planck time, 10^{-43} seconds after the Big Bang.
• 10^{-43} means a decimal point followed by 42 zeros and then a one.

BIG BANG

THE BIG BANG occurred some 14 billion years ago. It was the beginning of everything – time, space, and the building blocks of all matter. At first, the Universe was hot and dense. Then it began to expand and cool, and it is still expanding and cooling today.

EXPANSION REVERSED
If the expanding motion of the galaxies we see today is reversed, it leads back to an instant around 14 billion years ago when they all occupied a single point. This was the origin of the Big Bang.

Earliest possible date for Big Bang: 15 billion years ago

Most likely date for Big Bang: 14 billion years ago

Latest possible date for Big Bang: 11 billion years ago

Young, densely packed galaxies

Fuelled by the strong force, the Universe suddenly inflates

Just after creation, the Universe is infinitely hot and expands slowly

Increasing time

The Universe today

Big Bang

FUNDAMENTAL FORCES

Four forces control the Universe. Electromagnetism rules electricity and magnetism; the weak force governs how the stars shine; the strong force glues together the nuclei in atoms; and gravity keeps the planets and stars in orbit. The forces were once united in a single superforce, but as the Universe expanded and cooled, they split off, one by one.

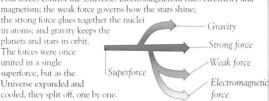

Superforce

Gravity

Strong force

Weak force

Electromagnetic force

Matter and antimatter particles have the same mass, and are equal and opposite to each other

The force of inflation works like antigravity, driving everything apart

The temperature drops rapidly to absolute zero, then rises again

INFLATION

Conditions in the early Universe turned energy into equal amounts of matter and antimatter – just 1 kg (2 lb) of material. Moments later, the Universe blew up, growing a hundred trillion quintillion quintillion times in a fraction of a second (cosmic inflation). This released huge amounts of energy, creating more matter and shaping the fundamental forces.

VIRTUAL PARTICLES

Energy from the Big Bang created virtual particle pairs – one of matter and one of antimatter – that almost immediately annihilated each other.

SCALE OF INFLATION

In a fraction of a second, the Universe grew from smaller than an atom to bigger than a galaxy.

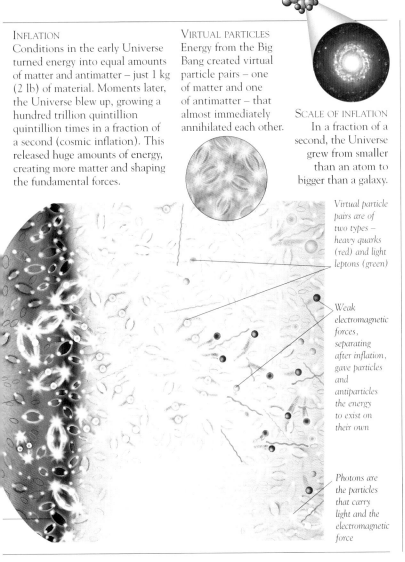

Virtual particle pairs are of two types – heavy quarks (red) and light leptons (green)

Weak electromagnetic forces, separating after inflation, gave particles and antiparticles the energy to exist on their own

Photons are the particles that carry light and the electromagnetic force

FIRST THREE MINUTES

THE HOT EARLY UNIVERSE contained subatomic particles of matter and antimatter. Most of these particles wiped each other out, but matter finally triumphed. As the Universe expanded and cooled, construction began. By the end of its third minute, the building blocks of all matter had been created – the nuclei of the first three elements: hydrogen, helium, and lithium.

DARK MATTER
Invisible, dark matter far exceeds visible matter, and probably consists of numerous WIMPs and neutrinos.

Particles and antiparticles destroy each other

Exotic particles include X bosons, Higgs bosons, and WIMPS

Quarks (red) and leptons (green) are released during inflation

Forces are carried between particles by W and Z bosons, gluons, photons, and gravitons

MATURING UNIVERSE
The early Universe had shortlived particles like quarks, leptons, and WIMPS, zooming about at temperatures of 10,000 trillion trillion°C (18,000 trillion trillion°F). Within three minutes, the temperature had dropped to less than 1 billion°C (1.8 billion°F) and the Universe was much calmer, with fewer, more stable particles.

SEARCHING FOR ANTIMATTER
An antimatter galaxy would look just like a normal one, except around its edge, where there would be flashes of energy as matter and antimatter met and annihilated each other. So far, none have been detected.

PROTONS AND NEUTRONS

As the Universe cooled, gluons pulled quarks together in threes to form protons and neutrons. Some neutrons decayed into protons. The remaining neutrons bonded with protons to form the nuclei of atoms. By the end of the first three minutes, there were no neutrons left.

Many subatomic particles from the early Universe no longer exist, or have changed into other particles. The most important early particles are listed below.

- X boson: very heavy particle predicted by theory but as yet undetected.

- Higgs boson: a very heavy particle proposed by British physicist Peter Higgs.

- WIMP: weakly interacting massive particle, thought to make up most of the Universe's dark matter.

- W and Z bosons: particles similar to photons – but with mass – that carry the weak force.

- Quark: building block of protons and neutrons, found in six varieties.

- Lepton: particle sensitive to the weak force – electrons are the lightest type of lepton.

- Neutrinos: low-mass, very common particles found in three types.

- Gluon: transmits the strong force that joins quarks together.

- Photon: massless particle carrying radiation and electromagnetism. This is the most common particle.

- Graviton: particle thought to carry gravitational force.

Protons

Neutron in helium nucleus

Neutron

Free protons (hydrogen nuclei)

COSMOS COMPOSITION

The first elements created were probably hydrogen (77%), helium (23%), and lithium (0.000,000,1%).

Photons carry radiation

Leptons still move freely

Quarks locked up in protons and neutrons

27

ECHOES OF THE BIG BANG

FOR A QUARTER of a million years, the ingredients
of space stayed the same, but were diluted as the
Universe expanded. Most of the energy was in the
form of radiation, but the early cosmos was foggy
so light could not travel far. Then the fog
lifted suddenly and space
became transparent.

Time

*At three minutes,
matter consists
of atomic nuclei,
electrons, and
dark matter
particles*

*Dark matter in the Universe,
unaffected by radiation, begins
to clump together under gravity*

*This division – "last scattering surface" – formed
300,000 years after the Big Bang. It separates
the opaque from the transparent Universe.
Background radiation comes from this "surface"*

*As the Universe
cools, heavier
leptons decay
into electrons.
Atomic nuclei
and electrons
soon dominate*

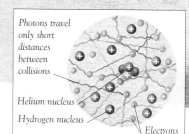

*Photons travel
only short
distances
between
collisions*

Helium nucleus

Hydrogen nucleus

Electrons

COOLING UNIVERSE

At three minutes, the Universe was filled
with high-energy gamma radiation. As
the Universe expanded and cooled, the
radiation lost energy, turning into X-rays,
light, and heat. Electrons slowed down,
combining with atomic nuclei to form
the first atoms. These atoms did not
interact with radiation, so light was able to
travel in straight lines over long distances,
and the Universe became transparent.

PHOTON SCATTERING

In the early Universe, photons of light kept
interacting with atomic nuclei and electrons,
so none got anywhere. Photons would bounce
off one particle, only to collide with another.
Light could never travel far in a straight line
and, as a result, the Universe was opaque.

AFTERGLOW

In 1965, physicists Arno Penzias and Robert Wilson discovered a weak radio signal coming from every direction in the sky. This signal was equivalent to that emitted by an object three degrees above absolute zero. The only possible source for this radiation was the dying heat of the Big Bang, cooled by the expansion of the Universe.

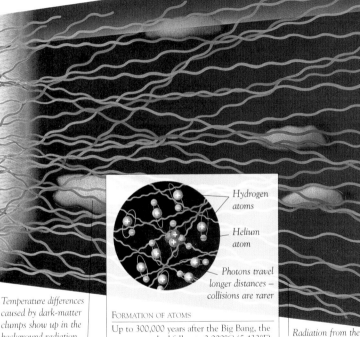

Hydrogen atoms

Helium atom

Photons travel longer distances – collisions are rarer

Temperature differences caused by dark-matter clumps show up in the background radiation

Galaxies begin to form as dark matter attracts hydrogen and helium clouds

FORMATION OF ATOMS

Up to 300,000 years after the Big Bang, the temperature had fallen to 3,000°C (5,432°F). The electrons had slowed down and could be pulled into orbit around the nuclei of hydrogen and helium, forming the first atoms.

Radiation from the "last scattering surface" continues to cool, turning from light and heat to radio waves

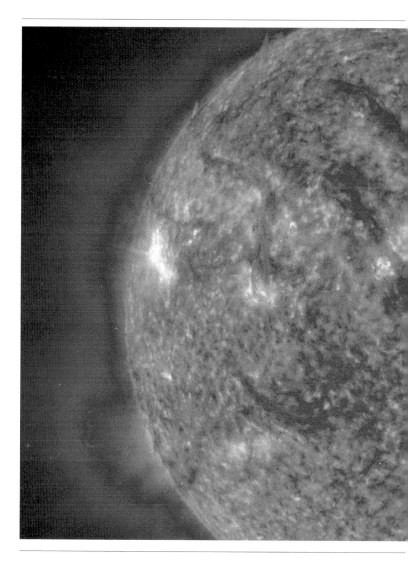

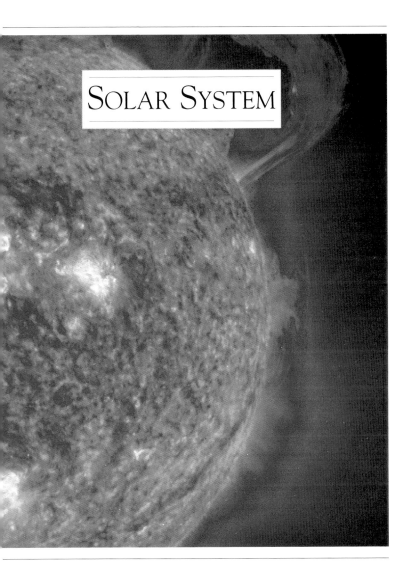

SOLAR SYSTEM

WHAT IS THE SOLAR SYSTEM?

THE SOLAR SYSTEM consists of the Sun and the many objects that orbit around it – nine planets, over 150 moons, and countless asteroids and comets. The system occupies a disc-shaped volume of space more than 12,000 million km (7,500 million miles) across. At the centre is the Sun, which contains more than 99 per cent of the Solar System's mass.

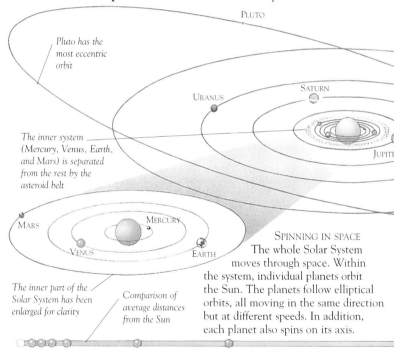

PLUTO

Pluto has the most eccentric orbit

URANUS

SATURN

The inner system (Mercury, Venus, Earth, and Mars) is separated from the rest by the asteroid belt

JUPITE

MARS

MERCURY

VENUS

EARTH

The inner part of the Solar System has been enlarged for clarity

Comparison of average distances from the Sun

SPINNING IN SPACE
The whole Solar System moves through space. Within the system, individual planets orbit the Sun. The planets follow elliptical orbits, all moving in the same direction but at different speeds. In addition, each planet also spins on its axis.

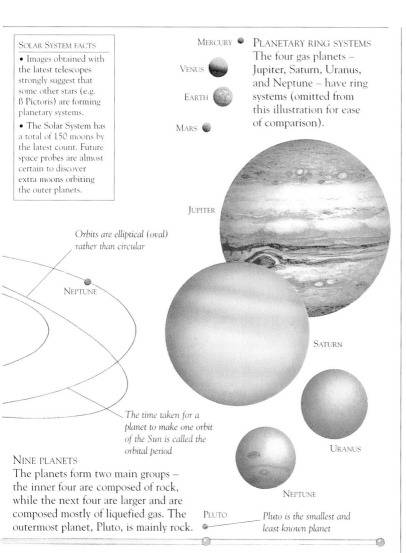

SOLAR SYSTEM FACTS

• Images obtained with the latest telescopes strongly suggest that some other stars (e.g. ß Pictoris) are forming planetary systems.

• The Solar System has a total of 150 moons by the latest count. Future space probes are almost certain to discover extra moons orbiting the outer planets.

MERCURY

VENUS

EARTH

MARS

PLANETARY RING SYSTEMS
The four gas planets – Jupiter, Saturn, Uranus, and Neptune – have ring systems (omitted from this illustration for ease of comparison).

JUPITER

Orbits are elliptical (oval) rather than circular

NEPTUNE

SATURN

The time taken for a planet to make one orbit of the Sun is called the orbital period

URANUS

NEPTUNE

NINE PLANETS
The planets form two main groups – the inner four are composed of rock, while the next four are larger and are composed mostly of liquefied gas. The outermost planet, Pluto, is mainly rock.

PLUTO

Pluto is the smallest and least known planet

BIRTH OF THE SOLAR SYSTEM

It is widely believed that the Solar System was born out of a vast, spinning cloud of gas and dust – the solar nebula. The process began 4.6 billion years ago with the Sun's birth. The planets and other objects formed from unused material. When the Solar System was nearly complete, 500 million years later, just 0.002 per cent of the solar nebula's original mass remained. The rest had fallen into the Sun or been blown out into space.

1 A giant, spinning cloud of gas and dust collected in space to form the solar nebula

Sun   Disc

2 The Sun formed as the solar nebula contracted, leaving a spinning outer disc of material

Dust and gas particles in the disc clumped together to form larger, grain-like particles

Grains collided to form ever larger, rocky particles, eventually producing planetesimals

SUPERNOVA SHOCK WAVE
A massive star may explode as a supernova at the end of its life. In some supernovas, the star's core collapses in on itself, causing a powerful shock wave. The contraction of the solar nebula may have been triggered by such a shock wave.

Gravity pulls the star's core in with force, sending out a shock wave

SOLAR NEBULA
As the vast cloud spun, its centre became denser and hotter, and the Sun was born. Rocky and metallic material near the Sun came together to form the inner planets. In the cooler, outer regions, snow combined with rock, metal, and gas to form the outer planets.

BIRTH OF THE PLANETS

The planets began to form about 4.6 billion years ago. Apart from Pluto, each planet came together from an initial, ring-shaped mass of material around the Sun. (Pluto was created from the leftovers.) As the planets formed, tiny particles stuck together to make grain-sized lumps, then pebbles and boulders, and eventually larger bodies called planetesimals. When they were a few kilometres (miles) across, the planetesimals' gravity was strong enough to attract more and more material.

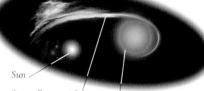

Sun

Sun pulls material off large cloud

Passing cloud of gas and dust

CAPTURE THEORY

This alternative theory suggests that part of a cloud of gas and dust, passing close to the Sun, was captured by the Sun's gravity. This then split into mini-clouds that contracted and formed the planets.

3 *The newborn Sun blew off excess material. Rings of material formed around it, in which planetesimals were born*

Rocky planets, such as Mercury, were molten when young. They developed a metallic core

Solar System debris consisted mainly of asteroids and comets

Rock and metal between Mars and Jupiter formed the Asteroid Belt

4 *Planetesimals joined to form larger bodies called protoplanets. These came together to form the rocky planets*

Rings produced planets

5 *Protoplanets also formed in the outer regions of the disc. As they grew larger, their gravity attracted vast amounts of gas, creating the gas giants*

Gas giants, such as Saturn, first formed a solid core and then captured a huge atmosphere

6 *Pluto formed from material not used in the gas giants. The remaining material formed the Oort Cloud of comets*

THE SUN

LIKE OTHER STARS, the Sun is a huge ball of spinning gas. Nuclear reactions take place at its core giving off energy. The Sun is the only star close enough to be studied in detail. Its surface features, such as sunspots and prominences, can be observed from Earth. Satellites and space probes are able to get a closer view and obtain even more information.

ECLIPSE OF THE SUN
During an eclipse, the outer layer of the Sun – the corona – becomes visible. Normally the corona is hidden by glare.

YEAR 1   YEAR 4   YEAR 7   YEAR 10   YEAR 12

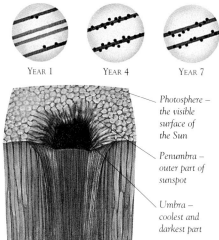

Photosphere – the visible surface of the Sun

Penumbra – outer part of sunspot

Umbra – coolest and darkest part

COOL AND DARK
Sunspots – dark patches on the surface – are regions of cooler gas caused by disturbances in the Sun's magnetic field. Sunspots follow an 11-year cycle that begins with the Sun being relatively spot-free. The spots appear at high latitude and gradually increase in number, moving towards the Sun's equator during the cycle.

SOLAR DATA	
Avg. distance from Earth	149,597,870 km (92,955,807 miles)
Distance from centre of galaxy	25,000 light years
Diameter (at equator)	1,391,980 km (864,976 miles)
Rotation period (at equator)	25.04 Earth days
Mass (Earth = 1)	330,000
Gravity (Earth = 1)	27.9
Avg. density (water = 1)	1.41
Absolute magnitude	4.83

SOLAR FACTS

• Never look directly at the Sun. Even with sunglasses, camera film, or smoked glass, you risk damaging your eyesight.

• The safe way is to project the Sun's image on to a piece of paper using a hand lens.

THE SUN: EXTERNAL AND INTERNAL FEATURES
(for details see pp 40–41)

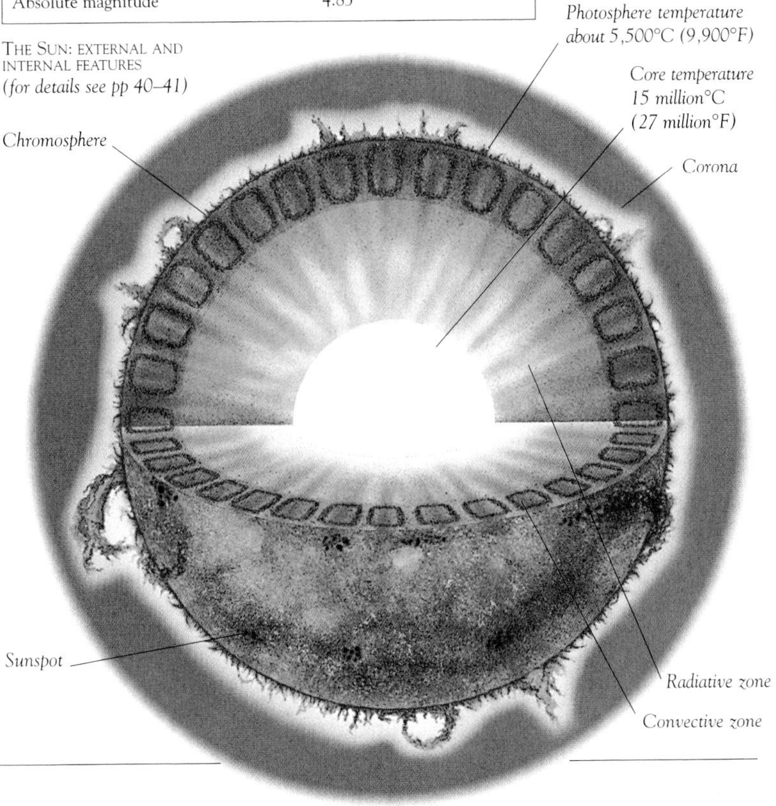

Photosphere temperature about 5,500°C (9,900°F)

Core temperature 15 million°C (27 million°F)

Chromosphere

Corona

Sunspot

Radiative zone

Convective zone

INSIDE THE SUN

OUR NEAREST STAR, the Sun, is a huge globe of hot gas that is 109 times the diameter of Earth, and 745 times greater in mass than all the other bodies in the Solar System put together. It has been blazing for 4.6 billion years and will continue to shine for about the same amount of time again.

The core is the centre where nuclear reactions occur

THE SUN'S STRUCTURE

The Sun's core is so hot – 15 million°C (27 million°F) – that atoms of gas are ripped apart, leaving just their bare nuclei, or centres. The energy travels through the radiative and convective zones to its photosphere, where it leaves the Sun.

NUCLEAR FUSION OF HYDROGEN

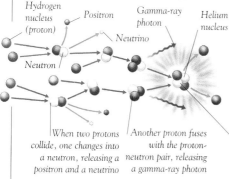

Hydrogen nucleus (proton) *Positron* *Gamma-ray photon* *Helium nucleus*

Neutrino

Neutron

When two protons collide, one changes into a neutron, releasing a positron and a neutrino *Another proton fuses with the proton-neutron pair, releasing a gamma-ray photon*

NUCLEAR REACTIONS

At the Sun's core, energy is produced when four hydrogen nuclei (protons) fuse to make one helium nucleus.

The two groups collide, forming a helium nucleus and releasing two photons

The radiative zone is where energy leaves the core in streams of photons

Photosphere – the Sun's visible surface

SOLAR NEUTRINOS
Neutrinos produced by nuclear reactions in the Sun's core travel out into space. Most of these pass through Earth, but a few can be detected by neutrino telescopes. The Sudbury Observatory lies 2 km (1.2 miles) underground to protect it from cosmic rays.

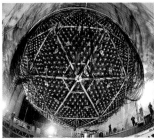

SUDBURY NEUTRINO OBSERVATORY, ONTARIO, CANADA

Area where the Sun's surface is falling

Area where the Sun's surface is rising

SOLAR OSCILLATIONS
The Sun's surface moves up and down in complex patterns of vibrations, or solar oscillations. Most are caused by sound waves generated in the convective zone and trapped inside the Sun. Studying them tells us about the Sun's internal structure.

COMPUTERIZED IMAGE OF SOLAR OSCILLATION PATTERNS

The convective zone is where energy is carried by convection cells

Beyond the photosphere is the solar atmosphere, with the corona extending millions of kilometres (miles) into space

VITAL STATISTICS	
Escape speed from surface	618 kps (384 mps)
Rate of conversion (hydrogen to helium)	615 million tonnes/s (605 million tons/s)
Time taken for light to reach Earth	8 minutes 19 seconds
Luminosity	390 quintillion megawatts
Surface temperature	5,500°C (9,900°F)
Core temperature	16 million°C (28 million°F)
Age	4.6 billion years
Remaining life	5 x 10^9 years

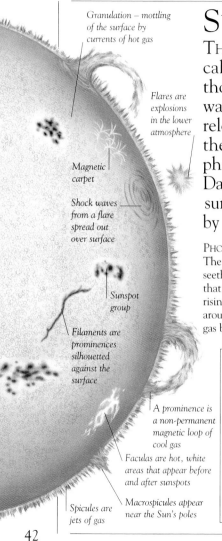

Granulation – mottling of the surface by currents of hot gas

Flares are explosions in the lower atmosphere

Magnetic carpet

Shock waves from a flare spread out over surface

Sunspot group

Filaments are prominences silhouetted against the surface

A prominence is a non-permanent magnetic loop of cool gas

Faculas are hot, white areas that appear before and after sunspots

Spicules are jets of gas

Macrospicules appear near the Sun's poles

SUN'S SURFACE

THE VISIBLE DISC OF THE SUN is called the photosphere. After thousands of years working its way up from the core, the energy released by nuclear reactions inside the Sun finally burst from the photosphere in a blaze of light. Dark markings on its surface – sunspots – were first noticed by Galileo 400 years ago.

PHOTOSPHERE

The photosphere is not solid like Earth's surface, but a seething sea of glowing gas 500 km (311 miles) thick that marks the tops of currents of hot, opaque gas rising from the Sun's interior. Its temperature averages around 5,500°C (9,932°F). At the photosphere, the gas becomes transparent, allowing light to escape.

SUNSPOTS

Dark blotches – sunspots – are shallow depressions in the photosphere where strong magnetic fields stop currents of hot gas from reaching the Sun's surface. They range

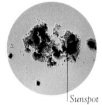

Sunspot

from small spots, known as pores, to large clusters called sunspot groups. They last from a few hours to many weeks. They are cooler than their surroundings and so they appear darker.

MAGNETIC SUNSPOTS

Sunspots occur in areas of violent magnetic activity called active regions. The magnetic fields inside the Sun are wound up and twisted by the different speeds at which the Sun's surface rotates. Churning gas currents in the photosphere cause loops of magnetism to break through the surface and form sunspots. One end of each loop is a north magnetic pole, while the other end is a south magnetic pole.

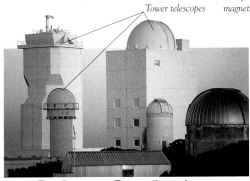

Yellow areas are south magnetic poles

Blue areas are north magnetic poles

A magnetogram is a map of the Sun's magnetic fields

MAGNETOGRAM OF A SUNSPOT GROUP

Tower telescopes

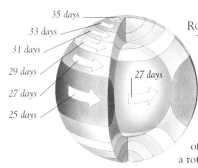

TIEDE OBSERVATORY, TENERIFE, CANARY ISLANDS

SOLAR TELESCOPES

A tower telescope tracks the Sun with a moving mirror (a heliostat) on top of a tower. The heliostat reflects light down a vertical shaft to measuring instruments at ground level. In a vacuum tower telescope, air is removed to stop the Sun's heat from stirring up air currents that may distort the image.

ROTATION SPEED

The Sun is a globe of gas, so it does not all rotate at the same speed as a solid object would. The Sun's equator makes one rotation roughly every 25 days, while areas near the poles turn once every 35 days. The way the Sun's surface oscillates, or vibrates, suggests that the inner part of the Sun spins like a solid ball, with a rotation period of 27 days.

35 days
33 days
31 days
29 days
27 days
25 days
27 days

SUN'S ATMOSPHERE

THE SUN'S THIN ATMOSPHERE consists of two main regions – the chromosphere and the corona. These regions are often rocked by enormous eruptions and explosions called prominences and flares. The corona is far hotter than the photosphere. As a result, hundreds of tonnes (tons) of the Sun's atmosphere evaporate into space every second.

PROMINENCES
These are vast loops or arches of gas extending from the chromosphere up into the corona. The gas may splatter down into the photosphere as coronal rain, or erupt into space.

This ultraviolet image of the chromosphere was taken by the SOHO spacecraft

CHROMOSPHERE
The chromosphere is a layer of hydrogen and helium gas above the photosphere, about 5,000 km (3,107 miles) thick. Its temperature is about 4,000°C (7,232°F) at the bottom, near the photosphere, and 500,000°C (900,000°F) at the top. Brush-like jets of gas – spicules – project from the chromosphere into the corona above.

Chromosphere can be seen as a blotchy pink ring around the edge of the Moon during a total eclipse

Hot hydrogen gas makes the chromosphere look pink in visible light

TOTAL ECLIPSE OF THE SUN

During a total eclipse, the dark disc of the Moon blots out the Sun, revealing the outer reaches of the solar atmosphere

44

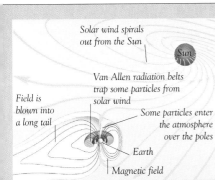

Solar wind spirals out from the Sun

Sun

Van Allen radiation belts trap some particles from solar wind

Field is blown into a long tail

Some particles enter the atmosphere over the poles

Earth

Magnetic field

SOLAR WIND

Made up of coronal electrons and protons, and the magnetic fields and electric currents generated, the solar wind passes Earth at 300 to 800 kps (186 to 497 mps). Earth's magnetic field deflects most of it and is squeezed into a long tail by the wind.

Density of corona is less than a trillionth the density of Earth's atmosphere

Dark patches are coronal holes – low-density regions from which high-speed streams of particles flow into the solar wind

The eclipse shows up the corona as a milky-white halo, often displaying wisps, loops, and streamers

AURORA SEEN FROM SPACE

Auroras are displays of coloured lights over Earth's magnetic poles. They occur when solar wind particles, trapped by Earth's magnetic field, collide with air molecules in the upper atmosphere.

The photosphere appears as a dark disc because it is not hot enough to produce X-rays

CORONA

The corona is the outermost region of the Sun's atmosphere, extending millions of kilometres (miles) into space. Even though temperatures can rise to more than 3 million°C (5.4 million°F), the corona is very faint because the gas is extremely thin. Bubbles containing billions of tonnes (tons) of gas sometimes erupt from the corona.

ECLIPSES OF THE SUN

IN ITS 27-DAY ORBIT OF EARTH, the Moon sometimes passes directly in front of the Sun causing a solar eclipse. Between two and five solar eclipses are visible from somewhere on Earth each year. Partial eclipses – when only a portion of the Sun is covered by the Moon – are visible over a wide area. Total eclipses – when the Sun is completely hidden – are seen from a far narrower region of Earth's surface.

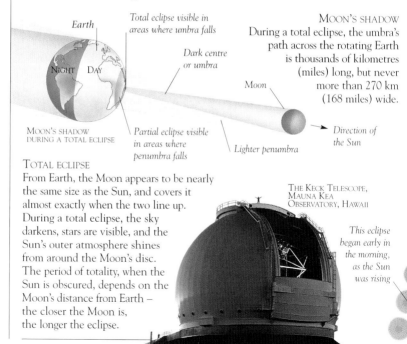

Earth

Total eclipse visible in areas where umbra falls

Dark centre or umbra

NIGHT DAY

Moon

MOON'S SHADOW DURING A TOTAL ECLIPSE

Partial eclipse visible in areas where penumbra falls

Lighter penumbra

MOON'S SHADOW
During a total eclipse, the umbra's path across the rotating Earth is thousands of kilometres (miles) long, but never more than 270 km (168 miles) wide.

→ *Direction of the Sun*

TOTAL ECLIPSE
From Earth, the Moon appears to be nearly the same size as the Sun, and covers it almost exactly when the two line up. During a total eclipse, the sky darkens, stars are visible, and the Sun's outer atmosphere shines from around the Moon's disc. The period of totality, when the Sun is obscured, depends on the Moon's distance from Earth – the closer the Moon is, the longer the eclipse.

THE KECK TELESCOPE,
MAUNA KEA
OBSERVATORY, HAWAII

This eclipse began early in the morning, as the Sun was rising

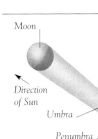

Moon

Direction
of Sun

Umbra

Penumbra

In the partial phase of the eclipse, the Sun looks as though a bite has been taken out of it

Umbra does not reach Earth

A total eclipse can last up to 7.5 minutes when the Earth and Moon are closest to each other, but it is usually much briefer

In the few minutes of totality, the Sun is completely hidden by the disc of the Moon

As an eclipse proceeds, the Moon covers more and more of the Sun

Warning: *Never look directly at the Sun during an eclipse. It should only be viewed through special filters or a projector*

TIME-LAPSE
PHOTOGRAPH OF
TOTAL ECLIPSE

ANNULAR ECLIPSE

During an annular eclipse, the Moon is at its farthest from Earth and is not big enough in the sky to cover the Sun completely. When the Moon is exactly in front of the Sun, the Sun's photosphere is still visible around its edges, like a ring of fire. Annular eclipses can last for more than 12 minutes.

Annular eclipse visible in area beneath tip of umbra

Day   Night

Earth

MOON'S SHADOW DURING
AN ANNULAR ECLIPSE

ECLIPSE EFFECTS

For a few seconds just before or after totality, the disappearing or emerging Sun shines between the mountains at the edge of the Moon's disc. Sometimes this produces a brilliant spot of light – the diamond ring. At other times, an arc of bright points, similar to a string of pearls – Baily's Beads – is visible.

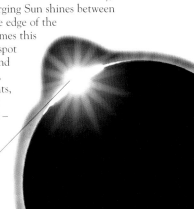

The last bright sliver of the Sun's disc shines like a diamond in a ring formed by the chromosphere

47

SOLAR ENERGY AND INFLUENCE

AT ITS CORE, the Sun converts hydrogen to helium at a rate of 600 million tonnes (590 million tons) every second. The energy produced eventually reaches the surface and travels through space.

Visible light and other radiation travels from the Sun's surface to Earth in about 8 minutes

Nuclear reactions at core produce gamma rays

Gamma rays take up to two million years to travel to the surface, losing energy in the process

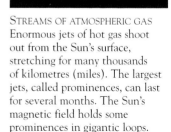

STREAMS OF ATMOSPHERIC GAS
Enormous jets of hot gas shoot out from the Sun's surface, stretching for many thousands of kilometres (miles). The largest jets, called prominences, can last for several months. The Sun's magnetic field holds some prominences in gigantic loops.

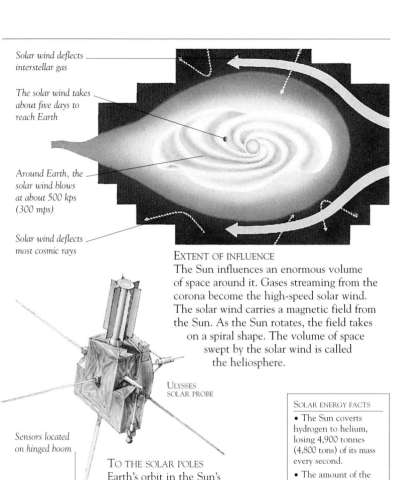

Solar wind deflects interstellar gas

The solar wind takes about five days to reach Earth

Around Earth, the solar wind blows at about 500 kps (300 mps)

Solar wind deflects most cosmic rays

EXTENT OF INFLUENCE
The Sun influences an enormous volume of space around it. Gases streaming from the corona become the high-speed solar wind. The solar wind carries a magnetic field from the Sun. As the Sun rotates, the field takes on a spiral shape. The volume of space swept by the solar wind is called the heliosphere.

ULYSSES
SOLAR PROBE

Sensors located on hinged boom

TO THE SOLAR POLES
Earth's orbit in the Sun's equatorial plane means that the Sun's poles cannot be studied from Earth. The Ulysses probe was launched in 1990 to study these hard-to-observe regions.

SOLAR ENERGY FACTS

• The Sun coverts hydrogen to helium, losing 4,900 tonnes (4,800 tons) of its mass every second.

• The amount of the Sun's energy reaching Earth's surface (known as the solar constant) is equivalent to 1.37 kw (kilowatts) per square metre (1.15 kw per square yard) per second.

EARTH

THE THIRD PLANET FROM THE SUN, Earth, combines many features of the other planets with some that are all its own. It has craters as on Mercury, volcanoes as on Venus and Mars, and swirling weather systems as on Jupiter and Neptune. But it is the only planet with both liquid water and frozen ice that has an atmosphere rich in oxygen, and on which life exists.

VITAL STATISTICS	
Diameter	12,756 km (7,930 miles)
Avg. distance from Sun	149,597,870 km (92,955,807 miles)
Orbital speed around Sun	27.8 kps (17.3 mps)
Sunrise to sunrise	24 hours
Mass	5.9742 x 1024 kg
Volume	1.087 x 1021 m3
Avg. density (water = 1)	5.52
Surface gravity	9.78 m/s2
Avg. surface temperature	15°C (59°F)
Number of moons	1

BLUE PLANET
From space, Earth is blue in colour. This is due to the vast expanses of water on its surface. It is the only planet with a surface temperature between 0°C (32°F) and 100°C (212°F), where water can be liquid at the surface.

Oceans and seas cover 71% of Earth's surface

Clouds condense from water vapour that evaporates from oceans

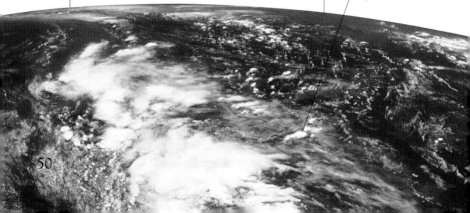

Earth is the largest of the rocky planets. It is the only planet with a crust split into moving plates, oxygen in its atmosphere, and liquid water and life on its surface.

TILT, SPIN AND ORBIT

Orbits the Sun in 365.25 days

Axis tilts from the vertical by 23.5°

Spins on its axis once every 23.93 hours

ATMOSPHERE

Argon, water vapour and trace gases (1%)

Oxygen (20.9%)

Nitrogen (78.1%)

SCALE

Crust

STRUCTURE

Mantle of silicate rock

Outer core (liquid iron)

Inner core (solid iron)

Earth is about four times the size of the Moon

Rain from clouds returns water to the oceans to complete the water cycle

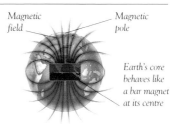

Magnetic field

Magnetic pole

Earth's core behaves like a bar magnet at its centre

EARTH AS A MAGNET

Earth's magnetism is caused by swirling currents of molten iron at its core. For its size, Earth has the strongest magnetic field of any planet. Over time, the magnetism changes direction, causing the magnetic poles to wander.

Magnetic field lines

Magnetosphere

Van Allen belts trap particles from solar wind

Solar wind

Earth

MAGNETOSPHERE

Earth is surrounded by a "magnetic bubble" or magnetosphere that protects it from the effects of the solar wind – electrified particles that sweep outwards from the Sun at high speeds. Some particles are trapped in the Van Allen belts – regions of radiation – close to Earth, while others stream to the magnetic poles causing auroras.

EARTH'S SURFACE

EARTH'S SURFACE IS SHAPED by unique geological forces. The crust (outer shell) is split into huge sections called plates, which float on a partially molten layer of rock, and are always on the move. As they collide or drift apart, the surface rocks are continually destroyed and renewed.

250 million years ago, all the continents are a single land mass, Pangaea

200 million years ago, Pangaea splits into Laurasia and Gondwanaland

135 million years ago, Gondwanaland splits into Africa and South America

60 million years ago, the North Atlantic splits into Europe and North America

DRIFTING CONTINENTS

Carried on top of the moving plates, the continents gradually drift over Earth's surface about as fast as a fingernail grows. In the process, continents split apart. India, Africa, Australia, and Antarctica were once part of a single continent. India smashed into Asia, causing the mighty Himalayas to be pushed up.

PLATE TECTONICS

Earth's surface is shaped by plate tectonics – the forces caused by the moving plates. There are eight large plates and many smaller ones. Some consist only of ocean floor, while others include continents. The edges of the plates are marked by long cracks, winding ridges, strings of volcanoes, and earthquake zones.

RING OF FIRE

ALEUTIAN TRENCH

EURASIAN PLATE

HIMALAYA

MARIANA TRENCH

PHILIPPINE PLATE

HAWAII

PACIFIC PLATE

INDO-AUSTRALIAN PLATE

TONGA TRENCH

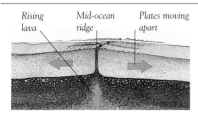

Rising lava | Mid-ocean ridge | Plates moving apart

WHERE PLATES MOVE APART
Where two plates move apart, lava wells up to form a mountain range called a mid-ocean ridge, which is part of the ocean floor. The Mid-Atlantic Ridge is the longest mountain range on Earth. Its highest peaks are islands such as Iceland, Ascension Island, and Tristan da Cunha.

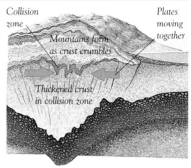

Collision zone | Plates moving together

Mountains form as crust crumbles

Thickened crust in collision zone

COLLIDING CONTINENTS
When continents collide, mountains are pushed up. The Alps are the result of the African Plate pushing northwards into the Eurasian Plate.

Pacific Ocean floor forced under South America

WHERE PLATES MEET
The Andes are part of a volcanic chain – the Ring of Fire – circling the Pacific Ocean. In a process called subduction, South America is riding up over the Nazca Plate, causing ocean floor rocks to melt and erupt as volcanos.

EARTH'S ATMOSPHERE

EARTH IS SURROUNDED by a thin layer of gas called the atmosphere, which keeps the planet at a comfortable temperature and protects the surface from dangerous radiation. Heated unevenly by the Sun and spun by Earth, it has ever-changing, swirling patterns, and is the most complex atmosphere in the Solar System.

STRUCTURE OF THE ATMOSPHERE
The atmosphere is a mixture of gases, water, and dust, with 98 per cent of the mass in the lowest 30 km (19 miles). At ground level, the circulating air produces strong winds. Between the wind systems lie swirling ovals of high pressure (anticyclones) and low pressure (depressions).

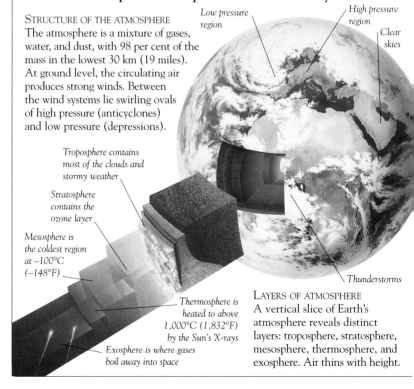

Low pressure region

High pressure region

Clear skies

Troposphere contains most of the clouds and stormy weather

Stratosphere contains the ozone layer

Mesosphere is the coldest region at −100°C (−148°F)

Thermosphere is heated to above 1,000°C (1,832°F) by the Sun's X-rays

Exosphere is where gases boil away into space

Thunderstorms

LAYERS OF ATMOSPHERE
A vertical slice of Earth's atmosphere reveals distinct layers: troposphere, stratosphere, mesosphere, thermosphere, and exosphere. Air thins with height.

SOLAR SYSTEM

GREENHOUSE EFFECT

Without the atmosphere, Earth would be 30°C (54°F) colder. Like a greenhouse, the air traps some of the heat generated by sunlight.

Some heat escapes

Earth's atmosphere

Gases in the atmosphere

Sunlight

Heat from Earth

Heat radiated back to Earth

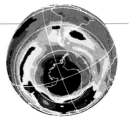

OZONE HOLE

The ozone layer protects Earth from the Sun's harmful ultraviolet rays. This layer has thinned above both poles.

CHANGING CLIMATE

Earth warms up by 0.02°C (0.04°F) per year, probably due to extra carbon dioxide, released by burning coal and oil, and the destruction of rainforests, enhancing the greenhouse effect.

THE WORLD'S TEMPERATURE IN THE TROPOSPHERE (RED IS HOTTER)

WIND CIRCULATION

At the equator, warm air rises, moves north and south, then descends and flows back at sea level. At each pole, cold air sinks and spreads. Then it warms up and rises to flow back at high altitude. Caught between these circulating currents, air at middle latitudes circulates the opposite way.

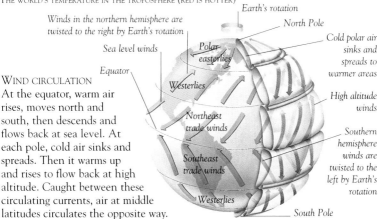

Winds in the northern hemisphere are twisted to the right by Earth's rotation

Sea level winds

Equator

Polar easterlies

Westerlies

Northeast trade winds

Southeast trade winds

Westerlies

Earth's rotation

North Pole

Cold polar air sinks and spreads to warmer areas

High altitude winds

Southern hemisphere winds are twisted to the left by Earth's rotation

South Pole

55

LIFE ON EARTH

IN 1990, THE GALILEO space probe swept past Earth and recorded a green covering over the land, a corrosive gas in the atmosphere, and some radio signals. The green covering was biological material absorbing sunlight, and in the process, releasing the corrosive gas oxygen. Earth has one special quality: it is the only place where life is known to exist.

EVOLUTION OF LIFE

Earth is home to more than a million species of living things, ranging from bacteria to giant trees and mammals. All have come about by the process of evolution, that is, changes in successive generations as species adapt to their surroundings and to competitors.

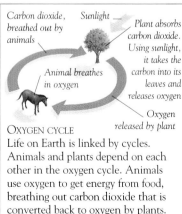

2 Large shallow pools concentrated chemicals to make the first cells 4 billion years ago

3 Dinosaurs and giant tree ferns flourished 200 million years ago

4 Today, life is still evolving but is threatened by destructive human activity

Carbon dioxide, breathed out by animals

Sunlight

Plant absorbs carbon dioxide. Using sunlight, it takes the carbon into its leaves and releases oxygen

Animal breathes in oxygen

Oxygen released by plant

OXYGEN CYCLE

Life on Earth is linked by cycles. Animals and plants depend on each other in the oxygen cycle. Animals use oxygen to get energy from food, breathing out carbon dioxide that is converted back to oxygen by plants.

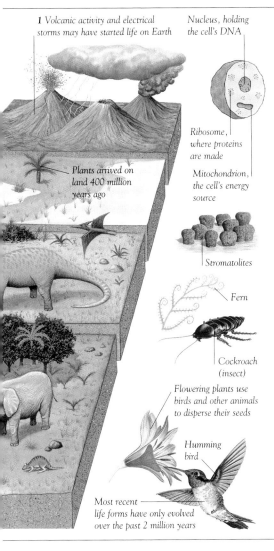

1 *Volcanic activity and electrical storms may have started life on Earth*

Plants arrived on land 400 million years ago

Nucleus, holding the cell's DNA

Ribosome, where proteins are made

Mitochondrion, the cell's energy source

Stromatolites

Fern

Cockroach (insect)

Flowering plants use birds and other animals to disperse their seeds

Humming bird

Most recent life forms have only evolved over the past 2 million years

LIVING CELLS

All life is made up of microscopic cells. Some organisms consist of a single cell, while the human body has 100 billion cells. Cells differ in detail, depending on their function, but all have the same parts.

SINGLE CELLS

Many species consist of a single cell, such as bacteria and pond-dwelling algae. Sometimes single cells group together in colonies, such as stromatolites.

SIMPLE LIFE-FORMS

Some simpler life-forms have survived for millions of years. Ferns were the first plants on dry land. Molluscs in the sea and insects on land have stayed the same for 350 million years.

COMPLEX SYSTEMS

Many life forms have evolved to become more complex. Some plants use insects to pollinate them. Mammals and birds are warm-blooded, so they can endure temperature changes.

THE MOON

THE MOON IS THE CLOSEST celestial object to Earth. The pair waltz through space together, with the Moon spinning around Earth, as Earth itself orbits the Sun. The Moon is larger and brighter than any other object in the night sky. It has no light of its own but shines by reflecting sunlight. Thrice a year, the Moon's face is eclipsed as it passes through Earth's shadow.

MOON AT A GLANCE

The Moon is a dusty, barren sphere of rock with no atmosphere or liquid water. It takes the same time to rotate on its axis as it does to orbit Earth.

TILT, SPIN, AND ORBIT

Orbits Earth in 27.32 days

Earth

Axis tilts from the vertical by 6.7°

Spins on its axis once every 27.32 days

STRUCTURE

Crust of granite-like rock

Rocky mantle

Probably solid inner core

SCALE

Moon is just over a quarter the diameter of Earth

VITAL STATISTICS	
Diameter	3,476 km (2,160 miles)
Avg. distance from Earth	384,400 km (238,866 miles)
Orbital speed around Earth	1.02 kps (0.63 mps)
New Moon to new Moon	29.53 days
Mass (Earth =1)	0.0123
Volume (Earth = 1)	0.0202
Avg. density (water = 1)	3.34
Surface gravity (Earth = 1)	0.17
Avg. surface temperature	–20°C (–4°F)

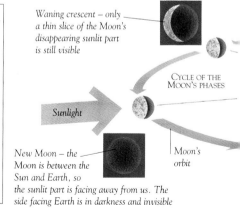

Waning crescent – only a thin slice of the Moon's disappearing sunlit part is still visible

CYCLE OF THE MOON'S PHASES

Sunlight

New Moon – the Moon is between the Sun and Earth, so the sunlit part is facing away from us. The side facing Earth is in darkness and invisible

Moon's orbit

LUNAR ECLIPSES

When the full Moon moves through Earth's shadow, a lunar eclipse occurs. In a total eclipse, the entire Moon is in the umbra, the central, darkest part of the shadow. In a partial eclipse, some of the Moon is in the umbra and the rest is in the penumbra – the paler, outer part.

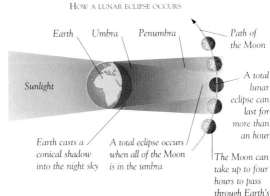

HOW A LUNAR ECLIPSE OCCURS

Earth   Umbra   Penumbra

Path of the Moon

Sunlight

A total lunar eclipse can last for more than an hour

Earth casts a conical shadow into the night sky

A total eclipse occurs when all of the Moon is in the umbra

The Moon can take up to four hours to pass through Earth's shadow completely

PHASES OF THE MOON

Just like Earth, one half of the Moon is always bathed in sunlight, while the other lies in darkness. As the Moon circles Earth, its shape seems to change as we see varying phases of its sunlit part. The phases follow a cycle, from new Moon, when the dark side is facing us, to full Moon, when we see all of the sunlit part.

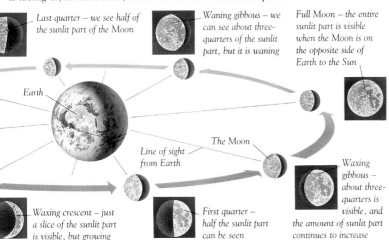

Last quarter – we see half of the sunlit part of the Moon

Waning gibbous – we can see about three-quarters of the sunlit part, but it is waning

Full Moon – the entire sunlit part is visible when the Moon is on the opposite side of Earth to the Sun

Earth

The Moon

Line of sight from Earth

Waxing gibbous – about three-quarters is visible, and the amount of sunlit part continues to increase

Waxing crescent – just a slice of the sunlit part is visible, but growing

First quarter – half the sunlit part can be seen

MOON'S SURFACE

FROM EARTH, THE MOON looks very grey, but the variations in its greyness tell us something about it. The lighter areas are older, higher land, covering about 85 per cent of the Moon, while the darker areas are younger, lowland plains. Only 7 per cent of the light falling on the Moon is reflected by its surface. By studying the surface, astronomers can date the different stages of the Moon's development.

Regolith is the surface layer of dust and rock created by meteorite bombardment

Mare, which means sea in Latin, is the name given to a dark plain on the Moon

Craters are bowl-shaped scars left by meteorites. Crater comes from the Greek word for bowl

Highlands, above the level of the maria, were the first parts of the crust to cool and solidify

Mountain ranges are uplifted areas of crust that ring some of the maria and large craters

The largest craters, several hundred kilometres (miles) across, are called basins

The rocky crust is 60–100 km (40–60 miles) thick

LUNAR LANDSCAPE

Two distinctive landscape forms on the Moon are dark grey plains, or maria (singular: mare) and lighter highlands. Covered with craters, the highlands are the oldest parts of the crust. The smooth plains are large craters that were filled with lava, and are usually surrounded by mountains.

HISTORY OF THE MOON

This vast crater will eventually become the Mare Imbrium

Meteorites pound the Moon's crust

The Mare Imbrium is created as lava floods the crater basin

Lava erupts through fractures in the crust

Copernicus forms about 800 million years ago

Volcanic activity has all but ceased

FOUR BILLION YEARS AGO
During its first 750 million years, the Moon went through a period of devastating bombardment by meteorites. Their impact punctured the crust and formed craters all over the surface.

THREE BILLION YEARS AGO
About 3.7 billion years ago, bombardment slowed and intense volcanic activity followed as deep craters filled with lava welling up from 100 km (62 miles) below the surface. The lava solidified to form maria.

THE MOON TODAY
The lunar surface has changed little in the past 1.6 billion years, though a few young craters, such as Copernicus, stand out. Most of the original crust has been destroyed by cratering.

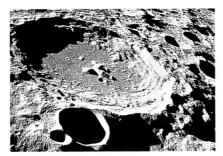

SURFACE TEMPERATURES
The Moon experiences extremes of temperature. The lunar surface is –180°C (–292°F) at its coldest, but reaches a searing maximum of 110°C (230°F). The Moon's lack of atmosphere means that there is nothing to regulate the surface temperature. When sunlit, its surface is fully heated, but when in shadow, the heat is lost.

NEARSIDE OF THE MOON

THE DOMINANT FEATURES on the Moon's nearside –
the side that always faces Earth – are the dark maria,
which early astronomers thought were seas. These
lava-filled basins formed when molten rock seeped
through the Moon's crust to fill depressions left by
meteorite impacts. The surface is pockmarked by
craters everywhere. All landings by spacecraft
have been on the Moon's nearside.

MONTES APENNINUS
One of the most
impressive ranges of
lunar mountains, the
Montes Apenninus,
along with the Montes
Carpatus, Caucasus,
Jura, and Alpes, make up the walls of the
Mare Imbrium. This broken ring of
mountains formed from a meteorite impact.

*Aristarchus, a 37-km (23-mile) diameter
crater, is the brightest point on the entire Moon*

COPERNICUS
Copernicus is a lunar
ray crater. It is 107 km
(66 miles) in diameter
and 4 km (2.4 miles)
deep, with rays of
bright rock fragments
leading out from it. Analysis of ray
material collected by the Apollo 12 crew
showed it to be 850 million years old.

Labels on the Moon map: MARE FR, Plato, MONTES JURA, MARE IMBRIUM, Aristillu, 17, Aristillu, Archimedes, Eratosthenes, OCEANUS PROCELLARUM, MONTES CARPATUS, 13, Kepler, Encke, 9, Hevelius, 1, 12, 3, Grimaldi, Flamsteed, 14, Fra Ma, 7, Ptolemae, MARE NUBIUM, Gassendi, MARE HUMORUM, MARE ORIENTALE, Schickard, Longomontanus, Clavius

NEARSIDE FEATURES

The extensive maria, the darkest of the nearside features, lie between 2 and 5 km (1.2 and 3.1 miles) below the average surface level. The most recently formed features are the bright ray craters. The southern area – the roughest part of the nearside surface – is mainly high, cratered land with a handful of large, walled plains. Both polar regions are highland areas.

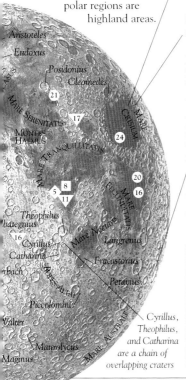

MARE CRISIUM

Separated from the main system of interlinked maria is the Mare Crisium, measuring 450 km (280 miles) by 563 km

(350 miles). The smooth, lava-filled floor of this oval-shaped basin contains two significant craters – Picard and Peirce – as well as smaller ones.

Maria are usually referred to by their Latin names, such as Mare Crisium, which means Sea of Crises

HUMBOLDT CRATER

Named after the German statesman Wilhelm Humboldt, the Humboldt crater is surrounded by a high mountain wall. A blanket of ejecta – material thrown out

at the time of a meteorite impact – covers the ground outside the walls. Inside the crater is a central peak, while a system of fractures runs across the floor.

LANDING SITES

Marked on the map are the landing sites of the 16 space probes and 6 crewed craft that reached the Moon between 1959 and 1976.

7	Ranger 7, 8, & 9
7	Surveyor 1, 3, 5, 6, & 7
13	Luna 2, 9, 13, 16, 17, 20, 21, & 24
11	Apollo 11, 12, 14, 15, 16, & 17

Cyrillus, Theophilus, and Catharina are a chain of overlapping craters

FARSIDE OF THE MOON

THE FARSIDE OF THE MOON is always turned away from Earth. It was a mystery until 1959, when the space probe Luna 3 was able to send back the first photographs. The farside has few maria, because the lunar crust is thicker here than on the nearside, making it difficult for lava to seep through into the impact basins left by colliding space rocks. The farside also has more craters.

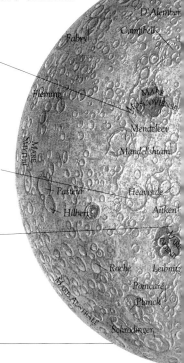

MARE MOSCOVIENSE
One of the few maria lying entirely on the farside, the 277-km (172-mile) long Mare Moscoviense is smaller than large farside crater basins such as Apollo. Its dark floor makes it stand out clearly against its surroundings.

Gagarin is a crater named after Yuri Gagarin, the first person to go into space

VAN DE GRAAFF
This irregularly shaped crater is about 233 km (145 miles) long and has several smaller craters inside it. Surprisingly, it is only 4 km (2.4 miles) deep. The basin has a stronger magnetism and is more radioactive than the land surrounding it, which may be because volcanic rock lies buried under it.

Schwarzschild
D'Alembert
Campbell
Fabry
Fleming
MARE MOSCOVIENSE
Mendeleev
Mandel'shtam
MARE SMYTHII
Pasteur
Heaviside
Hilbert
Aitken
Tsiolkovsky
Roche
Leibnitz
Poincaré
Planck
MARE AUSTRALE
Schrödinger

FARSIDE FEATURES

The two prominent farside maria are the Mare Orientale and Mare Moscoviense. Craters abound but they are smaller and not as dark as those on the nearside. The most noticeable craters are the circular depressions such as Hertzsprung, Apollo, and Korolev. Hertzsprung's outer ring has smaller craters.

LUNAR
SOUTH POLE

Schrödinger
Crater

POLAR REGIONS

The polar regions were the last parts of the Moon to be mapped. Mosaic maps, made by assembling the images sent back in 1994 by the space probe Clementine, suggest that some polar craters are permanently in shadow.

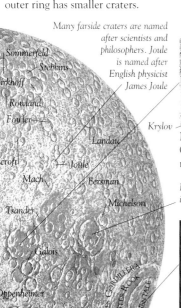

Many farside craters are named after scientists and philosophers. Joule is named after English physicist James Joule

Sommerfeld
Stebbins
Birkhoff
Rowland
Fowler
Krylov
Landau
croft
Joule
Mach
Fersman
Tsander
Michelson
Galois
Oppenheimer
MONTES CORDILLERA
MONTES ROOK
MARE ORIENTALE
Minkowski
Mendel
Lemaître

The Apollo crater was named in honour of the Apollo missions to the Moon

KOROLEV

Measuring 437 km (271 miles) across, the Korolev Crater is among the largest ringed formations on the farside of the Moon. Many smaller craters lie inside it. One of these, Krylov, has a central peak and measures about 50 km (31 miles) across.

Hertzsprung, a 591-km (367-mile) crater basin, is one of the major features on the farside

MARE ORIENTALE

This huge mare is the Moon's youngest and measures 327 km (200 miles) across. It straddles the farside and nearside boundary and is surrounded by concentric rings of mountains about 900 km (560 miles) wide. Beyond them lies ejected material. Only the centre of the impact basin filled with lava.

LUNAR INFLUENCES

ALTHOUGH THE MOON IS much smaller than Earth, it still has an influence on it. Just as Earth's gravity pulls on the Moon, the gravity of the Moon pulls on Earth, stretching it into a slight ovoid (egg-shape). This barely affects the landmasses, but makes the oceans bulge on either side of Earth, producing tides along coastlines. The tides also affect the speed of Earth's spin and the distance between Earth and Moon.

TIDES

The oceans rise in a high tide and then fall back in a low tide twice each day. This tidal cycle lasts 24 hours and 50 minutes, because the Moon arrives above a given spot 50 minutes later each day. The actual height of the tides depends on the position of the Moon on its orbit and on local geography.

Tidal bulge also forms on side facing away from the Moon

Earth's orbit

Water forms a tidal bulge

Earth

The Moon's gravity pulls Earth's oceans

The Moon

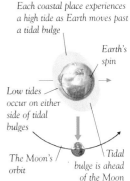

Each coastal place experiences a high tide as Earth moves past a tidal bulge

Earth's spin

Low tides occur on either side of tidal bulges

The Moon's orbit

Tidal bulge is ahead of the Moon

HIGH TIDE, SEVERN ESTUARY, ENGLAND

LOW TIDE, SEVERN ESTUARY, ENGLAND

CAUSES OF TIDES

Water on the side of Earth closest to the Moon feels the Moon's gravitational pull most strongly. Two bulges of tidal water form and follow the Moon as it orbits Earth. Earth's rotation causes the tidal bulges to be carried around slightly ahead of the Moon, rather than directly in line with it.

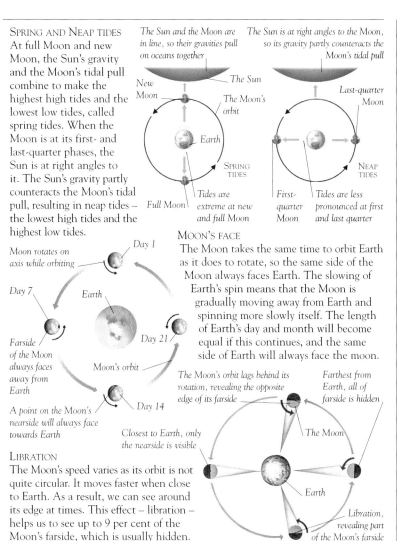

SPRING AND NEAP TIDES

At full Moon and new Moon, the Sun's gravity and the Moon's tidal pull combine to make the highest high tides and the lowest low tides, called spring tides. When the Moon is at its first- and last-quarter phases, the Sun is at right angles to it. The Sun's gravity partly counteracts the Moon's tidal pull, resulting in neap tides – the lowest high tides and the highest low tides.

The Sun and the Moon are in line, so their gravities pull on oceans together

The Sun is at right angles to the Moon, so its gravity partly counteracts the Moon's tidal pull

New Moon

The Sun

The Moon's orbit

Earth

Last-quarter Moon

SPRING TIDES

NEAP TIDES

Full Moon

Tides are extreme at new and full Moon

First-quarter Moon

Tides are less pronounced at first and last quarter

Moon rotates on axis while orbiting

Day 1

Day 7

Earth

Day 21

Farside of the Moon always faces away from Earth

Moon's orbit

Day 14

A point on the Moon's nearside will always face towards Earth

Closest to Earth, only the nearside is visible

MOON'S FACE

The Moon takes the same time to orbit Earth as it does to rotate, so the same side of the Moon always faces Earth. The slowing of Earth's spin means that the Moon is gradually moving away from Earth and spinning more slowly itself. The length of Earth's day and month will become equal if this continues, and the same side of Earth will always face the moon.

The Moon's orbit lags behind its rotation, revealing the opposite edge of its farside

Farthest from Earth, all of farside is hidden

The Moon

Earth

Libration, revealing part of the Moon's farside

LIBRATION

The Moon's speed varies as its orbit is not quite circular. It moves faster when close to Earth. As a result, we can see around its edge at times. This effect – libration – helps us to see up to 9 per cent of the Moon's farside, which is usually hidden.

EXPLORING THE MOON

THE FIRST SPACECRAFT to leave Earth's gravity, Luna 1, was launched towards the Moon in 1959. Over the next decade, many probes, robots, and crewed craft were sent to investigate and land there. Scientists are now planning lunar bases, where astronauts will live and work for months at a time.

8 *The Command Module enters the atmosphere 120 km (75 miles) above Earth*

7 *Approaching Earth, the Command Module separates from the Service Module*

3 *The rest of the rocket is discarded and the modules continue to the Moon*

4 *Lunar Module descends to the Moon*

1 *Lift-off from Cape Canaveral*

5 *The Command and Service Modules orbit the Moon, waiting for the Lunar Module to return*

6 *The astronauts link up and the Lunar Module is abandoned*

9 *Craft parachutes into the ocean*

2 *Saturn V's engines fire to send the Apollo craft to the Moon*

Apollo 15's Jim Irwin

APOLLO PROGRAMME

In 1961, the United States set up the Apollo programme with the aim of sending astronauts to the Moon by the end of the decade. A powerful rocket, the Saturn V, was designed, built, and tested. In July 1969, Neil Armstrong and Buzz Aldrin touched down on the Moon. Their third crew member, Mike Collins, remained in orbit in the Command and Service Module.

CREWED APOLLO MOON LANDINGS				
Mission	Date of landing	Landing site	Activity	Time outside vehicle
Apollo 11	20 Jul 1969	Mare Tranquillitatis	First astronaut on the Moon	2.5 hours
Apollo 12	19 Nov 1969	Oceanus Procellarum	First major scientific experiments set up	7.8 hours
Apollo 14	5 Feb 1971	Fra Mauro	First landing in lunar highlands	9.3 hours
Apollo 15	30 Jul 1971	Hadley-Apennines	First lunar rover excursions	18.6 hours
Apollo 16	21 Apr 1972	Descartes region	Explored highlands	20.2 hours
Apollo 17	11 Dec 1972	Taurus-Littrow	Longest and last stay on the Moon	22.1 hours

APOLLO SCIENTIFIC EXPERIMENTS
Astronauts left behind experiments and equipment to measure moonquakes, the soil temperature, the amount of dust in space, and the number of solar particles reaching the Moon.

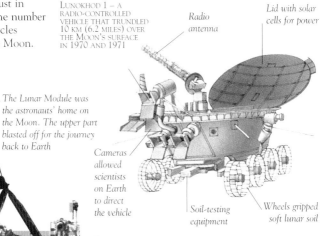

LUNOKHOD 1 – A RADIO-CONTROLLED VEHICLE THAT TRUNDLED 10 KM (6.2 MILES) OVER THE MOON'S SURFACE IN 1970 AND 1971

Radio antenna

Lid with solar cells for power

The Lunar Module was the astronauts' home on the Moon. The upper part blasted off for the journey back to Earth

Cameras allowed scientists on Earth to direct the vehicle

Soil-testing equipment

Wheels gripped soft lunar soil

LUNAR PROBES
Besides the Apollo missions, many remote-controlled crafts, such as the US Ranger and Surveyor probes, also made the journey to the Moon. The Russian Luna probes were the first to land on its surface, followed by Lunokhod 1 and 2.

OTHER SOLAR SYSTEMS

IS OUR SOLAR SYSTEM UNIQUE? Until recently, astronomers could only guess whether there were extrasolar planets – those that orbit stars other than the Sun. Such planets are difficult to detect, being about one-billionth the brightness of their parent stars. But since 1995, sensitive instruments have discovered a number of extrasolar planets.

EXTRASOLAR ORBITS
The orbits of Earth and the first 10 extrasolar planets discovered can be compared as if they were all orbiting the same parent star. Most are closer to their parent stars than Earth is to the Sun, and have far more elliptical orbits.

ORBITS OF EARTH AND
EXTRASOLAR PLANETS,
AND AVERAGE DISTANCES
FROM PARENT STAR

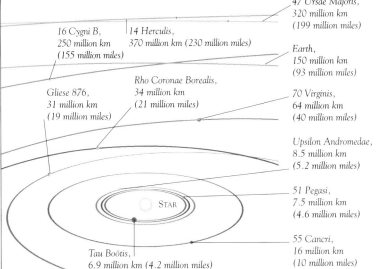

16 Cygni B,
250 million km
(155 million miles)

14 Herculis,
370 million km (230 million miles)

Gliese 876,
31 million km
(19 million miles)

Rho Coronae Borealis,
34 million km
(21 million miles)

STAR

Tau Boötis,
6.9 million km (4.2 million miles)

47 Ursae Majoris,
320 million km
(199 million miles)

Earth,
150 million km
(93 million miles)

70 Virginis,
64 million km
(40 million miles)

Upsilon Andromedae,
8.5 million km
(5.2 million miles)

51 Pegasi,
7.5 million km
(4.6 million miles)

55 Cancri,
16 million km
(10 million miles)

FIRST 10 EXTRASOLAR PLANETS DISCOVERED				
Name of parent star	Distance of parent star from Sun (ly)	Year of discovery	Minimum mass (Earth = 1)	Time to orbit star in days
51 Pegasi	50	1995	150	4.2
55 Cancri	44	1996	270	14.6
47 Ursae Majoris	46	1996	890	1,090
Tau Boötis	49	1996	1,230	3.3
Upsilon Andromedae	54	1996	220	4.6
70 Virginis	59	1996	2,100	117
16 Cygni B	72	1996	480	804
Rho Coronae Borealis	55	1997	350	39.6
Gliese 876	15	1998	670	60.8
14 Herculis	55	1998	1,050	1,620

WHAT ARE OTHER PLANETS LIKE?

Most extrasolar planets that have been detected are as big as, or bigger than, Jupiter. They are believed to be gas giants, and most are close to their parent stars so they will also be very hot. Astronomers have so far discovered 134 extrasolar planetary systems, containing a total of 154 known planets.

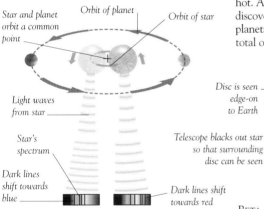

Star and planet orbit a common point

Orbit of planet

Orbit of star

Light waves from star

Star's spectrum

Dark lines shift towards blue

Dark lines shift towards red

WOBBLING STARS

Extrasolar planets can be found by observing how their gravity causes their parent stars to wobble slightly. If the star's light is split into a spectrum, the dark lines in the spectrum shift to the blue end as the star wobbles towards us, and to the red end as it wobbles away.

Disc of gas and dust

Disc is seen edge-on to Earth

Telescope blacks out star so that surrounding disc can be seen

BETA PICTORIS

Astronomers have discovered planets that are being formed around newborn stars. It is thought planets may be forming in the swirling disc of gas and dust around the young star Beta Pictoris.

MERCURY

SCORCHED AND BLASTED by solar radiation, Mercury is the planet closest to the Sun. This dry, rocky world has an extremely thin atmosphere. Of all the planets in the Solar System, it travels around the Sun the fastest, but spins slowly on its axis. From Earth, faint markings can be seen on its surface, and astronomers are puzzled as to why this small planet has such a vast iron core.

Red and hot areas, near the equator

FALSE-COLOUR TEMPERATURE MAP OF MERCURY

Mauve regions out of direct sunlight are coolest

Craters vary from a few metres (feet) to hundreds of kilometres (miles) across

Younger craters are surrounded by light-coloured streaks of ejected material

Brontë crater

Craters are generally shallower than those on the Moon

SCARRED SURFACE
About 4 billion years ago, in the early history of the Solar System, the young Mercury's surface was punctured by meteorite impacts. Lava flooded out from the interior to form extensive plains, giving the planet an appearance that, at first glance, resembles the Moon. With no wind or water to shape its crater-scarred landscape, Mercury has remained virtually unchanged since then.

In this image taken by the Mariner 10 space probe, ultraviolet light from the Sun causes the surface to look bleached

74

TEMPERATURE

Mercury, being closest to the Sun, has the greatest variation in day and night temperatures of any planet. The average surface temperature is 167°C (333°F). It can soar to 450°C (842°F) when it is closest to the Sun. At night, because the atmosphere is too thin to retain heat, temperatures fall to as low as –180°C (–292°F).

VITAL STATISTICS	
Diameter	4,880 km (3,030 miles)
Avg. distance from Sun	58 million km (36 million miles)
Orbital speed around Sun	48 kps (30 mps)
Sunrise to sunrise	176 days
Mass (Earth=1)	0.0553
Volume (Earth=1)	0.0560
Avg. density (water=1)	5.43
Surface gravity (Earth=1)	0.38
Avg. surface temperature	167°C (333°F)
Number of moons	0

MERCURY AT A GLANCE

A dense, fast-moving, rocky planet with a large metal core, Mercury has weak gravity and a thin atmosphere. It is the second smallest planet, after Pluto.

TILT, SPIN, AND ORBIT

Orbits the Sun in 87.97 days

Axis of rotation is almost vertical

Spins on its axis once every 58.65 days

ATMOSPHERE

Potassium and other gases 1%

Helium 6%

Hydrogen 22%

Sodium 29%

Oxygen 42%

Crust of silicate rock

Rocky silicate mantle

Iron core

STRUCTURE

SCALE

Diameter is 3,600 km (2,237 miles) less than Earth's

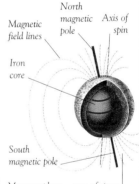

North magnetic pole

Axis of spin

Magnetic field lines

Iron core

South magnetic pole

Magnetosphere – area of space affected by planet's magnetism

MAGNETIC CORE

Mercury is believed to have a solid iron core, surrounded by a layer of liquid iron and sulphur. The core produces the planet's magnetic field, which is about 1 per cent as strong as Earth's.

75

MERCURY'S SURFACE

BECAUSE MERCURY IS CLOSE to the Sun,
even a space-based observatory like the
Hubble Space Telescope would get damaged
by the Sun's rays if it tried to obtain
views of it. In the 1970s, Mariner 10
used protective sunshields to
produce detailed images of
parts of its surface, but more
than half is still unexplored.

*Sobkou Planitia,
a large lava plain
formed after the
Caloris impact*

CALORIS BASIN

A crater about 1,300 km
(808 miles) wide, Caloris
Basin formed about 3.6
billion years ago when a
space rock about 100 km
(62 miles) across

crashed into Mercury. There are similar,
smaller impact craters on the crater floor.

*Space rock strikes
Mercury*

*Caloris Montes mountain chain
was formed by the Caloris impact*

IMPACT SHOCK WAVES

Mercury's crust and upper
mantle were still cooling
and compressing when the
vast space rock that formed the
Caloris Basin struck it. This
made its surface buckle into
ranges of hills and mountains.

*Shock waves spread
throughout planet*

*Shock waves converge and crumple
surface opposite the impact site*

*Tolstoj, a huge, flooded
crater in Mercury's
southwestern quarter*

CRATERED WORLD

Mercury's surface is covered with craters, including the Caloris Basin, ringed by the Caloris Montes. Beyond are rock-strewn areas, smooth lava-flooded plains, wrinkles, and ridges that formed as the planet cooled.

TRANSIT OF MERCURY

Mercury's path across our sky usually takes it just above or below the Sun. But every few years, when the Sun, Earth, and Mercury are aligned, a transit occurs and Mercury travels across the Sun's face. The planet appears as a black dot, and can take several hours to cross from one side of the Sun to the other.

Mercury

This part of Mercury and all of its opposite side were not photographed by Mariner 10 and remain unmapped

Petrarch is one of the younger craters on Mercury. Its smooth floor contains a few, more recent craters

DISCOVERY RUPES

This is a vast ridge that stretches about 500 km (311 miles) across Mercury's surface, towering up to 2 km (1.2 miles) above its surroundings. So far 16 such features have been detected on Mercury.

SOUTH POLAR REGION

Mercury's polar regions include areas that are always shaded from the Sun's heat. Scientists, studying these regions by reflecting radar off them, believe there may be water-ice at Mercury's poles, but other substances like sulphur can produce similar results.

Craters cover about 60% of the known surface. The rest is mostly lava plains

Labels on Mercury image: Monteverdi, Stravinsky, Velázquez, Holbein, Al-Hamádhání, Praxiteles, Mussorgskij, Kuan Han-Ch'eng, Pigalle, Wren, Levnation, To Po, Vivaldi, Giotto, Yeats, Handel, Dolignotes, Madham, Titian, Homer, Renoir, Repin, Ibsen, Chekhov, Amaru, Schubert, ridge, Dostoevskij

VENUS

CALLED AN INFERIOR PLANET

because it orbits closer to the Sun than Earth does, Venus is a sphere of rock similar in size to Earth. A dark, hostile world of volcanoes and suffocating atmosphere, its average temperature is higher than that of any other planet. From Earth, we can only see cloud tops. Hidden under this thick blanket of gas is a landscape moulded by volcanic eruption.

CLOUD-TOP
VIEW OF VENUS

Venus is visible before sunrise at western elongation

Venus is lost in the Sun's glare at inferior conjunction

Venus

The Sun

Earth

Venus is visible after sunset at eastern conjunction

Venus is hidden behind the Sun at superior conjunction

ORBIT OF VENUS
The Venusian orbit sometimes passes between Earth and the Sun. During this inferior conjunction, it is hidden by the Sun's glare. It is brightest when the angle of elongation is about 39°, and it is visible after sunset or before sunrise.

VOLCANOES

The Venusian surface has long lava flows, volcanic craters, and dome- and shield-shaped volcanoes. There are 156 large volcanoes that are more than 100 km (62 miles) across, nearly 300 that are between 20 and 100 km (12 and 62 miles) across, and at least 500 clusters of smaller volcanoes.

Pancake dome volcanoes have flat tops and steep sides, like these in Alpha Regio

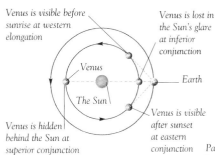

Eistla Regio, a spider-like Arachnoid volcano

VITAL STATISTICS	
Diameter	12,104 km (7,521 miles)
Avg. distance from Sun	108 million km (67 million miles)
Orbital speed around Sun	35.02 kps (21.76 mps)
Sunrise to sunrise	117 days
Mass (Earth = 1)	0.82
Volume (Earth = 1)	0.86
Avg. density (water = 1)	5.2
Surface gravity (Earth = 1)	0.9
Avg. surface temperature	464°C (867°F)
Number of moons	0

VENUS AT A GLANCE

Venus is a rocky planet, with a structure and size similar to Earth's. Its atmosphere helps make it the hottest planet of all. It spins slowly, in the opposite direction to most planets.

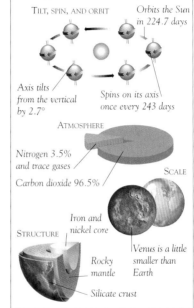

TILT, SPIN, AND ORBIT

Orbits the Sun in 224.7 days

Axis tilts from the vertical by 2.7°

Spins on its axis once every 243 days

ATMOSPHERE

Nitrogen 3.5% and trace gases

Carbon dioxide 96.5%

SCALE

STRUCTURE

Iron and nickel core

Rocky mantle

Silicate crust

Venus is a little smaller than Earth

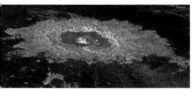

IMPACT CRATERS

More than 900 impact craters have been identified on Venus. About 60 per cent are undamaged, a handful of the other 40 per cent have been damaged by volcanic lava, and the rest have been altered by the cracking and movement of the planet's crust.

VENUSIAN PLAINS

Over three-quarters of Venus is covered by plains that were largely formed by volcanic processes. The plains are marked by volcanic and impact craters, lava flows, and features sculpted by the Venusian wind.

Belts of narrow ridges, a few hundred metres (feet) high, stretch across the plain

Lavinia Planitia is one of the main plains of Venus

79

VENUSIAN ATMOSPHERE

SOME FOUR BILLION YEARS AGO, Venus and Earth
had similar atmospheres. Today, the Venusian
atmosphere is mainly carbon dioxide, with sulphur
dust and droplets of sulphuric acid from the many
volcanic eruptions. It is also very thick, making
Venus hot, gloomy, and suffocating.

STRUCTURE OF THE ATMOSPHERE

Probes that have survived the corrosive Venusian
atmosphere show it to be clear up to 45 km (28 miles).
Above this is a thick, 20-km (12-mile)
layer of cloud consisting of droplets
of sulphuric acid (75 per cent) and
water (25 per cent). The pressure and
density decrease in proportion to
distance above the clouds.

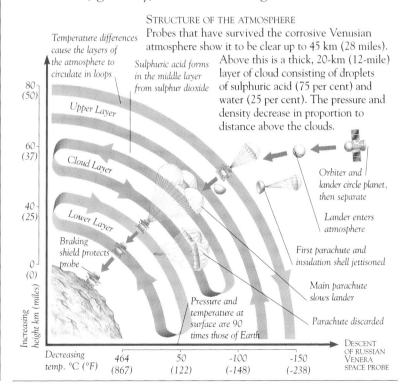

Temperature differences cause the layers of the atmosphere to circulate in loops

Sulphuric acid forms in the middle layer from sulphur dioxide

80 (50)

Upper Layer

60 (37)

Cloud Layer

40 (25)

Lower Layer

Braking shield protects probe

0 (0)

Increasing height km (miles)

Orbiter and lander circle planet, then separate

Lander enters atmosphere

First parachute and insulation shell jettisoned

Main parachute slows lander

Parachute discarded

Pressure and temperature at surface are 90 times those of Earth

Decreasing temp. °C (°F)

| 464 (867) | 50 (122) | -100 (-148) | -150 (-238) |

DESCENT
OF RUSSIAN
VENERA
SPACE PROBE

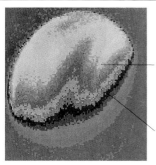

Hot gases from the equator spiral up to polar region

Orange shows the presence of sulphur dioxide

Bands show pattern of cloud-top movement

VENUS IN ULTRAVIOLET
The Pioneer Venus space probe took many ultraviolet pictures, which showed cloud patterns in the atmosphere that were studied to understand its winds.

CLOUD MOVEMENT
The Sun warms the gases in the Venusian atmosphere at the equator. These rise and move towards the cooler polar regions, and then sink to the lower cloud layer as they cool, moving back to the equator.

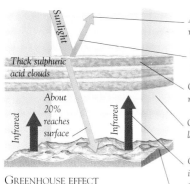

Sunlight

Thick sulphuric acid clouds

About 20% reaches surface

Infrared   Infrared

About 80% reflects away

Sunlight bounces off cloud tops

Clouds block out most of the sunlight

Carbon dioxide layer holds in heat

Only some of the infrared released by the ground escapes

Surface temperature, 462°C (864°F) – 466°C (870°F), is higher than if there was no atmosphere

GREENHOUSE EFFECT
The Venusian atmosphere traps only some of the Sun's heat. The infrared is absorbed by the carbon dioxide in the atmosphere, reflecting some of it back to the surface, while a small amount is radiated into space.

PHASES OF VENUS
We never see the full Venus, because when the whole of the sunlit side points towards Earth, Venus is obscured by the Sun. As it moves around the Sun and gets closer to Earth, it grows larger in Earth's sky, but we see less and less of its sunlit side.

81

VENUSIAN SURFACE

ALTHOUGH VENUS IS THE CLOSEST planet to Earth, it is only in the last 30 years that scientists have successfully pierced its cloud layers using radar techniques. The data collected by Earth-based instruments and orbiters have been combined to produce a global map of Venus. The orbiter Magellan added about 4,000 surface features to this map.

Ishtar Terra is an elevated plateau encircled by narrow mountain belts

Lakshmi Planum is a smooth volcanic plain dominated by two large shield volcanoes, Colette and Sacajawea

MAXWELL MONTES
A steep mountain range lies in the middle of Ishtar Terra, a highland region about the size of Australia. This is Maxwell

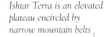

Montes – the highest part of the Venusian surface, rising up to 12,000 m (39,400 ft).

ALPHA REGIO
This was the first feature to be identified on the Venusian surface using Earth-based radar. It is located in the southern hemisphere. It is an area of volcanic highland measuring about 1,300 km (800 miles) across. It includes low, domed hills, intersecting ridges, and troughs and valleys.

Lavinia Planitia, a lava plain

SURFACE FEATURES

Venus is a largely smooth planet, covered by rolling planes that rise or dip by no more than 3 km (2 miles). Lowland volcanic plains, or planitia, cover 85 per cent of the surface. The remaining 15 per cent consists of highland areas, named terra or regio.

Danu Montes, a 5,000-m (16,400-ft) high mountain

Waterfall-like flows of solidified lava

LAKSHMI PLANUM

This is a high plateau rising about 4 km (2.5 miles), bounded by the mountain ranges Danu, Akna, Freyja, and Maxwell Montes. The eastern side has several lava flows.

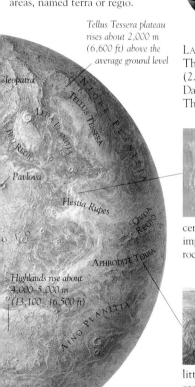

Tellus Tessera plateau rises about 2,000 m (6,600 ft) above the average ground level

Cleopatra

LEDA PLANITIA

TELLUS TESSERA

NIOBE PLANITIA

BELL REGIO

Pavlova

Hestia Rupes

OVDA REGIO

APHRODITE TERRA

Highlands rise about 4,000-5,000 m (13,100-16,500 ft)

AINO PLANITIA

MEAD CRATER

The largest impact crater on Venus, Mead crater has a diameter of 280 km (170 miles). Inside, the terrain is rough, with a hilly central region. Outside, material ejected on impact has been eroded by winds into narrow rock ridges separated by wind-eroded corridors.

APHRODITE TERRA

The most extensive highland region of Venus, Aphrodite Terra stretches for 6,000 km (3,700 miles). The western part shows little evidence of volcanic activity, but the eastern part is occupied by Atla Regio, a large volcanic rise with rifts and volcanic peaks.

MARS

NAMED AFTER THE ROMAN GOD OF WAR because of its dusty red appearance, Mars is also known as the Red Planet. Along with Mercury, Venus, and Earth, it is one of the four terrestrial – or Earth-like – planets of the inner Solar System. It is one and a half times more distant from the Sun than Earth is. In recent years, scientists have begun to study Mars in detail, and they may yet uncover fossils, or even show that primitive life exists.

The northern lowlands contain many fewer craters than the southern hemisphere. This indicates that the region has been smoothed off by volcanic lava flow and is younger, having been exposed to asteroidal bombardment for a lesser amount of time

The pale areas around the rims of impact craters are wind-blown dust deposits

Dark areas are thought to correspond to regions of fine-grained rock formed from solidified lava

SURFACE FEATURES
Much of the Red Planet's surface is a frozen, rock-strewn desert interrupted by dunes and craters. But Mars also has some of the most spectacular and diverse features of the Solar System. Its volcanoes and canyons dwarf those found on Earth. The planet's red colour comes from soil rich in iron oxide (rust).

MOONS AND THEIR ORBITS

The Martian moons – Phobos and Deimos – first observed in 1877, are small, lumpy satellites with a lower density than Mars, and both are heavily cratered. They may be asteroids captured by the Martian gravity. They orbit Mars in an easterly direction. Phobos is 26 km (16 miles) in diameter and Deimos is 16 km (10 miles) at its widest.

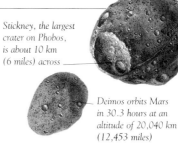

Stickney, the largest crater on Phobos, is about 10 km (6 miles) across

Deimos orbits Mars in 30.3 hours at an altitude of 20,040 km (12,453 miles)

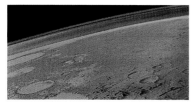

ATMOSPHERE

Mars has a thin atmosphere, mainly composed of carbon dioxide. At times, one-third of the atmosphere is frozen at the poles. Each day solar winds carry away a little more of the atmosphere.

MARS AT A GLANCE

Mars is a rocky planet with a small iron core. It is about half the size of Earth, with a similar rotation time. Its atmosphere is thin, and pressure at the surface is 1 per cent of Earth's.

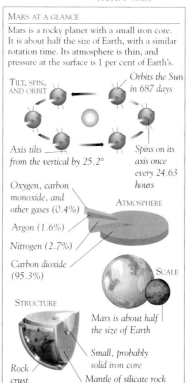

TILT, SPIN, AND ORBIT

Orbits the Sun in 687 days

Axis tilts from the vertical by 25.2°

Spins on its axis once every 24.63 hours

Oxygen, carbon monoxide, and other gases (0.4%)

ATMOSPHERE

Argon (1.6%)

Nitrogen (2.7%)

Carbon dioxide (95.3%)

SCALE

Mars is about half the size of Earth

STRUCTURE

Small, probably solid iron core

Rock crust

Mantle of silicate rock

VITAL STATISTICS	
Diameter	6,794 km (4,222 miles)
Avg. distance from Sun	228 million km (142 million miles)
Orbital speed around Sun	24.13 kps (15 mps)
Sunrise to sunrise	24.63 hours
Mass (Earth=1)	0.11
Volume (Earth=1)	0.15
Avg. density (water=1)	3.93
Surface gravity (Earth=1)	0.38
Avg. surface temperature	−63°C (−81.4°F)
Number of moons	2

SURFACE OF MARS

THE MARTIAN SURFACE IS cratered by meteorite impacts and has no vegetation and no water. It is probably made up of one plate and lacks movement. This explains the huge volcanoes and volcanic flood plains, which build up to great sizes because molten rock continues to pour from the same spot for millions of years.

This view shows the northern ice cap and the volcanoes and canyons near the equator

VASTITAS BOREALI
Milankovic
Arcadia Planitia
Alba Fossae
Tantalus Fossae
Mareotis Fossae
Uranius Thol
Geraunius Thöl
Tharsis
Olympus Mons
Ascraeus Mons
Amazonis Planitia
Tharsis Montes
Valles M
Tith
Ch
Pavonis Mons
Syria Planum
Arsia Mons
Sirenum Fossae

LAND STRUCTURES

Highlands dominate the planet's southern hemisphere, and vast lowland plains lie to the north. There are long cliffs between the two regions. In and around Tharsis Rise, just north of the equator, there are huge volcanoes, the Valles Marineris canyon system, and many ridges and fractures.

Tharsis Rise extends 8,000 km (5,000 miles)

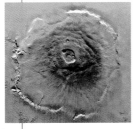

OLYMPUS MONS

The largest volcano in the Solar System, Olympus Mons is situated in Tharsis Rise. It is 24,000 m (78,740 ft) high and 600 km (370 miles) across. Its crater is 90 km (56 miles) across.

Valles Marineris is a vast canyon system near Tharsis Rise

Water-ice clouds sometimes develop, but dust and carbon dioxide clouds cause most of the planet's weather

Dark, low-reflective patches

Polar ice cap

SPOTTING SURFACE FEATURES
Some surface details on Mars can be distinguished with a relatively inexpensive 15-cm (6-in) telescope. The viewer can see polar ice caps and, occasionally, clouds. Some parts of the surface reflect less light and are seen as dark patches.

A Martian storm, in which wind speeds can rise to 300 kph (186 mph), whips up dust storms that sometimes envelop the whole planet

POLAR ICE CAP
The north and south poles on Mars are capped with carbon dioxide ice, dust, and water-ice. In the summer, the ice caps shrink as the frozen carbon dioxide evaporates, leaving behind mainly water-ice. This picture, taken by the Viking Orbiter, shows the southern ice cap in summer, when it retreats to 400 km (250 miles) across.

Floods of lava have created smooth plains in the otherwise cratered southern highlands

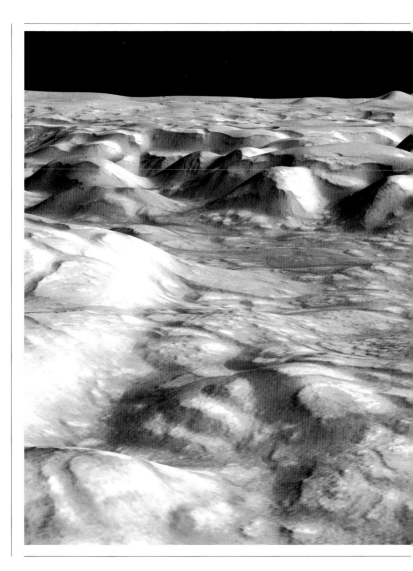

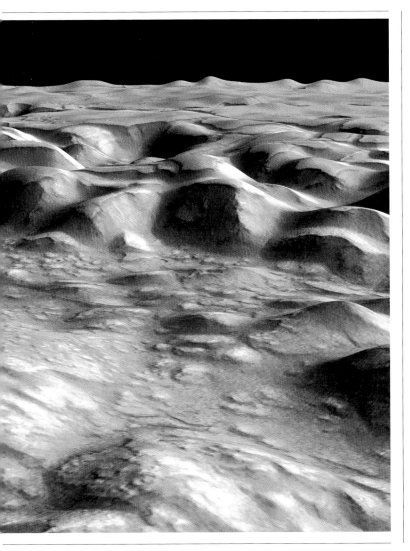

JUPITER

THE FIFTH PLANET FROM the Sun is very different from the terrestrial (Earth-like) planets. Jupiter, the largest planet in the Solar System, is a gas giant. It is all gas and liquid except for a very small rocky core. Its mass is 2.5 times that of all the other planets combined, and 1,300 Earths would fit into its volume.

RING SYSTEM
Jupiter's faint ring system was first seen in images sent to Earth by the Voyager 1 space probe in 1979. The rings are formed from dust knocked off its four inner moons by meteorites. There is a "cloudy" inner ring, a flattened central ring, and an outer ring, which is actually one ring embedded within another.

Substances including sulphur give Jupiter its multicoloured appearance

Jupiter is also called the banded planet due to its bands of different coloured clouds

If Jupiter had been 50 times more massive, its core would have been hot enough to fuse hydrogen and it would have become a star

JUPITER AT A GLANCE

Jupiter has no crust. Its atmosphere is a 1,000-km (600-mile) thick gaseous shell surrounding inner layers of liquid hydrogen, liquid metallic hydrogen, and a solid core.

TILT, SPIN, AND ORBIT

Orbits Sun in 11.87 years

Axis tilts 3.1° from vertical

Rotates once every 9.93 hours

ATMOSPHERE

Helium (10%), traces of methane and ammonia

Hydrogen (90%)

Diameter is 11 times that of Earth

STRUCTURE

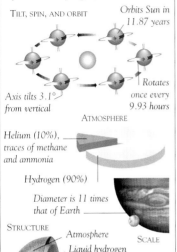

Atmosphere

SCALE

Liquid hydrogen and helium

Metallic hydrogen

Probably solid core

STRUCTURE

Jupiter is a giant ball of hydrogen and helium, compressed into a liquid inside, and probably into a solid at the core. Its core is likely to be 10–15 times more massive than Earth's. Pressure and temperature 20,000 km (12,400 miles) below the cloud tops are so intense that hydrogen turns into a liquid that behaves like a metal.

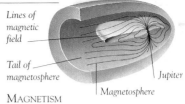

Lines of magnetic field

Tail of magnetosphere

Jupiter

Magnetosphere

MAGNETISM

Jupiter's magnetic field is 20,000 times stronger than Earth's. It surrounds the planet in a huge magnetic bubble, or magnetosphere. It was most likely created by electric currents in the fast-spinning metallic hydrogen within the planet.

OBSERVING JUPITER

Jupiter is the fourth brightest object in the night sky. It can easily be seen by the naked eye, and details such as its banding can be seen with a 15-cm (6-in) telescope.

VITAL STATISTICS	
Diameter (equator)	142,984 km (88,850 miles)
Diameter (poles)	133,708 km (83,086 miles)
Distance from Sun	778 million km (483 million miles)
Speed around Sun	13 kps (8 mps)
Sunrise to sunrise (at cloud tops)	9.84 hours
Mass (Earth = 1)	318
Volume (Earth = 1)	1,321
Density (water = 1)	1.33
Gravity at cloud tops (Earth = 1)	2.36
Cloud-top temperature	–110°C (–166°F)
Number of moons	60

JUPITER'S ATMOSPHERE

JUPITER'S ATMOSPHERE IS TURBULENT, with huge swirling storm systems and giant superbolts of lightning. Its rapid rotation helps whip up winds, measured by the Galileo probe at 650 kph (404 mph). Jupiter formed from the same ancient gas cloud as the Sun, so scientists study its deep atmosphere to understand the Solar System's earliest history.

CLOUD TOPS

Jupiter is a giant gas ball, compressed into a liquid and then into a solid, with increasing depth. It has no solid surface, so astronomers often refer to properties such as its temperature at a certain level in the atmosphere, where the pressure is the same as Earth's atmospheric pressure at sea level.

North Temperate Belt is bounded on its southern edge by red ovals

Violent winds give the North Equatorial Belt a twisted look

Damp air in GRS rises and is whipped into a spiral

GREAT RED SPOT

A storm system three times the size of Earth has raged in Jupiter's atmosphere for more than 300 years. Known as the Great Red Spot (GRS), it rotates anti-clockwise every six Earth days.

ZONES AND BELTS

Bright bands (zones) in the atmosphere are areas of rising gas, while dark bands (belts) are regions of falling gas. The tops of the belts are about 20 km (12 miles) lower than the tops of the zones.

Charged particles from the moon Io strike Jupiter just below its poles

North Polar Region

CLOUD PROFILE

At the edge of Jupiter's 1,000-km (621-mile) thick atmosphere are three layers of cloud that reach down to a depth of about 80 km (50 miles).

Water-ice appears about 30 km (19 miles) below the cloud tops

The hazy cloud tops are made of ammonia ice

About 20 km (12 miles) below the cloud tops are ammonium sulphide clouds

Increasing temperature and pressure lower in the atmosphere cause simple, colourless gases to react, forming complex coloured molecules

Equatorial Zone

South Equatorial Belt

Bands are windstreams travelling in opposite directions at more than 600 kph (373 mph)

One of the sites of impact

COMET IMPACT

In July 1994, 21 fragments of the comet Shoemaker-Levy-9 hit Jupiter at about 210,000 kph (130,500 mph), sending 4,000-km (2,500-mile) wide fireballs 2,000 km (1,200 miles) into the atmosphere.

South Polar Region

JUPITER'S MOONS

JUPITER AND ITS 60 known moons are like a mini Solar System. Some of the moons are rocky, some icy, and some may have had the conditions needed to foster primitive life. They may be asteroids or comets captured by Jupiter's gravity. The four largest moons were first investigated by the Italian astronomer Galileo in 1610. There may be many more moons yet undiscovered.

The volcanoes on Io can send up plumes of gas 250 km (155 miles) high

| JUPITER'S MOONS | | | | |
Name	Diameter in km (miles)	Distance to Jupiter in km (miles)	Orbit in days	Year of discovery
Metis	40 (25)	127,960 (79,514)	0.29	1979
Adrastea	20 (12)	128,980 (80,148)	0.30	1979
Amalthea	200 (124)	181,300 (112,660)	0.50	1892
Thebe	100 (62)	221,900 (137,889)	0.67	1979
Io	3,643 (2,264)	421,600 (261,982)	1.77	1610
Europa	3,130 (1,945)	670,900 (416,897)	3.55	1610
Ganymede	5,268 (3,274)	1,070,000 (664,898)	7.15	1610
Callisto	4,806 (2,986)	1,883,000 (1,170,096)	16.69	1610
Leda	10 (6)	11,094,000 (6,893,812)	239	1974
Himalia	170 (106)	11,480,000 (7,133,672)	251	1904
Lysithea	24 (15)	11,720,000 (7,282,808)	259	1938
Elara	80 (50)	11,737,000 (7,293,372)	260	1905
Ananke	20 (12)	21,200,000 (13,173,680)	631	1951
Carme	30 (19)	22,600,000 (14,043,640)	692	1938
Pasiphae	36 (22)	23,500,000 (14,602,900)	735	1908
Sinope	28 (17)	23,700,000 (14,727,180)	758	1914

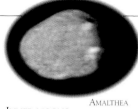

AMALTHEA

INNER MOONS

Jupiter's innermost moons, Metis and Adrastea, will eventually spiral into the planet. The largest of the non-Galilean moons is the potato-shaped Amalthea.

GANYMEDE

Jupiter's largest satellite is bigger than the planet Mercury. The space probe Galileo discovered that it had a magnetosphere of its own. It is thought to have a core of molten iron surrounded by a rocky mantle with an icy shell.

Ganymede's surface has faults similar to the San Andreas fault in California, USA, where grooves have slipped sideways

IO

Io has a thin atmosphere of sulphur dioxide. The gravities of Jupiter, Europa, and Ganymede bend Io's crust back and forth, causing heat to be generated. As a result, Io is the most volcanically active body in the Solar System.

CALLISTO

Callisto's surface is completely covered with craters, dating from the birth of Jupiter's system. Callisto consists of about 60 per cent rock and iron and 40 per cent ice and water. Scientists believe that it has a salty ocean beneath its icy crust.

EUROPA

Europa's surface is smooth ice. Data gathered by the Galileo probe suggests that a liquid ocean may exist beneath the ice and aquatic life may have arisen in the warmer parts of the ocean. A very thin atmosphere, composed of both molecular oxygen and hydrogen, has been detected.

SATURN

THE SECOND-LARGEST PLANET, Saturn is the easiest to recognize because of the bright rings around its equator. Like Jupiter, it is a large ball of gas and liquid topped by clouds. Nearly 10 times farther from the Sun than we are, it was the most distant planet known before the invention of the telescope.

Rings are made of particles and larger pieces of ice

BUTTERSCOTCH PLANET
Saturn, like Jupiter, has a surface of clouds, drawn out into bands by the planet's spin. The clouds are calmer and less colourful but also lower and colder at −140°C (−220°F) in the topmost layer. Above the clouds is a layer of haze, which gives Saturn its butterscotch colour and makes it look smoother than Jupiter.

Saturn's cloud patterns are hidden by a haze of ammonia crystals

White clouds
Dark orange clouds
Blue clouds

Saturn is nine times wider than Earth

ATMOSPHERE
Saturn has three main cloud layers and a haze above them. The clouds have the same gases as Jupiter's clouds, but the layers are farther apart because its gravity is weaker than Jupiter's.

Clouds form bright belts and dark zones

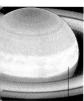

STORMS ON SATURN

Every 30 years or so, during summer in the northern hemisphere, storms break out on Saturn, producing large white spots near the equator.

A storm cloud broke out in 1990 and spread right around the planet

BULGING PLANET

Saturn spins every 10 hours 39 minutes at the equator, but takes nearly half an hour longer at the poles. Its low density and fast spin mean that Saturn's equator bulges more than any other planet.

If we could find an ocean large enough, Saturn would float

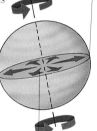

At the equator, Saturn spins every 10 hours 39 minutes

Saturn's core spins every 10 hours 14 minutes

PLANET DENSITY

Saturn is the least dense of the planets. Its average density is 70 per cent that of water (its centre is more dense than its surface), which means that it would float in water.

SATURN AT A GLANCE

Nine times the diameter of Earth, Saturn has a rocky centre, with outer layers of liquid and gas. Bright rings of icy particles circle the planet's equator.

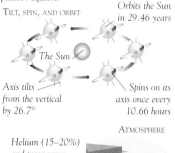

TILT, SPIN, AND ORBIT

Orbits the Sun in 29.46 years

The Sun

Axis tilts from the vertical by 26.7°

Spins on its axis once every 10.66 hours

ATMOSPHERE

Helium (15–20%) and trace gases

Hydrogen (80–85%)

Atmosphere

Liquid hydrogen and helium

Liquid metallic hydrogen and helium

SCALE

Core of rock and ice

STRUCTURE

Saturn is nine times wider than Earth

VITAL STATISTICS	
Avg. diameter	114,632 km (71,232 miles)
Avg. distance from the Sun	1.4 billion km (0.9 billion miles)
Orbital speed around the Sun	10 kph (6 mph)
Sunrise to sunrise (at cloud tops)	10.23 hours
Mass (Earth=1)	95
Volume (Earth=1)	763.59
Avg. density (water=1)	0.69
Cloud-top temperature	−140°C (−220°F)
Number of known moons	46

SATURN'S RINGS

Four planets have rings – Jupiter, Saturn, Uranus, and Neptune – but Saturn's are the brightest. They are visible from Earth even through small telescopes. They consist of chunks of ice and rock, ranging from specks of dust to large icebergs, and are probably the remains of a failed satellite production process.

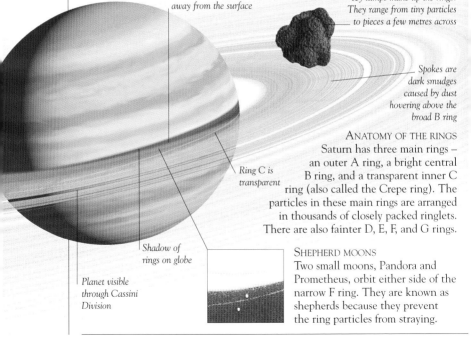

Ring D is 6,000 km (3,700 miles) away from the surface

Icy lumps make up the rings. They range from tiny particles to pieces a few metres across

Spokes are dark smudges caused by dust hovering above the broad B ring

ANATOMY OF THE RINGS
Saturn has three main rings – an outer A ring, a bright central B ring, and a transparent inner C ring (also called the Crepe ring). The particles in these main rings are arranged in thousands of closely packed ringlets. There are also fainter D, E, F, and G rings.

Ring C is transparent

Shadow of rings on globe

Planet visible through Cassini Division

SHEPHERD MOONS
Two small moons, Pandora and Prometheus, orbit either side of the narrow F ring. They are known as shepherds because they prevent the ring particles from straying.

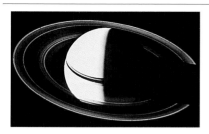

GLORIOUS RINGS

This view of Saturn cannot be seen from Earth. It was taken by Voyager 2 in 1981, looking back as it left the planet on its way to more distant Uranus and Neptune. The rings are lit up by sunlight shining through from behind. Saturn's globe shows through the inner part of the rings.

Each particle is a satellite of Saturn

Smaller particles are up to several centimetres in size

Dust from the moon Enceladus may be found in the E ring, which is the farthest from Saturn

INNER RINGS

D ring
C ring
B ring
Cassini Division
A ring
Encke Division
F ring

Ring B is the brightest and the broadest of the rings visible from Earth. The Cassini Division, 5,000 km (3,100 miles) wide, lies between the A and B rings. A narrower gap, the Encke Division, splits the A ring. The fainter G and E, farther from Saturn, are not shown here.

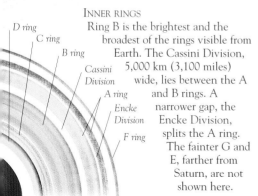

CASSINI CLOSE-UP

The Cassini orbiter reached Saturn in July 2004. It will complete 74 orbits of Saturn, 44 close fly-bys of its moon Titan, and numerous fly-bys of the other icy moons.

SATURN'S MOONS

SATURN HAS 49 KNOWN moons, most of which were discovered by the Cassini probe in 2004. Except for Titan, which is the largest, all of them have a low density and are thought to consist of a mixture of rock and frozen water. Some of them share the same orbits.

HUYGENS PROBE
This probe, built by the European Space Agency (ESA), was carried to Saturn as part of the Cassini mission. In January 2005, it parachuted to the surface of Titan to report on conditions beneath the moon's orange clouds.

Titan

Titan's density is increased by gravitational compression

DIONE
Dione is Saturn's fourth largest moon and has a diameter of 1,118 km (695 miles). The Cassini space probe sent images of a heavily cratered surface, and the bright, wispy streaks first noticed by Voyager 2 were found to be bright ice cliffs created by tectonic fractures.

TITAN

Titan is Saturn's largest moon, the second largest in the Solar System. It is even larger and more massive than the planet Pluto. Its dense, fully developed atmosphere contains complex hydrocarbons, including benzene, and the surface pressure is one and a half times that of Earth's. Its surface temperature is about −180°C (−292°F).

VITAL STATISTICS

Satellite	Diameter in km (miles)	Distance to Saturn in km (miles)	Orbit (days)	Year of discovery
Pan	20 (12)	133,583 (83,008)	0.57	1990
Atlas	34 (21)	137,640 (85,530)	0.60	1980
Prometheus	100 (62)	139,350 (86,592)	0.61	1980
Pandora	88 (55)	141,700 (88,052)	0.63	1980
Epimetheus	110 (68)	151,422 (94,094)	0.69	1966
Janus	191 (119)	151,472 (94,125)	0.69	1966
Mimas	398 (247)	185,520 (115,282)	0.94	1789
Enceladus	498 (309)	238,020 (147,906)	1.37	1789
Tethys	1,060 (659)	294,660 (183,102)	1.89	1684
Telesto	25 (16)	294,660 (183,102)	1.89	1980
Calypso	16 (10)	294,660 (183,102)	1.89	1980
Dione	1,120 (696)	377,400 (234,516)	2.74	1684
Helene	32 (20)	377,400 (234,516)	2.74	1980
Rhea	1,528 (950)	527,040 (327,503)	4.52	1672
Titan	5,150 (3,200)	1,221,850 (759,258)	15.95	1655
Hyperion	280 (174)	1,481,100 (920,356)	21.28	1848
Iapetus	1,436 (892)	3,561,300 (2,212,992)	79.33	1671
Phoebe	220 (137)	12,952,000 (8,048,373)	550.48	1898

Dione

Epimetheus

EPIMETHEUS AND JANUS

Janus and Epimetheus are two small moons with orbits only 50 km (31 miles) apart near the edge of Saturn's rings. Every four years, when the inner moon overtakes the outer, the two swap orbits, one moving farther away from Saturn and the other dropping closer, thus avoiding a collision. These two small moons may be halves of a former moon that broke apart.

Janus

ENCELADUS

Parts of this moon's icy surface are cratered, but other parts are so smooth they seem to have melted, wiping out any craters.

URANUS

URANUS, THE FIRST PLANET discovered through a telescope, was spotted in 1781. Its most remarkable feature is that it appears to lie on its side, so that first one pole and then the other points to the Sun as it moves along its orbit. It has 27 known moons and faint rings.

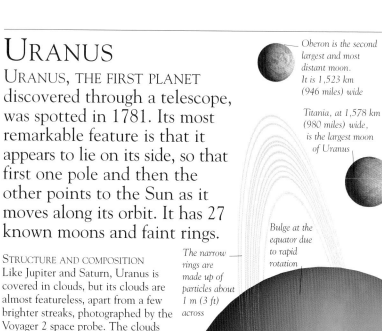

Oberon is the second largest and most distant moon. It is 1,523 km (946 miles) wide

Titania, at 1,578 km (980 miles) wide, is the largest moon of Uranus

Bulge at the equator due to rapid rotation

STRUCTURE AND COMPOSITION

Like Jupiter and Saturn, Uranus is covered in clouds, but its clouds are almost featureless, apart from a few brighter streaks, photographed by the Voyager 2 space probe. The clouds of Uranus consist of methane ice crystals and appear blue-green.

The narrow rings are made up of particles about 1 m (3 ft) across

RINGS

Uranus has 11 known rings, which circle the planet's equator. These dark rings, and the equator, appear to be almost upright, because Uranus is tilted on its side. Two tiny moons, Cordelia and Ophelia, orbit either side of the outermost ring (the Epsilon ring).

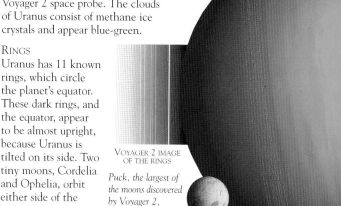

VOYAGER 2 IMAGE OF THE RINGS

Puck, the largest of the moons discovered by Voyager 2, is just 150 km (93 miles) across

VITAL STATISTICS	
Diameter	51,118 km (31,763 miles)
Avg. distance from Sun	2.871 billion km (1.8 billion miles)
Speed around Sun	6.82 kps (4.2 mps)
Sunrise to sunrise	17.24 hours
Mass (Earth=1)	14.5
Volume (Earth=1)	63.1
Avg. density (water=1)	1.32
Gravity at cloud tops (Earth=1)	0.89
Cloud-top temperature	−197°C (−323°F)
Number of known moons	27

ARIEL AND UMBRIEL

These two moons are similar in size – about 1,160 km (720 miles) – but look very different. Ariel is the brightest of the major moons, while Umbriel is the darkest. Ariel has valleys on its surface, caused by its crust cracking. Uranus's moons are named after characters from the writings of William Shakespeare and Alexander Pope.

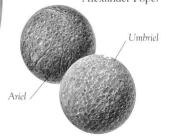

Umbriel

Ariel

MIRANDA

Miranda, the smallest of the five main moons with a diameter of 470 km (292 miles), has a jumbled surface with a bright tick mark and grooves. One theory for this is that Miranda broke apart and then came together again.

URANUS AT A GLANCE

The extreme tilt of Uranus gives it unusually long seasons. As the planet follows its 84-year orbit around the Sun, each pole has 42 years of continuous sunlight, followed by 42 years of darkness.

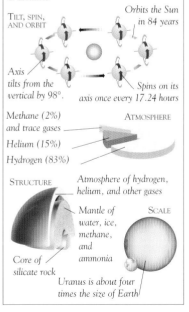

TILT, SPIN, AND ORBIT

Orbits the Sun in 84 years

Axis tilts from the vertical by 98°.

Spins on its axis once every 17.24 hours

ATMOSPHERE

Methane (2%) and trace gases

Helium (15%)

Hydrogen (83%)

STRUCTURE

Atmosphere of hydrogen, helium, and other gases

Mantle of water, ice, methane, and ammonia

Core of silicate rock

SCALE

Uranus is about four times the size of Earth

SOLAR SYSTEM

NEPTUNE

THE MOST DISTANT OF the four giant planets in the
Solar System, Neptune is 30 times farther from the
Sun than Earth. It was discovered by Johann Galle
in 1846, but its existence was predicted earlier,
from the fact that its gravity was pulling Uranus off
course. It has 13 known moons, and a faint set of
rings. It is similar to Uranus in many ways.

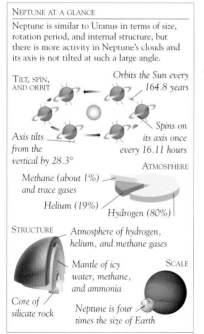

NEPTUNE AT A GLANCE

Neptune is similar to Uranus in terms of size,
rotation period, and internal structure, but
there is more activity in Neptune's clouds and
its axis is not tilted at such a large angle.

TILT, SPIN, AND ORBIT

Orbits the Sun every 164.8 years

Spins on its axis once every 16.11 hours

Axis tilts from the vertical by 28.3°

ATMOSPHERE

Methane (about 1%) and trace gases

Helium (19%)

Hydrogen (80%)

STRUCTURE

Atmosphere of hydrogen, helium, and methane gases

Mantle of icy water, methane, and ammonia

Core of silicate rock

SCALE

Neptune is four times the size of Earth

At least four rings surround the planet

ATMOSPHERE

Methane gas high up in Neptune's
atmosphere makes its clouds appear
blue. Most of the gas in its atmosphere
is helium and hydrogen. Its clouds are
stormier than Uranus's because the
inside of the planet is warmer, stirring
up the gas to produce white and dark
clouds that appear and disappear.

CLOUDS
Bright streaks of
cloud, similar to
cirrus clouds on
Earth but made
of methane, were
photographed by
Voyager 2.

The blue colouring is due to methane in the planet's atmosphere

GREAT DARK SPOT
A large oval cloud, about the size of Earth, was discovered by Voyager 2 in 1989, but had vanished when the Hubble Space Telescope looked at Neptune in 1994.

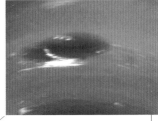

Triton is 2,706 km (1,681 miles) across

South polar ice cap on Triton

VITAL STATISTICS	
Diameter	49,532 km (30,779 miles)
Avg. distance from Sun	4.498 billion km (2.795 billion miles)
Orbital speed around Sun	5.48 kps (3.4 mps)
Sunrise to sunrise	16.11 hours
Mass (Earth=1)	17.2
Volume (Earth=1)	57.74
Avg. density (water=1)	1.64
Gravity at cloud tops (Earth=1)	1.13
Cloud-top temperature	−200°C (−328°F)
Number of known moons	13

TRITON
Neptune's largest moon, Triton, is bigger than the planet Pluto. Triton was once a minor planet that was captured by Neptune's gravity. It has the coldest surface in the Solar System, −235°C (−391°F), and is covered with frozen nitrogen and methane.

PLUTO

Pluto's surface is covered in frozen nitrogen and methane

PLUTO IS THE SMALLEST planet of all, and the most distant from the Sun. Clyde Tombaugh discovered it in 1930. Its orbit is the least circular of all the planets. It is so small and unusual that some wonder if it is a true planet at all, or simply the largest of a family of icy bodies in the Kuiper Belt.

The elliptical and angled Pluto orbit

Orbit of Uranus

Orbit of Neptune

Pluto's orbit is more tilted than other planets

ANATOMY OF PLUTO
Pluto is just 2,274 km (1,413 miles) in diameter, smaller than Earth's Moon. It has bright markings that may be made by patches of ice on its otherwise dark reddish surface. There may also be craters.

UNUSUAL ORBIT
Pluto's orbit takes it from 4.4 to 7.4 billion km (2.7 to 4.6 billion miles) from the Sun. On each 248-year orbit, Pluto comes nearer to the Sun than Neptune. This lasts for about 20 years and brings it closer to Uranus than Neptune for that 20-year period.

MOST DISTANT PLANET
From Pluto, the Sun is a thousand times fainter than from Earth, but still much brighter than the stars. Pluto's temperature is about –220°C (–364°F), but when it is closest to the Sun, its surface warms up and some of the ice turns to gas and produces a thin atmosphere.

ARTIST'S IMPRESSION OF SUN FROM SURFACE OF PLUTO

Sun

Pluto's surface is dotted with impact craters

Surface covered by water-ice and scarred with impact craters

Charon's density is less than Pluto's

PLUTO AT A GLANCE

Pluto is a tiny ball of ice and rock much smaller than Earth. The tilt of its axis is greater than that of Uranus. It is thought that a collision knocked off ice from Pluto to make Charon.

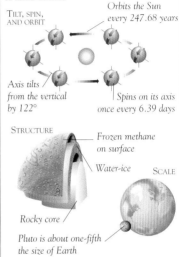

TILT, SPIN, AND ORBIT

Orbits the Sun every 247.68 years

Axis tilts from the vertical by 122°

Spins on its axis once every 6.39 days

STRUCTURE

Frozen methane on surface

Water-ice

SCALE

Rocky core

Pluto is about one-fifth the size of Earth

DOUBLE WORLD

Pluto's moon, Charon, has a diameter of 1,150 km (714 miles) – over half of Pluto's. The two bodies are so similar in size that they are often thought of as a double planet.

VITAL STATISTICS	
Diameter	2,274 km (1,413 miles)
Avg. distance from Sun	5.9 billion km (3.6 billion miles)
Orbital speed around Sun	4.75 kps (3 mps)
Sunrise to sunrise	6.39 days
Mass (Earth=1)	0.00251
Volume (Earth=1)	0.00658
Avg. density (water=1)	2.05
Surface gravity (Earth=1)	0.067
Surface temperature	–223°C (–387°F)
Number of moons	1

COMETS AND ASTEROIDS

MINOR MEMBERS

NEARLY ALL THE MASS of the Solar System is found in the Sun, planets, and their moons. The remaining tiny proportion of material is distributed among a huge number of small objects – the minor members. They are lumps of rock, or combinations of rock, dust, ice, and snow. The rocky bodies – asteroids – lie in the planetary region of the Solar System, while most of the snow and dust objects – comets – form the Oort Cloud on its outer edge.

OUTER SOLAR SYSTEM

The Oort Cloud marks the outer edge of the Solar System. The spherical cloud is made of orbiting comets that surround the planetary region of the Solar System out to 0.8 light years. Between the Cloud and the planets, a belt of comet-like objects orbit the Sun – the Kuiper Belt.

The Oort Cloud extends a fifth of the distance to the nearest star

KUIPER BELT

At least 70,000 objects, with diameters of more than 100 km (62 miles), are believed to exist in the Kuiper Belt, which stretches from the orbit of Neptune into the outer Solar System. More than 80 of these comet-like objects have been found, although none have been seen close up.

ARTIST'S IMPRESSION OF KUIPER BELT OBJECT

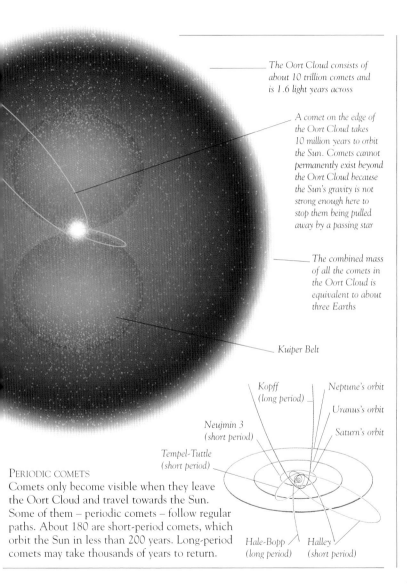

The Oort Cloud consists of about 10 trillion comets and is 1.6 light years across

A comet on the edge of the Oort Cloud takes 10 million years to orbit the Sun. Comets cannot permanently exist beyond the Oort Cloud because the Sun's gravity is not strong enough here to stop them being pulled away by a passing star

The combined mass of all the comets in the Oort Cloud is equivalent to about three Earths

Kuiper Belt

Kopff (long period)

Neptune's orbit

Uranus's orbit

Neujmin 3 (short period)

Saturn's orbit

Tempel-Tuttle (short period)

PERIODIC COMETS

Comets only become visible when they leave the Oort Cloud and travel towards the Sun. Some of them – periodic comets – follow regular paths. About 180 are short-period comets, which orbit the Sun in less than 200 years. Long-period comets may take thousands of years to return.

Hale-Bopp (long period)

Halley (short period)

COMETS

A COMET is a "dirty snowball" composed of snow and dust. Billions of comets orbit the Sun at a distance of about one light year. A few comets have orbits that take them closer to the Sun. As they near the Sun and are heated, the snow turns to gas and forms a long, bright tail.

COMET HALLEY
Most comets that approach the Sun are seen only once, but a few return periodically. Comet Halley travels out beyond Neptune and returns to the Sun about every 76 years.

ORBITING THE SUN
A periodic comet has an elliptical orbit that brings it close to the Sun. For most of its orbit, the comet has no tail. The tail only develops as the comet nears the Sun and its surface is heated. The tail gets longer and longer, and then disappears as the comet moves away from the Sun.

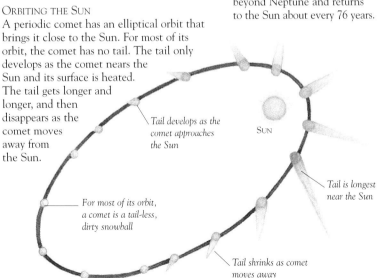

Tail develops as the comet approaches the Sun

SUN

Tail is longest near the Sun

For most of its orbit, a comet is a tail-less, dirty snowball

Tail shrinks as comet moves away

GLOWING GAS

The nucleus of a typical comet is about 1 km (0.62 miles) across. When heated by the Sun, jets of gas and dust erupt from the surface of the nucleus to form a glowing cloud called a coma, which surrounds the nucleus. The coma can be ten times larger than Earth. The comet's tail may be millions of kilometres (miles) long.

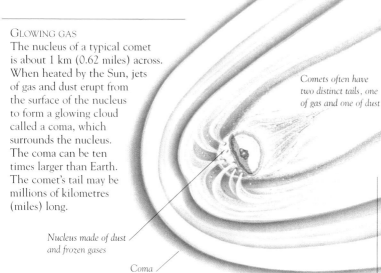

Comets often have two distinct tails, one of gas and one of dust

Nucleus made of dust and frozen gases

Coma

Dust reflects sunlight

HEART OF A COMET

This photograph of the nucleus of Comet Halley was taken by the Giotto probe from a distance of about 1,700 km (1,060 miles). Bright gas jets can be seen on the comet's sunlit surface. Instruments aboard Giotto showed that the main constituent of the nucleus was water-ice.

COMET FACT

• The planet Jupiter is so massive that its gravity can affect the orbit of comets. In 1992, Comet Shoemaker-Levy passed close to Jupiter and was broken into several fragments by gravitational forces. During July 1994, these fragments crashed into Jupiter, causing a series of huge explosions in Jupiter's atmosphere.

EXPLORING COMETS

BILLIONS OF COMETS exist at the edge of the Solar System, forming the large Oort Cloud. Comets are small, irregularly shaped lumps of snow and rocky dust orbiting the Sun. Occasionally, one leaves the Cloud and travels into the inner Solar System. About 1,000 comets have been seen in Earth's sky, and another 60 to 80 are added to the list yearly.

COMET HALE-BOPP
About three times a century, a spectacular comet can be seen from Earth. Comet Hale-Bopp was clearly visible by eye during much of 1997.

ANATOMY OF A COMET
A comet's nucleus is a loose collection of snow and rocky dust. When it crosses the inner Solar System, the Sun's heat turns the snow to gas and forms a glowing head – the coma. Solar wind and radiation also sweep away gas and dust from the nucleus into two tails – one gas, the other dust.

Coma can grow to 100,000 km (62,150 miles) across

Inside the coma, the nucleus of snow and dust (usually only a few kilometres (miles) in size) is too small to be seen

COMET WATCHING WITH TELESCOPES

SPOTTING COMETS
Some comets are bright enough to see with the naked eye; others can only be seen using binoculars or a telescope. Comets look like fuzzy patches of light, and travel at speed. Their nightly progress can be observed and charted.

Gas tail is characteristically blue and narrow

Gas and dust released from the nucleus are blown away from the Sun and form tails

A tail typically stretches for 100 million km (62 million miles)

Dust tail, which is yellowish-white, is the broader of the two tails

Camera

The Giotto space probe used 10 instruments to analyse and take images of Comet Halley

SPACE PROBES TO COMETS
Astronomers are keen to study cometary material, as it dates from the origin of the Solar System. In 2004, the space probe Stardust collected dust and gas samples from Comet Wild 2, after five years of travel.

COMETARY BREAK-UP
A comet loses its dust and gas after 10,000 orbits. It may also be pulled off its path by the gravity of the Sun or a planet, and then may die spectacularly like Shoemaker-Levy-9, which crashed into Jupiter.

METEORS

EVERY NIGHT, BRIGHT STREAKS of light can be seen in the sky. These meteors, or shooting stars, are caused by pieces of rock and dust – meteoroids – that are lost by comets or colliding asteroids. They burn up as they travel through Earth's atmosphere. Each year, Earth sweeps up 200,000 tonnes (196,850 tons) of meteoroids that appear as random meteors, or as part of a meteor shower.

LIFE OF A METEOR
Comets lose material when they travel close to the Sun, and pieces of asteroid break off when asteroids collide. When a meteoroid enters Earth's atmosphere, it is heated by friction and evaporates, producing a trail of light – a meteor – along its path.

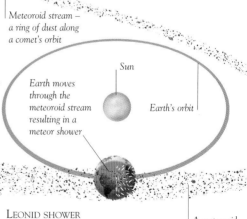

Meteoroid stream – a ring of dust along a comet's orbit

Sun

Earth moves through the meteoroid stream resulting in a meteor shower

Earth's orbit

LEONID SHOWER
This long-exposure photograph shows the stars as short trails of light. The longer trails in the foreground are meteors that fell as part of the Leonid meteor shower in November 1966.

A meteoroid stream can take tens to hundreds of years to form

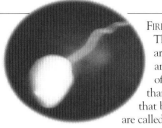

FIREBALLS AND BOLIDES
The brightest meteors are known as fireballs, and have a magnitude of at least −5, brighter than Venus. Fireballs that break up and explode are called bolides.

FROM METEOROID TO METEOR
The greater a meteoroid's speed, the faster and higher up it will burn out while travelling through Earth's atmosphere. The core of a massive one may survive the atmospheric friction and fall to the ground as a meteorite.

A meteoroid enters the atmosphere at 11–74 kps (7–46 mps)

Meteors occur between 120 and 80 km (75 and 50 miles) above Earth

Meteors with magnitudes of 5 or brighter are visible to the naked eye

Fireballs occur lower in the atmosphere

Meteoroid break-ups occur between 30 and 10 km (19 and 6 miles) above the ground

Very large rocks punch through the atmosphere producing explosion craters

SINGLE METEOR
About 10 single meteors – that are not part of a shower and fall on their own – can be seen per hour, each lasting less than a second.

METEOR SHOWERS		
Name	Date	Constellation
Quadrantids	1–6 Jan	Boötes
April Lyrids	19–24 April	Lyra
Eta Aquarids	1–8 May	Aquarius
Delta Aquarids	15 July–15 Aug	Aquarius
Perseids	25 July–18 Aug	Perseus
Orionids	16–27 Oct	Orion
Taurids	20 Oct–30 Nov	Taurus
Leonids	15–20 Nov	Leo
Geminids	7–15 Dec	Gemini

Aerogel used on aircraft

COLLECTING DUST
Aircraft with gel-coated panels cruise 20 km (12.4 miles) high. Fast-moving meteoroid particles slow down within the aerogel and become buried inside it to be studied later.

METEORITES

EACH YEAR ABOUT 3,000 space rocks, weighing more than 1 kg (2.2 lb) and too big to burn up in the atmosphere, land on Earth's surface. They are called meteorites. Most fall in the sea and are never discovered. Some meteorites are seen to fall on land and are quickly collected. Others are discovered centuries later. Many are never found.

METEORITE TYPES
Meteorites are usually made of materials commonly found on Earth, but in different proportions. They are believed to represent the solid material in the early Solar System. Meteorites are divided into three types: iron, stony, and stony-iron.

Canyon Diablo meteorite, which collided with Earth 50,000 years ago

ASTRONAUT JACK SCHMITT INVESTIGATES THE SITE OF A METEORITE IMPACT ON THE MOON

Meteorite consists of iron-nickel alloy

IRON METEORITE
The second most common meteorites consist mainly of iron-nickel metal with small amounts of other minerals. Most were originally molten and formed in the cores of asteroids.

METEORITE ORIGINS
Statistics indicate that 24,000 different meteorites have been discovered on Earth. Of these, 39 have come from the Moon, and 34 from Mars. Meteorites are also found on the Moon; most of these are believed to come from asteroids.

STONY METEORITE

Most meteorites found on Earth are lumps of stone. About 20,000 of them have been collected. They can be subdivided into chondrites that contain "drops" of solidified rock, and achondrites that do not.

Piece broken off reveals lighter original rock

Melted surface solidifies into a thin black crust

Dark fusion crust formed as meteorite fell through Earth's atmosphere

This 6-cm (2.3-in) stony-iron was found in Antarctica

Molten rock flows away from direction of fall

ANATOMY OF A METEORITE

Friction with the atmosphere causes the outer surface of a falling space rock to heat up and melt. Some meteorites have a uniform outer surface, while others have a leading and a shielded surface.

STONY-IRON METEORITE

These are the rarest meteorites. Some were formed from molten iron-nickel and olivine, and others by impact and welding of metal and stony fragments.

Pale-green olivine crystals set in iron-nickel

SEARCHING FOR METEORITES

Scientists find about 400 meteorites a year by searching undisturbed areas of Earth, including Antarctica, the Sahara Desert, and parts of Australia. It is easy to spot the dark meteorite falls against the snow and ice.

NOTABLE METEORITES		
Name and site	Tonnes (tons)	Year of find
Iron meteorites:		
Hoba West, Namibia	60 (59)	1920
Ahnighito, Greenland	30.4 (30)	1895
Bacuberito, Mexico	27 (26)	1871
Mbosi, Tanzania	26 (25)	1930
Stone meteorites:		
Jilin, China	1.77 (1.74)	1976
N. County, Kansas, USA	1 (0.98)	1948
Long Island, Kansas, USA	0.56 (0.55)	1891
Paragould, Arkansas, USA	0.4 (0.39)	1930
Bjurbole, Finland	0.3 (0.29)	1899
Recent finds:		
Algeria NwA 3171 (Mars)	0.5 kg (1.1 lb)	2004
Dhofar 1180 Oman (Moon)	0.115 kg (0.25 lb)	2005

ASTEROIDS

BILLIONS OF SPACE ROCKS – ASTEROIDS – orbit the Sun within the inner Solar System. They are sometimes called minor planets because they have their own orbits around the Sun. Most are in the Asteroid Belt, or Main Belt, which lies between the orbits of Mars and Jupiter. Asteroids range in size, shape, and colour. Only one, Vesta, is large and bright enough to be seen with the naked eye.

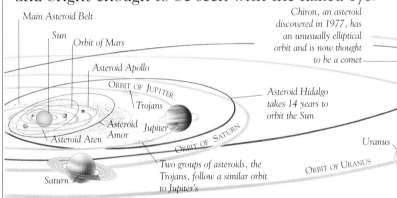

Main Asteroid Belt

Sun

Orbit of Mars

Asteroid Apollo

ORBIT OF JUPITER

Trojans

Asteroid Amor

Asteroid Jupiter

Asteroid Aten

ORBIT OF SATURN

Saturn

Two groups of asteroids, the Trojans, follow a similar orbit to Jupiter's

Chiron, an asteroid discovered in 1977, has an unusually elliptical orbit and is now thought to be a comet

Asteroid Hidalgo takes 14 years to orbit the Sun

Uranus

ORBIT OF URANUS

ASTEROID BELT
The Main Belt contains billions of asteroids, all moving independently around the Sun. It stretches from about 254 million km (158 million miles) to 598 million km (372 million miles) from the Sun.

NEAR-EARTH ASTEROIDS
Some asteroids follow orbits that bring them close to Earth's orbit. These are members of the Apollo, Amor, and Aten groups, with each group following a particular orbit.

Ceres contains about
one-third of the total
mass of all asteroids

Vesta is the third
largest asteroid

Psyche has an
irregular shape

185 km (115 miles) wide

SIZES OF ASTEROIDS

The first asteroid discovered – Ceres –
is also the biggest, with a diameter of
932 km (579 miles), and spherical in
shape. However, Ceres is not typical.
Most asteroids measure less
than 300 km (185 miles)
across, and are
irregular in shape.

ORBIT OF PLUTO

Pluto

OF NEPTUNE

Neptune

TYPES OF ASTEROIDS

There are three main types of asteroids –
those made of rock, those made of
metal, and those that are a mixture of
the two. Gaspra is a rock asteroid, the
first to be seen close up. It is about
19 km (12 miles) long, orbits the Sun
every 3.3 years, and was photographed
by the Galileo space probe in 1991.

COLLISIONS BETWEEN ASTEROIDS

The Main Belt has changed over time.
When the Solar System was forming,
over 600 rocky bodies larger than Ceres
inhabited the Belt. These protoplanets
collided and broke up, and a large
amount of material was lost. Remaining
asteroid pieces collided and formed the
present-day Main Belt. There are three
types of collisions that still occur today.

When the
impacting asteroid is
less than 1/50,000th of
the larger body, a
crater forms

When the impacting body is
1/50,000th of the body it hits, the
larger asteroid breaks up and forms
a ball of rubble

When an asteroid is hit by an object more
than 1/50,000th of its mass, it breaks
up and forms a family of asteroids

Stream of dust forms

IMPACTS

WHEN A METEORITE COLLIDES with Earth, it can form an impact crater on its surface. Craters up to 1,000 km (621 miles) wide exist in very large numbers on moons and planets throughout the Solar System. About 150 have been found on Earth, dating back to 4 billion years ago when the planet was young.

IMPACT ON MIMAS
The surface of Mimas, Saturn's moon, is full of impact craters. One of them, Herschel, covers an area that is a third of Mimas's diameter.

CRATERS ON EARTH
Impact craters are found on every continent on Earth, and are being formed all the time. They are most common in parts of Australia, Europe, and North America. This is not because more have fallen there, but because the surface of these areas has changed so little that craters have been preserved.

MANICOUAGAN CRATER
This huge crater, one of the largest in Canada, can even be seen by astronauts orbiting Earth. Two semicircular lakes form its outline.

METEOR CRATER
This 1.2-km (0.7-mile) wide crater in the Arizona Desert, USA, has been known since 1871. It was formed about 50,000 years ago when an iron meteorite about 30 m (98 ft) wide struck Earth.

HOW CRATERS ARE FORMED

All craters are formed in much the same way. An impacting meteorite blasts surface material from the point of impact and produces a crater. The size of the crater depends on the size of the original rock.

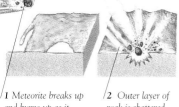

1 *Meteorite breaks up and burns up as it meets the friction of the atmosphere*

2 *Outer layer of rock is shattered as the meteorite impacts with Earth*

3 *Shock waves move through the surface as the meteorite burrows into Earth*

4 *An explosion, caused by heat and compression, blasts a crater in Earth's surface*

HENBURY CRATERS
A cluster of 11 craters in northern Australia includes the smallest craters on Earth. The craters are thought to have been formed by a meteorite that broke up in the atmosphere no more than 5,000 years ago. The smallest crater is 6 m (20 ft) across.

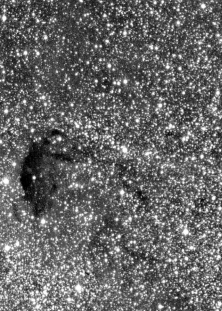

STARS

WHAT IS A STAR?

A STAR IS an enormous spinning
ball of hot and luminous gas.
Most stars contain two main
gases – hydrogen and helium.
These gases are held together
by gravity, and at the core they
are very densely packed. Within
the core, immense amounts of
energy are produced.

STAR CLUSTER
The cluster M13 in the
constellation of Hercules
contains hundreds of
thousands of stars
orbiting the
central point.

STRUCTURE
OF A STAR

*Temperature
and pressure
increase towards
the core*

*Energy is
released at the surface
as light and heat*

*Energy is produced
by nuclear reactions
in the core*

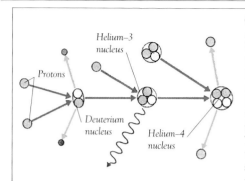

Core Fusion

A star produces energy by nuclear fusion. Within the core, hydrogen nuclei (protons) collide and fuse to form first deuterium (heavy hydrogen) and then two forms of helium. During fusion, energy is given off. This type of reaction, which is found in most stars, is called the proton-proton chain.

Varying Sizes

Stars differ greatly in the amount of gas they contain, and in their size. The largest stars are 1,000 times the diameter of the Sun, while white dwarf stars are just a fraction of its size – not much bigger than the planet Earth.

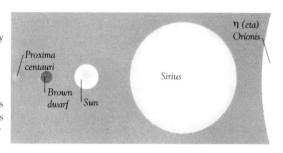

Prominent Stars: Data	(see p 153 for more on Greek lettering)	
Name	**Designation**	**Distance**
Vega	α Lyrae	26 light years
Pollux	β Geminorum	36 light years
Capella	α Aurigae	45 light years
Aldebaran	α Tauri	68 light years
Regulus	α Leonis	84 light years
Canopus	α Carinae	98 light years
Spica	α Virginis	260 light years
Betelgeuse	α Orionis	520 light years
Polaris	α Ursa Minoris	700 light years

Star Facts

• All the chemical elements that exist in the Universe and are heavier than hydrogen, helium, and lithium were made by nuclear reactions inside stars 14 billion years ago.

• The mass of the Sun (1 solar mass) is used as a standard for measuring other stars.

LIFE CYCLE OF A STAR

A STAR'S LIFE CYCLE depends on its mass. Stars of the same mass as the Sun shine steadily for about 10,000 million years. More massive stars convert their hydrogen more quickly, and have shorter lives. The Sun is halfway through its life. In about 5,000 million years, it will expand to become a red giant star, and then collapse and end its life as a white dwarf star.

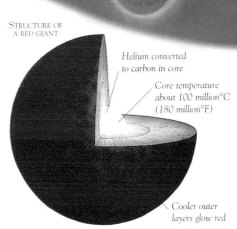

All stars converting hydrogen are called main sequence stars

STRUCTURE OF
A RED GIANT

Helium converted to carbon in core

Core temperature about 100 million°C (180 million°F)

Cooler outer layers glow red

RED GIANTS

When most of the hydrogen has been converted to helium, the star becomes a red giant – converting helium to carbon. The core heats up causing the surface to expand and cool. A red giant may expand to more than 100 times its former size.

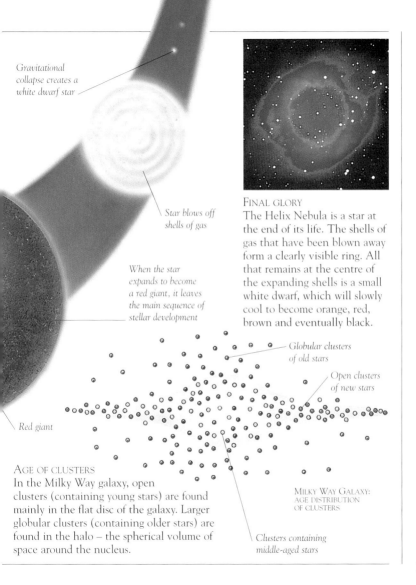

Gravitational collapse creates a white dwarf star

Star blows off shells of gas

When the star expands to become a red giant, it leaves the main sequence of stellar development

Red giant

FINAL GLORY

The Helix Nebula is a star at the end of its life. The shells of gas that have been blown away form a clearly visible ring. All that remains at the centre of the expanding shells is a small white dwarf, which will slowly cool to become orange, red, brown and eventually black.

Globular clusters of old stars

Open clusters of new stars

AGE OF CLUSTERS

In the Milky Way galaxy, open clusters (containing young stars) are found mainly in the flat disc of the galaxy. Larger globular clusters (containing older stars) are found in the halo – the spherical volume of space around the nucleus.

MILKY WAY GALAXY:
AGE DISTRIBUTION
OF CLUSTERS

Clusters containing middle-aged stars

WHERE STARS ARE BORN

STARS ARE BORN DEEP within dark molecular clouds of gas and dust. When newborn stars – protostars – light up, they heat this cloud with their radiation. The glowing cloud is called a nebula. The stars' gravitation causes the cloud to collapse, and eventually the whole cloud turns into stars.

Radiation from nearby stars disperses thinner parts of the cloud

Dense globules with protostars become detached as parts of the cloud disperse

HEART OF A NEBULA
The Orion Nebula, 1,500 light years away, is the star-forming region nearest to Earth. It is heated by UV radiation from a tiny cluster of young stars – the Trapezium. Many stars and protostars lie within it. The nebula is itself burning its way through a giant molecular cloud.

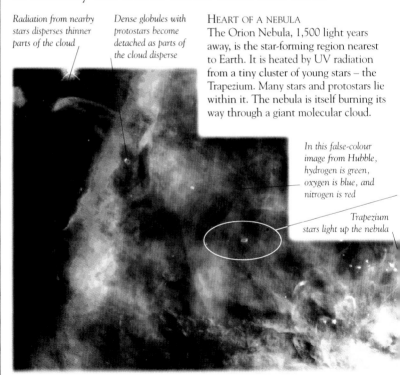

In this false-colour image from Hubble, hydrogen is green, oxygen is blue, and nitrogen is red

Trapezium stars light up the nebula

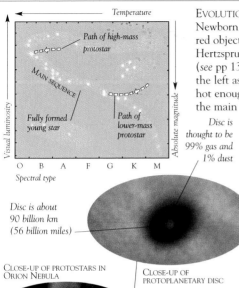

Temperature

Path of high-mass protostar

MAIN SEQUENCE

Fully formed young star

Path of lower-mass protostar

Visual luminosity

Absolute magnitude

O B A F G K M

Spectral type

EVOLUTION OF YOUNG STARS
Newborn stars appear as glowing red objects on the right of the Hertzsprung-Russell diagram (*see* pp 138–139). They move to the left as they shrink and become hot enough to burn hydrogen on the main sequence.

Disc is thought to be 99% gas and 1% dust

Disc is about 90 billion km (56 billion miles)

PROTOPLANETARY DISC
A new star is being formed inside this small, dark disc of dust and gas. The protostar, which is only a few hundred thousand years old, has about one-fifth the mass of the Sun. The surrounding disc contains about seven times the mass of Earth.

CLOSE-UP OF PROTOSTARS IN ORION NEBULA

CLOSE-UP OF PROTOPLANETARY DISC

PROTOSTAR GROUP
Astronomers have identified more than 150 protostars within the Orion Nebula. The five protostars in this group are surrounded by the swirling discs of dust and gas out of which they were formed. These discs are called protoplanetary discs, because planets may be forming inside them.

OBSERVING THE ORION NEBULA
Several star-forming regions are bright enough to be seen with binoculars, appearing as misty patches against the sky. The Orion Nebula is the brightest of all. It is visible to the naked eye between November and March, and is easy to find, as it forms part of Orion's Sword.

135

PROPERTIES OF STARS

THERE ARE DIFFERENT STAR types that vary in size, age, and mass. Some are white dwarfs the size of Earth and some are supergiants big enough to engulf the Solar System. Some stars are only a few million years old, while others are as ancient as the Universe itself. To sort out different star types, astronomers use a special graph called a Hertzsprung-Russell (H-R) diagram.

LUMINOSITY AND ABSOLUTE MAGNITUDE
The total energy that a star radiates in a second is called its luminosity. Compared with the Sun, we find stars with luminosities ranging from 100,000 times to 1/100,000 that of the Sun. Luminosity also refers to a star's absolute magnitude – the magnitude the star would appear if it were 10 parsecs (32.6 light years) from Earth.

Two white dwarfs are heavier than the Sun

Sun

About 10 low-mass, hydrogen-burning type M stars would balance the Sun

Sun

A red giant has about the same mass as the Sun

Sun

The apparent brightness of stars depends on the luminosity and distance from Earth

MASSES COMPARED
The masses of stars are not usually measured in kilograms (pounds) or tonnes (tons), but in relation to the mass of the Sun. The lightest stars are less than one-tenth of a solar mass, while the heaviest may be more than 50 solar masses. Like pebbles on a beach, there are uncountable small stars, but few big ones.

About 30 Suns are needed to balance a high-mass, hydrogen-burning type B star

Type B star

HERTZSPRUNG-RUSSELL DIAGRAM

Astronomers plot stars on a graph, with spectral type along the bottom and visual luminosity up the side. Absolute magnitude and temperature may also be given. Each star has a place on this H-R diagram, according to what point it has reached in its life. Most stars fall into a band called the main sequence, while others fall into groups called giants, supergiants, and white dwarfs.

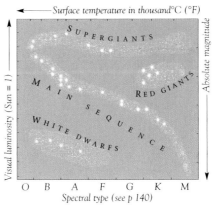

Surface temperature in thousand°C (°F)

Absolute magnitude

Visual luminosity (Sun = 1)

SUPERGIANTS
MAIN SEQUENCE
RED GIANTS
WHITE DWARFS

O B A F G K M
Spectral type (see p 140)

AVERAGE SIZES OF STARS

Stars vary greatly in size, from supergiants 300 times the size of the Sun to neutron stars, and black holes that are very much smaller than Earth.

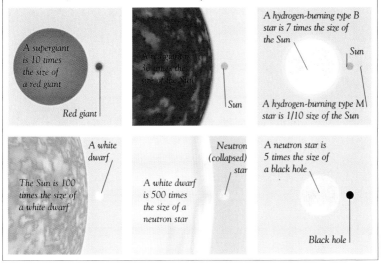

A supergiant is 10 times the size of a red giant

Red giant

A red giant is 30 times the size of the Sun

Sun

A hydrogen-burning type B star is 7 times the size of the Sun

Sun

A hydrogen-burning type M star is 1/10 size of the Sun

A white dwarf

The Sun is 100 times the size of a white dwarf

A white dwarf is 500 times the size of a neutron star

Neutron (collapsed) star

A neutron star is 5 times the size of a black hole

Black hole

STELLAR CLASSIFICATION

THE MASS OF A STAR affects its other properties – its colour, temperature, and luminosity. By studying their properties, astronomers have been able to devise a system that enables them to classify all stars.

TYPE O	◯	40,000–29,000°C (72,032–52,232°F)
TYPE B	◯	28,000–9,700°C (50,432–17,492°F)
TYPE A	◯	9,600–7,200°C (17,312– 12,992°F)
TYPE F	◯	7,100–5,800°C (12,812–10,472°F)
TYPE G	◯	5,700–4700°C (10,292–8,492°F)
TYPE K	●	4,600–3,300°C (8,312–5,972°F)
TYPE M	●	3,200–2,100°C (5,792–3,812°F)

SPECTRAL TYPES

A star's colour depends on its temperature – the hottest are blue-white and the coolest orange-red. Stars are classified into seven spectral types – O, B, A, F, G, K, and M – where O is the hottest and M the coolest. Each type has 10 subdivisions, 0 to 9, from hottest to coolest. The Sun is type G2.

Continuous spectrum

Distinctive absorption lines

Lines from several elements

PURE WHITE LIGHT

SODIUM LIGHT

SUNLIGHT

CHEMICAL LINES

Each star emits its own particular light. Splitting this light into a spectrum reveals the chemical elements that make up the star. The different elements are indicated by dark absorption lines that run across the spectrum. Sodium atoms absorb light only in the yellow part of the spectrum. Sunlight displays hundreds of absorption lines, but only the most prominent are shown here.

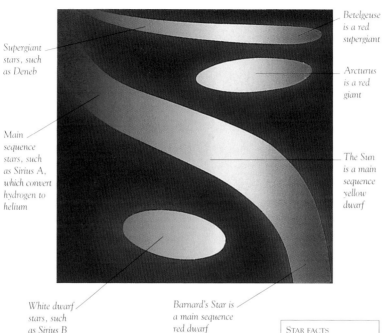

Betelgeuse
is a red
supergiant

Arcturus
is a red
giant

The Sun
is a main
sequence
yellow
dwarf

Supergiant
stars, such
as Deneb

Main
sequence
stars, such
as Sirius A,
which convert
hydrogen to
helium

White dwarf
stars, such
as Sirius B

Barnard's Star is
a main sequence
red dwarf

COLOUR-CODED DIAGRAM

The H-R diagram plots a star's temperature against its
luminosty (the amount of light it gives off). The
brightest stars are at the top, and the dimmest are
near the bottom. The hottest stars are to the left, and
the coolest to the right. Most stars spend some part of
their lives on the main sequence, which runs from top
left to bottom right across the diagram. Brown dwarfs
are the smallest stars on the main sequence, with
giant stars above them, and white dwarf stars below.

STAR FACTS

• Hot, bright young
stars are found in large
groups known as OB
associations.

• By the standards of
space, the Sun is very
small. Astronomers
refer to it as a type G
dwarf star.

• The smallest stars,
cooler and fainter than
red dwarfs, are known
as brown dwarfs.

BRIGHTNESS

HOW BRIGHTLY A STAR shines in the sky depends on its luminosity (the amount of light energy it produces), and on its distance from Earth. Astronomers use two different scales to measure a star's magnitude (brightness). Absolute magnitude compares stars from a standard distance. Apparent magnitude describes how bright a star appears as viewed from Earth.

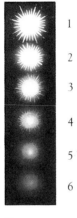

1
2
3
4
5
6

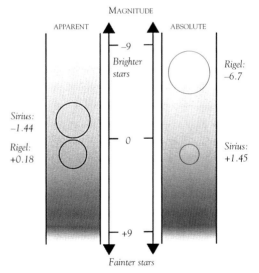

MAGNITUDE

APPARENT

ABSOLUTE

−9

Brighter
stars

Rigel:
−6.7

Sirius:
−1.44

Rigel:
+0.18

0

Sirius:
+1.45

+9

Fainter stars

OBSERVED BRIGHTNESS
On the scale of apparent magnitude for stars viewed with the naked eye, brighter stars have lower numerical values.

APPARENT VS ABSOLUTE
Sirius is the brightest star in our sky (apparent magnitude −1.46) and is brighter than Rigel (apparent magnitude +0.12). However, in reality, Rigel is by far the more luminous star with an absolute magnitude of −7.1, as opposed to Sirius which has an absolute magnitude of +1.4.

Calcium Hydrogen Hydrogen Sodium Hydrogen

SPECTRUM SHOWING DARK LINES OF 3 ELEMENTS

Wavelengths are longest at the red end

SPECTRAL ANALYSIS

Light consists of electromagnetic waves of varying lengths. In spectral analysis, a spectrograph splits the light from a star into its different wavelengths, producing a band of colours called a spectrum. Elements in the star's atmosphere absorb light at some wavelengths, producing dark absorption lines on the spectrum. Each element gives a different pattern of lines, so by studying the lines on the spectrum, astronomers can tell what a star is made of.

BRIGHTEST STARS			
Name	Apparent magnitude	Spectral type	Distance in ly
Sirius	−1.4 (double star)	A0, white dwarf	8.6
Canopus	−0.6	F0	310
Alpha Centauri	−0.3 (triple star)	G2, K1, M5	4.4
Arcturus	0.0	K2	36.8
Vega	0.0	A0	25.3
Capella	0.1 (double star)	G2, G6	42.2
Rigel	0.2	B8	800
Procyon	0.4 (double star)	F5, white dwarf	11.4
Achernar	0.5	B3	144
Betelgeuse	0.5 (variable star)	M2	400

BRIGHTNESS FACTS

• With both scales of magnitude, each whole number step (e.g., from +3 to +4) means that the star is 2½ times brighter or fainter.

• The Sun's apparent magnitude is −26.7.

• The brightest planet is Venus, with a maximum apparent magnitude of −4.7.

THE COLOUR OF HEAT

Anything that is hot will glow, whether it is a star or an iron bar – temperature determines its colour, not what it is made of. As the temperature increases, it will glow red, then yellow and then white-hot, and ultimately takes on a bluish tinge.

VARIABLE STARS

STARS DO NOT ALWAYS shine constantly. Some vary in brightness and are called variable stars. Pulsating, eclipsing, and rotating variables have a regular pattern or period to their variation. Others, such as eruptive and cataclysmic variables, are more unpredictable. A star may vary because it gives out changing amounts of light, or because its light is obscured by shifting dust clouds or a companion star.

CONSTELLATION OF CYGNUS, DURING AND AFTER THE 1975 NOVA

CATACLYSMIC VARIABLES
Stars that burst into brilliance due to sudden, violent changes are called cataclysmic variables. They include novas and supernovas. A nova occurs when a white dwarf in a binary star (two-star) system pulls hydrogen gas off its companion. The gas builds up until there is a nuclear explosion.

ETA CARINAE
As an eruptive variable, Eta Carinae's brightness has fluctuated dramatically, from magnitude –0.8 in the mid-19th century, to below magnitude 6. It puffed out an obscuring cloud of dust – the Homunculus Nebula. The shifting dust and unstable outer layers account for the variations in brightness.

Homunculus Nebula envelops star in dust

Eta Carinae is a luminous supergiant, 100 times the mass of the Sun

Today, most of Eta Carinae's energy is in the form of infrared radiation

PULSATING VARIABLES

Towards the end of their lives, stars often pulsate, varying in brightness, temperature, and size. Mira stars are red giants that pulsate over a period of up to 1,000 days. Cepheid variables are yellow supergiants that pulsate in cycles of 1–50 days.

ECLIPSING VARIABLES

Some pairs of stars are so close to each other, they look like a single star. If their orbits are angled edge-on to Earth, each star periodically passes in front of the other and eclipses it, so that the total light reaching Earth is reduced and the star appears to fade.

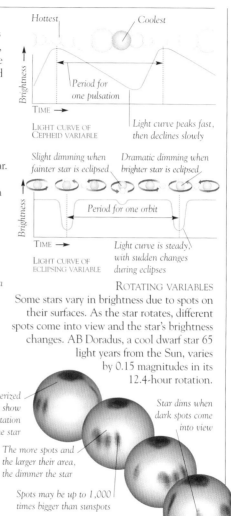

Hottest

Coolest

Brightness

Period for one pulsation

TIME →

LIGHT CURVE OF CEPHEID VARIABLE

Light curve peaks fast, then declines slowly

Slight dimming when fainter star is eclipsed

Dramatic dimming when brighter star is eclipsed

Brightness

Period for one orbit

TIME →

LIGHT CURVE OF ECLIPSING VARIABLE

Light curve is steady, with sudden changes during eclipses

ROTATING VARIABLES

Some stars vary in brightness due to spots on their surfaces. As the star rotates, different spots come into view and the star's brightness changes. AB Doradus, a cool dwarf star 65 light years from the Sun, varies by 0.15 magnitudes in its 12.4-hour rotation.

Keyhole Nebula is a dark cloud of gas and dust silhouetted against the bright Carina Nebula

Carina Nebula, about 300 light years across, includes the Keyhole Nebula

Computerized images show half a rotation of the star

Star dims when dark spots come into view

The more spots and the larger their area, the dimmer the star

The Keyhole Nebula is about 9,000 light years away

Spots may be up to 1,000 times bigger than sunspots

ETA CARINAE AND KEYHOLE NEBULA

STARSPOTS ON AB DORADUS

145

HOW FAR ARE THE STARS?

ASTRONOMERS HAD LITTLE IDEA of the true size of the Universe until 1838, when Friedrich Bessel used the parallax method to make the first successful measurement of the distance to a star. Our knowledge of stellar distances was revolutionized

ALPHA CENTAURI
4.4 LIGHT YEARS AWAY

further by the Hipparcos survey satellite, which used parallax to pinpoint many thousands of stars.

Statue of Liberty in New York, USA

Eiffel Tower in Paris, France

NEAREST STAR
The Sun's nearest neighbour is Proxima Centauri, one of the three stars that make up the Alpha Centauri system. It is 4.2 light years away. If the Sun were the size of a football, the distance to Proxima Centauri would be the same as the distance from Paris, France, to New York, USA.

LIGHT YEARS AND PARSECS
Distances are measured in light years and parsecs. One light year (ly) equals 9.5 trillion kilometres (5.9 trillion miles) – the distance light travels in a year. One parsec is 3.26 ly, the distance at which a star shows a parallax angle of one arc second.

NEAREST STARS AND STAR SYSTEMS

Name of star or star system	Magnitude	Spectral type	Distance in ly
Alpha Centauri A, B, C	0.1, 1.4, 11.0	G2, K1, M5	4.4
Barnard's Star	9.5	M5	5.9
Lalande 21185	7.5	M2	8.3
Sirius A, B	–1.4, 8.5	A0, white dwarf	8.6
Ross 154	10.4	M4	9.7
Epsilon Eridani	3.7	K2	10.5
HD 217987	7.4	M2	10.7
Ross 128	11.1	M4	10.9
61 Cygni A, B	5.2, 6.1	K5, K7	11.4
Procyon	0.4, 10.7	F5, white dwarf	11.4

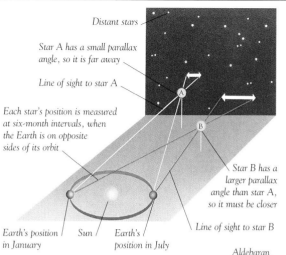

Distant stars

Star A has a small parallax angle, so it is far away

Line of sight to star A

Each star's position is measured at six-month intervals, when the Earth is on opposite sides of its orbit

Star B has a larger parallax angle than star A, so it must be closer

Line of sight to star B

Earth's position in January

Sun

Earth's position in July

PARALLAX METHOD

As Earth orbits the Sun, the stars that are nearer seem to move from side to side against the background of more distant stars. The angle through which a star moves over a period of six months is called its parallax, which is used to calculate the star's distance. The smaller the parallax, the farther the star.

INVERSE SQUARE LAW

A more distant star looks dimmer than a nearby one of a similar luminosity. This is because its light spreads out over a larger area before it reaches Earth, making it appear fainter. The inverse square law states that a star's apparent brightness decreases with the square of its distance.

The larger sphere has twice the radius of the smaller sphere

Light from the star spreads over this area of the smaller sphere

Star

When the light reaches the larger sphere it is spread over 4 times the area (the square of the distance, or 2 x 2).

Aldebaran

Hyades

ALDEBARAN AND HYADES

Stars that seem close in the sky are not necessarily neighbours in space. The red giant Aldebaran appears to be a member of the Hyades star cluster in Taurus. In fact, Aldebaran is much nearer to us than the cluster. It lies 65.1 light years from the Sun, compared with 150 light years for the Hyades cluster.

147

MEASURE OF THE STARS

AS IT TAKES SO LONG to travel any significant distance outside the Solar System, we have to study the stars from afar. Astronomers can tell a star's brightness, colour, and temperature by analysing its light. By splitting starlight into its constituent colours, they can find out what stars are made of and how fast they are moving. With accurate measurements of position, astronomers can predict where stars will wander through the sky, thousands of years from now.

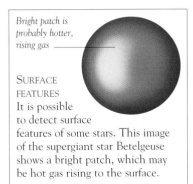

Coalsack Nebula

Hadar – magnitude 0.6, type B1

Alpha Centauri (triple star) – magnitude 0.1, 1.4, and 11.0, types G2, K1, and M5

PANORAMIC VIEW OF THE SOUTHERN MILKY WAY

STARRY SKY
The stars appear to our eyes as little more than twinkling points of light. Some are brighter than others, some are grouped in clusters, and here and there a red or blue star stands out. It may seem hard to believe, but everything we understand about the stars has been learned by studying starlight. We know that they are suns and that they are powered by nuclear energy. We know how they are born, how they live their lives, and how they die. Stars are classified according to their magnitude (luminosity) and colour.

Bright patch is probably hotter, rising gas

SURFACE FEATURES
It is possible to detect surface features of some stars. This image of the supergiant star Betelgeuse shows a bright patch, which may be hot gas rising to the surface.

Mimosa – magnitude
1.3, type B0

Lambda Centauri –
magnitude 3.6, type A7

Open Cluster
NGC 3532

Carina
Nebula

Theta Carinae
– magnitude 2.8,
type B0

Lambda Muscae –
magnitude 3.6, type A7

Mu Muscae –
magnitude 4.8, type K4

Alpha Muscae –
magnitude 2.7, type B2

The wavelengths of dark lines in a
star's spectrum are affected by the star's
motion – this is the Doppler effect.
Motion towards Earth shortens the
wavelengths, shifting the lines towards
the spectrum's blue end (blue shift).
Motion away from Earth stretches the
wavelengths and shifts the lines
towards the red end (red shift). By
measuring the changes in wavelength,
astronomers can calculate the star's
speed along the line of sight.

Wavelengths are squeezed
by star's motion

Star   Earth

BLUE SHIFT OF STAR   Dark lines shift
MOVING TOWARDS EARTH   towards blue end
of spectrum

Wavelengths are stretched
by star's motion

Star   Earth

RED SHIFT OF STAR MOVING   Dark lines shift
AWAY FROM EARTH   towards red end
of spectrum

PROPER MOTION

Stars are so far away, we are not
normally aware of their movement
through space. Over time, however, this
movement – called proper motion –
changes the shapes of constellations
dramatically. Astronomers can work
out a constellation's past and future
shape by accurately measuring the
positions of its stars over several years.

The Plough 100,000
years ago – the "shaft"
was much straighter

The Plough today –
the end of the shaft is
beginning to drop

The Plough in 100,000
years time

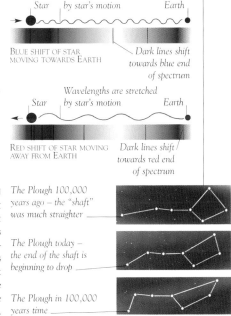

149

CONSTELLATIONS

SEEN FROM EARTH, the stars seem to form patterns in the sky. These patterns are known as constellations. The skies around Earth have been divided into 88 different constellations, each one of which is supposed to represent a mythological person, creature, or object.

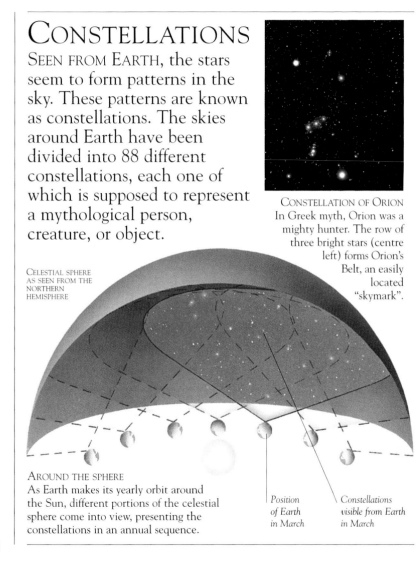

CONSTELLATION OF ORION
In Greek myth, Orion was a mighty hunter. The row of three bright stars (centre left) forms Orion's Belt, an easily located "skymark".

CELESTIAL SPHERE
AS SEEN FROM THE
NORTHERN
HEMISPHERE

AROUND THE SPHERE
As Earth makes its yearly orbit around the Sun, different portions of the celestial sphere come into view, presenting the constellations in an annual sequence.

Position
of Earth
in March

Constellations
visible from Earth
in March

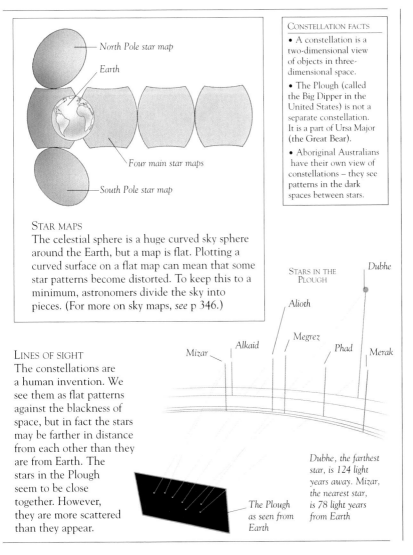

North Pole star map

Earth

Four main star maps

South Pole star map

STAR MAPS

The celestial sphere is a huge curved sky sphere around the Earth, but a map is flat. Plotting a curved surface on a flat map can mean that some star patterns become distorted. To keep this to a minimum, astronomers divide the sky into pieces. (For more on sky maps, see p 346.)

LINES OF SIGHT

The constellations are a human invention. We see them as flat patterns against the blackness of space, but in fact the stars may be farther in distance from each other than they are from Earth. The stars in the Plough seem to be close together. However, they are more scattered than they appear.

STARS IN THE PLOUGH

Dubhe

Alioth

Megrez

Mizar   Alkaid   Phad   Merak

The Plough as seen from Earth

Dubhe, the farthest star, is 124 light years away. Mizar, the nearest star, is 78 light years from Earth

STARS

151

CATALOGUING STARS

STARS ARE catalogued according to the constellation in which they appear. Within each constellation, the individual stars are identified by means of letters or numbers. Other objects are catalogued separately.

ORION NEBULA
In Earth's sky, the Orion Nebula appears as a faint, fuzzy patch of light just below Orion's Belt.

The constellation "figure" is drawn around the stars

ORION

POSSESSIVE NAMES
Constellations have been given Latin names, and when referring to particular stars, the possessive case of the Latin name is used – stars in the constellation of Orion are designated Orionis. (For more on Orion and other constellations *see* REFERENCE SECTION, p 312.)

MAPPING THE SKIES
The constellations fit together to map the sky. All the stars inside a constellation's boundaries belong to that constellation, even if they appear to be unconnected to the stars making up the main "title" figure.

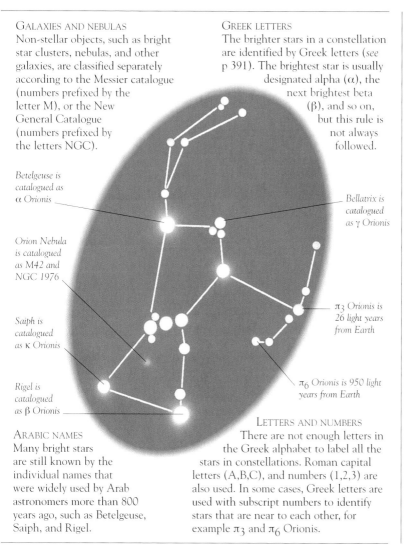

GALAXIES AND NEBULAS

Non-stellar objects, such as bright star clusters, nebulas, and other galaxies, are classified separately according to the Messier catalogue (numbers prefixed by the letter M), or the New General Catalogue (numbers prefixed by the letters NGC).

GREEK LETTERS

The brighter stars in a constellation are identified by Greek letters (see p 391). The brightest star is usually designated alpha (α), the next brightest beta (β), and so on, but this rule is not always followed.

Betelgeuse is catalogued as α Orionis

Bellatrix is catalogued as γ Orionis

Orion Nebula is catalogued as M42 and NGC 1976

Saiph is catalogued as κ Orionis

π_3 *Orionis is 26 light years from Earth*

Rigel is catalogued as β Orionis

π_6 *Orionis is 950 light years from Earth*

ARABIC NAMES

Many bright stars are still known by the individual names that were widely used by Arab astronomers more than 800 years ago, such as Betelgeuse, Saiph, and Rigel.

LETTERS AND NUMBERS

There are not enough letters in the Greek alphabet to label all the stars in constellations. Roman capital letters (A,B,C), and numbers (1,2,3) are also used. In some cases, Greek letters are used with subscript numbers to identify stars that are near to each other, for example π_3 and π_6 Orionis.

CLUSTERS AND DOUBLES

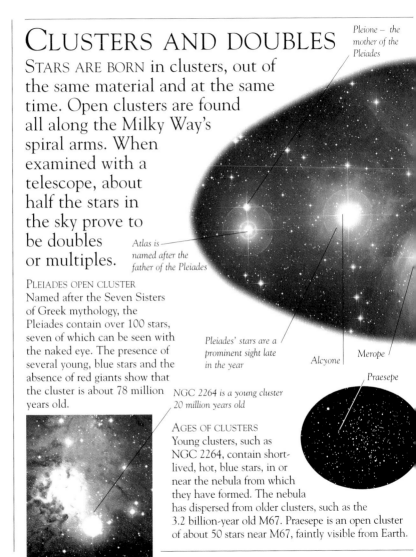

STARS ARE BORN in clusters, out of the same material and at the same time. Open clusters are found all along the Milky Way's spiral arms. When examined with a telescope, about half the stars in the sky prove to be doubles or multiples.

Pleione – the mother of the Pleiades

Atlas is named after the father of the Pleiades

Pleiades' stars are a prominent sight late in the year

Alcyone   Merope

Praesepe

PLEIADES OPEN CLUSTER

Named after the Seven Sisters of Greek mythology, the Pleiades contain over 100 stars, seven of which can be seen with the naked eye. The presence of several young, blue stars and the absence of red giants show that the cluster is about 78 million years old.

NGC 2264 is a young cluster 20 million years old

AGES OF CLUSTERS

Young clusters, such as NGC 2264, contain short-lived, hot, blue stars, in or near the nebula from which they have formed. The nebula has dispersed from older clusters, such as the 3.2 billion-year old M67. Praesepe is an open cluster of about 50 stars near M67, faintly visible from Earth.

Asterope

Maia

Taygeta

Celaeno

Electra

Streaks in the dust clouds are due to interstellar magnetic fields

Clouds of dust around the stars are lit up by starlight

In a double binary system, each star orbits its companion, and the two pairs orbit the same balance point

OPEN CLUSTERS				
Name	Constellation	Age in millions of years	Distance in light years	Number of bright stars
Double Cluster (h and chi Persei)	Perseus	3.2 + 5.6	7,400	150 + 200
Jewel Box	Crux	7.1	7,600	100
NGC 2264	Monoceros	20	2,400	40
Butterfly Cluster	Scorpius	51	2,000	80
M47	Puppis	78	1,600	30
Pleiades	Taurus	78	375	100
M41	Canis Major	190	2,300	100
Praesepe	Cancer	660	520	50
Hyades	Taurus	660	150	200
M67	Cancer	3,200	2,600	200

DOUBLE STARS

In optical pairs, two stars that are not really close look like a pair when they lie along the same line of sight. Two stars bound together by their gravities form a true binary system. They orbit a shared point of balance, determined by their masses. In visual binaries, two separate stars can be seen; in spectroscopic binaries, the stars are so close, they appear as one star; and in eclipsing binaries, the stars pass in front of each other, causing the brightness to change.

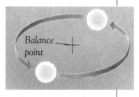

In a binary system with stars of equal mass, the balance point is in the middle

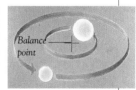

If one star in a binary system is more massive than the other, the balance point is closer to the heavier star

MULTIPLE STARS

Sometimes three or more stars are grouped in a multiple system. The stars are usually arranged in pairs, or as a pair orbited by a single star.

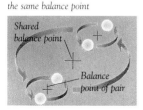

Shared balance point

Balance point of pair

A STARBURST REGION
A cluster of bright young stars in the Tarantula Nebula of our galactic neighbour, the Large Magellanic Cloud

GLOBULAR CLUSTERS

GLOBULAR CLUSTERS are tight-knit swarms of up to a million stars that inhabit the lonely outer reaches of the Milky Way. Our galaxy may contain as many as 200 of them. Their stars are among the oldest in the Milky Way and help in determining the age of the Universe.

WHAT GLOBULARS LOOK LIKE

Globular clusters are bigger and brighter than open clusters and contain about a thousand times more stars, bound tightly by gravity. While open clusters are irregular in shape, globulars are roughly spherical and measure about 100 light years in diameter.

IMPORTANT GLOBULAR CLUSTERS

Name	Constellation	Distance in light years	Diameter in light years
M4	Scorpius	7,000	50
M22	Sagittarius	10,000	70
47 Tucanae	Tucana	15,000	140
Omega Centauri	Centaurus	17,000	180
M13 (Great Cluster)	Hercules	23,000	110
M92	Hercules	25,000	85
M5	Serpens	25,000	130
M15	Pegasus	31,000	110
M3	Canes Venatici	32,000	150
M2	Aquarius	37,000	140

47 Tucanae is the second-brightest globular cluster

At the core, about 1,000 stars are packed into each cubic light year

Stars in the centre of a globular cluster are packed about a million times more densely than the stars near the Sun

47 TUCANAE
GLOBULAR CLUSTER

47 Tucanae measures 140 light years across and has a mass of about a million Suns

R136, in the Tarantula Nebula in the Large Magellanic Cloud, may become a globular cluster in 100 million years

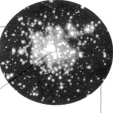

FORMATION OF GLOBULARS

Globulars are typically 10 billion years old. It was originally thought they were created as their parent galaxies first started to form, but the Hubble Space Telescope has found much younger globulars, especially in galaxies colliding with each other. Some of the globulars in the Milky Way may have been brought here by smaller galaxies that collided with it in the past. The giant open cluster, R136, is so big that it may be in the process of becoming a globular.

Globulars probably contain many white dwarfs, but they are too faint to see

Most globulars move in long, elliptical orbits around the galactic centre, journeying far out into the halo

A few globulars orbit close to the bulge

Most of the bright stars are giants

OMEGA CENTAURI

Three globular clusters can easily be seen with the naked eye – M13, 47 Tucanae, and Omega Centauri. Of these, Omega Centauri in the constellation of Centaurus is the brightest, being highly luminous and relatively close to Earth.

The Sun

Omega Centauri looks like a fuzzy, bright star

MAPPING GLOBULARS

While open clusters lie in the disc of the Milky Way, globulars occupy a spherical region around its central bulge. Distances to globulars are found using the RR Lyrae stars – a type of pulsating variable star – in the same cluster.

RED GIANTS

STARS DO NOT LIVE FOREVER. Their supply of hydrogen dwindles and the nuclear reactions in the core die down. The star balloons into a brilliant red giant, hundreds of times its former diameter, as its core begins to tap helium as a new energy source.

Helium-burning inner shell at 100 million°C (1.8 million°F)

INSIDE A RED GIANT STAR

Carbon and oxygen products of helium burning

Helium produced by main sequence hydrogen burning

INSIDE A RED GIANT

With its hydrogen almost gone, a red giant's core shrinks to a tenth of its size. Enormous temperatures and pressures are generated, and helium – produced in the core when the star was on the main sequence – is fused into carbon and oxygen, producing energy.

Hydrogen continues to burn in a shell on the outside of the core

Enlarged view of core region

High-mass stars use fuel rapidly

Instability strip, where stars pulsate and vary in brightness

Temperature

Supergiants

MAIN SEQUENCE

Red giants

Absolute magnitude

Visual luminosity

O   B   A   F   G   K   M
SPECTRAL TYPE

Smaller stars burn hydrogen slowly, becoming red giants over billions of years

EVOLUTION OF GIANT STARS

When a star runs out of hydrogen, it swells and cools, moving away from the main sequence, and entering the giant phase. Lower-mass stars brighten dramatically and become red giants. High-mass stars remain about the same brightness but become supergiants. A giant star's colour depends on its surface temperature – blue (hottest), white, yellow, or red.

Hotspots – where large currents of hot gas reach the surface

Sooty grains of dust condense in the outer atmosphere of the star, and can give rise to a new generation of stars

Convection cells carry heat from the core to the surface in rising and falling currents of hot gas. Some of the elements made in the core are carried to the surface as well

Sun is less than 10% the diameter of a typical red giant

GIANT STAR STATISTICS			
Name	Magnitude	Spectral type	Distance in light years
Canopus	–0.6	F0 White supergiant	310
Arcturus	0.0	K2 Orange giant	37
Capella	0.1	G6 & G2 Yellow giants	42
Rigel	0.2	B8 Blue supergiant	800
Betelgeuse	0.5	M2 Red supergiant	400
Hadar	0.6	B1 Blue giant	530
Aldebaran	0.9	K5 Red giant	65
Antares	1.1	M1 Red supergiant	500
Pollux	1.2	K0 Orange giant	129
Deneb	1.2	A2 White supergiant	1,500
Mimosa	1.2	B0 Blue giant	350
Gacrux	1.6	M4 Red giant	88

SIZES OF RED GIANTS

When a typical star first leaves the main sequence, it can swell up to 200 times the diameter of the Sun, eventually settling down to between 10 and 100 times the diameter of the Sun once helium starts burning. Supergiants may exceed 1,000 times the Sun's diameter.

Large red giant star at the centre of the Solar System could engulf Mercury, Venus, and Earth

Orbit of Earth

Orbit of Saturn

Orbit of Mars

Orbit of Jupiter

STELLAR WINDS

A giant star's outer atmosphere can drift into space across many light years as a stellar wind. The Toby Jug Nebula is a cloud of gas and dust which has been blown out by the giant star situated at its heart.

Sun

Typical supergiant at the centre of the Solar System could engulf the planets as far out as Mars and Jupiter

PLANETARY NEBULAS

WHEN A RED GIANT dies, it puffs off its outer
layers in a planetary nebula – an expanding
cloud that shines for tens of thousands
of years. Stars with a mass up to eight
times that of the Sun end their lives
this way. The nebula gradually
fades while the white dwarf at
its heart slowly cools.

*Outer lobes
of older gas*

CAT'S EYE NEBULA
When a red giant has no helium left to burn, its core
shrinks and the outer layers are blown away into space.
The departing gas is lit up by the intensely hot core,
creating a planetary nebula. These nebulas are quite
rare, with only about 1,500 known in the Milky Way.

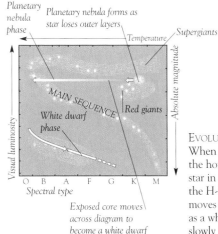

*Planetary
nebula
phase*

*Planetary nebula forms as
star loses outer layers*

Temperature

Supergiants

Absolute magnitude

MAIN SEQUENCE

*White dwarf
phase*

Red giants

Visual luminosity

O B A F G K M
Spectral type

*Exposed core moves
across diagram to
become a white dwarf*

CAT'S EYE
NEBULA

*Green and blue areas
are heavier elements, such
as oxygen and nitrogen*

*The glowing nebula is made of gas blown
off the star during its red giant phase. It is
kept hot by the white dwarf in the middle*

EVOLUTION OF WHITE DWARFS
When a red giant puffs off its outer layers,
the hot core is seen as the bright central
star in a planetary nebula, on the far left of
the H-R diagram. As the core cools, it
moves into the bottom left of the diagram
as a white dwarf. With no more fuel, it
slowly fades, moving down and to the right.

Inner shell of
recently ejected gas

Red areas are
hydrogen, which
makes up most
of the material in
the nebula

NOTABLE PLANETARY NEBULAS

Name	Constellation	Distance in light years	Size in light years
Helix	Aquarius	450	1.0
Dumbbell	Vulpecula	1,000	1.5
Owl	Ursa Major	1,300	1.0
Bug	Scorpius	2,000	0.5
Ring	Lyra	2,000	1.5
Saturn	Aquarius	3,000	1.5
Clown	Gemini	3,000	0.5
Blinking Planetary	Cygnus	3,500	2.5
Little Dumbbell	Perseus	3,500	5.0
Cat's Eye	Draco	3,500	6.0

White dwarf at the
centre – the burned-out
core of a red giant,
which astronomers
think may be part of
a double star system

Less massive
white dwarf
is larger

More massive white dwarf
is smaller and denser

CHANDRASEKHAR LIMIT

In 1930, Subrahmanyan
Chandrasekhar showed that the mass of a white
dwarf cannot exceed 1.4 times that of the Sun. If
it does, it will collapse into a neutron star or black
hole. The more massive the white dwarf, the
smaller it is as it is crushed under its own gravity.

DENSITY OF A WHITE DWARF

White dwarf material is
extremely dense – a million
times more so than water. This
means that the gravitational
field around a white dwarf is
intense. A person standing on
a white dwarf would weigh
about 600 tonnes (590 tons).
A matchbox of white dwarf
material would weigh as
much as an elephant.

163

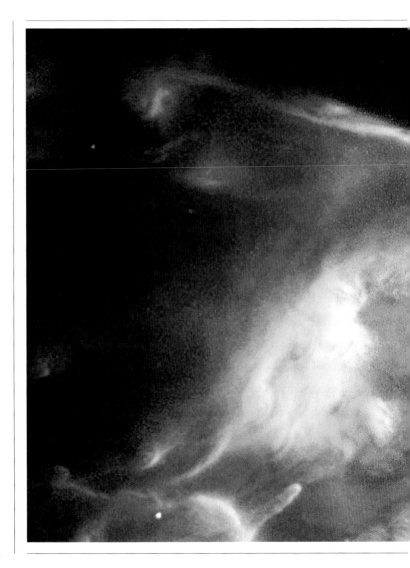

DYING STAR
A star's outer envelope is blasted into space as it transforms itself into a white dwarf.

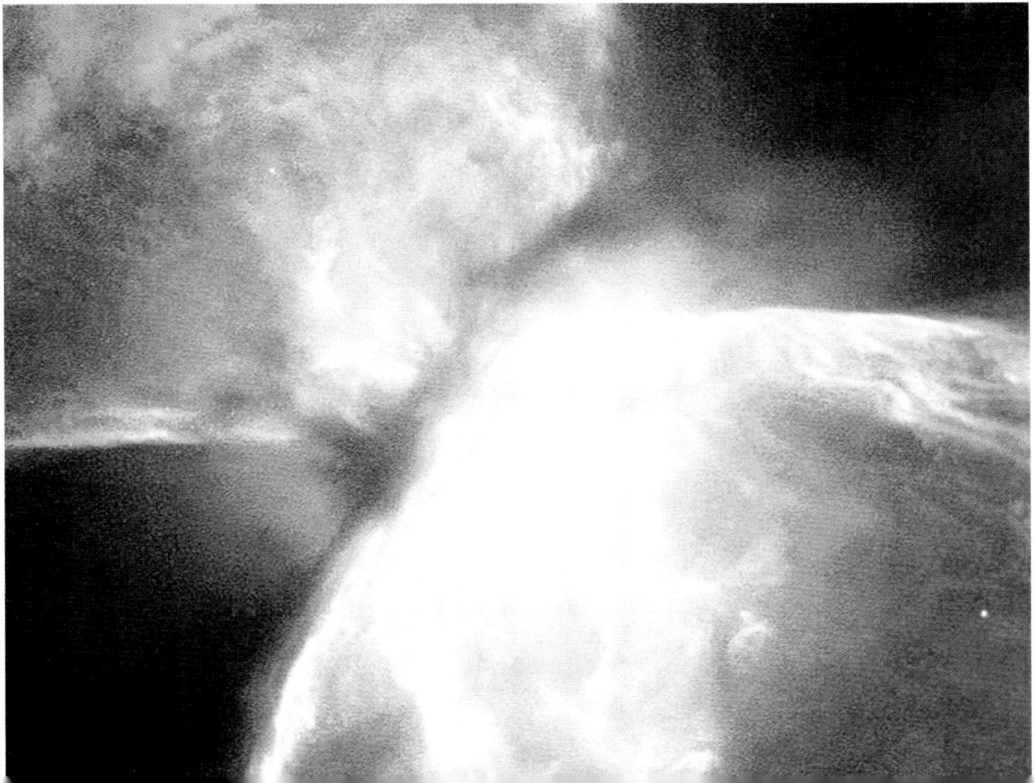

SUPERNOVAS

THE MOST MASSIVE STARS end their lives in a huge explosion called a supernova. Supernovas are rare – only two or three are expected in our galaxy each century, and most will be hidden by interstellar dust. The last one seen in the Milky Way was in 1604, but many more have been found in other galaxies.

Hydrogen makes up most of star

Supergiant may be more than a thousand times the Sun's size

Dense core

Other heavy elements

Iron at the centre

Core has onion-like layers of elements. Nuclear fusion cannot create elements heavier than iron, which builds up at the core

Core reaches 1.4 solar masses and collapses in on itself

Subatomic neutrinos burst from iron at centre

COLLAPSE OF A STAR
When a very massive star uses up most of its available hydrogen, it becomes a supergiant. Unlike red giants, supergiants are hot and can use carbon and oxygen – made by helium-burning – as fuel to make heavier elements, like iron.

Outer layers of core collapse inward

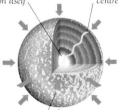

White dwarf

Large companion star

Material being pulled from companion star

OTHER KINDS OF SUPERNOVAS
An exploding supergiant is a Type II supernova. A Type Ia supernova is even more powerful – a small, dense white dwarf star pulls gas from a larger companion, and increases its mass until it cannot support itself and collapses in a huge explosion.

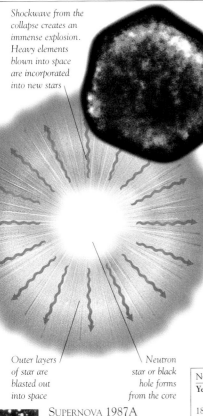

Shockwave from the collapse creates an immense explosion. Heavy elements blown into space are incorporated into new stars

Outer layers of star are blasted out into space

Neutron star or black hole forms from the core

SUPERNOVA REMNANTS

There are about 150 known supernova remnants. They are extremely hot, and continue to expand and glow for thousands of years. This X-ray image shows the remnants of a supernova that exploded in Cassiopeia in 1572. It was named after Tycho Brahe, who studied it.

STELLAR REMAINS

The Vela supernova remnant is the remains of a star that exploded about 11,000 years ago. The centre is about 1,500 light years from the Sun. Expanding material collided with gas lying in space, heating it and making it glow. The red light comes from hydrogen and the blue from oxygen.

SUPERNOVA 1987A

The brightest supernova in Earth's skies for four centuries appeared on 23 February 1987 in the Large Magellanic Cloud – a satellite galaxy of the Milky Way. At magnitude 2.8, it was faint compared with those in distant galaxies.

NOTABLE SUPERNOVAS			
Year	Constellation	Magnitude	Distance in light years
185	Centaurus	–8	9,800
386	Sagittarius	1.5	16,000
393	Scorpius	0	34,000
1006	Lupus	–9.5	3,500
1054	Taurus	–5	6,500
1181	Cassiopeia	0	8,800
1572	Cassiopeia	–4	7,500
1604	Ophiuchus	–3	12,500
1987	Dorado	2.8	160,000

NEUTRON STARS

A SUPERNOVA EXPLOSION MARKS the death of a star, but also its rebirth in another form. As the outer parts of the star are flung off, the core collapses into a tiny, superdense neutron star. Because of their intense magnetic and gravitational fields, neutron stars often become radio or X-ray pulsars. The Milky Way may be strewn with the dark remains of pulsars.

Ripples spread out from the pulsar as its radio beams heat the gas around them

Gas from the explosion, driven outward at 1,000 kps (621 mps)

CRAB NEBULA
The best-known neutron star is at the heart of the Crab Nebula – the remains of a star that exploded as a supernova almost 1,000 years ago. Although most of the star's material has been flung over a region of space 15 light years across, the collapsed core of the star remains. Spinning furiously 30 times a second, the neutron star is the powerhouse of the nebula, pouring out energy in the form of light, radio waves, and X-rays.

CRAB NEBULA

The central star is a pulsar, a spinning neutron star with a powerful magnetic field whose energy makes the nebula glow

Beams of radiation from the pulsar light up the surrounding gas

PULSARS

More than a thousand pulsars have been discovered since the first one was found in 1967. They are strongly magnetic, spinning neutron stars, which send out rhythmic bursts of radio waves. The fastest pulses 642 times a second, while the slowest pulses every 8.51 seconds. Most lie in the Milky Way Galaxy. Magnetars are a recently discovered type of neutron star with an even stronger magnetic field, which may be linked to gamma-ray bursts from space.

STRUCTURE OF A PULSAR

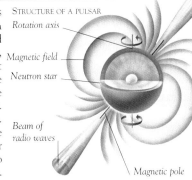

Rotation axis

Magnetic field

Neutron star

Beam of radio waves

Magnetic pole

HOW PULSARS WORK

A neutron star sends out a radio beam from each magnetic pole, which is detected each time it sweeps past Earth. It gradually radiates away its energy and slows down. Eventually it stops emitting radio waves and fades away.

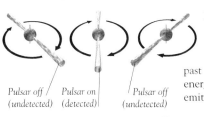

Pulsar off / (undetected)   Pulsar on (detected)   Pulsar off (undetected)

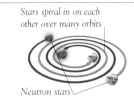

Stars spiral in on each other over many orbits

Neutron stars

BINARY PULSARS

Pulsars often orbit other stars, which may be a normal star, a white dwarf, or another neutron star. In binary pulsar systems with two neutron stars, the stars slowly spiral towards each other. They may eventually collide or may even form a black hole.

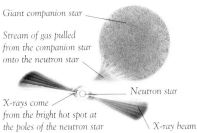

Giant companion star

Stream of gas pulled from the companion star onto the neutron star

Neutron star

X-rays come from the bright hot spot at the poles of the neutron star

X-ray beam

X-RAY BINARIES AND RECYCLED PULSARS

A neutron star in a binary system pulls gas from its normal companion star. An X-ray-emitting hot spot forms where the gas hits the surface. X-ray binaries may be recycled pulsars – old, dead pulsars, spun up again by gas from a companion red giant.

BLACK HOLES

THE MOST BIZARRE OBJECTS in the Universe, black holes emit no visible light at all. Most are the end state of brilliant giant stars that go supernova. The supercompressed core that remains has such strong gravity that even light cannot escape, so it is black. As nothing travels faster than light, whatever falls in is trapped forever – so it is also a hole in space.

Small, slow orbit of visible star shows it is close to the balance point of the system, and that it must be heavier than its invisible companion

Large, fast orbit of visible star shows it is farther from the balance point, and therefore lighter than its invisible companion

Streamer hits the gas orbiting the black hole, creating a bright hot spot

Neutron star

Balance point

Small orbit

Black hole

Companion star

WEIGHING A BLACK HOLE

When a star is in orbit with an invisible companion, the companion is weighed to see if it is a neutron star or black hole. The visible star's mass, visible by its colour and brightness, is used to work out its companion's mass. Anything more than three solar masses is a black hole.

Dust ring feeding the accretion disc

Region of black hole

NGC 4261

SUPERMASSIVE BLACK HOLES

Some black holes were made by the collapse of huge gas clouds in the past. Their great gravity attracts dust and gas from space, forming massive accretion discs. They can appear dark, as in NGC 4261, or shine, as in quasars.

DETECTION

Black holes can be detected only if they are close to another star. The hole's powerful gravity pulls gas off its companion at high speeds. The gas pours down the black hole, forming a spiral vortex around it called an accretion disc. Friction makes the swirling gas hot, and it emits X-rays.

Gas is torn away from the companion star by the black hole's powerful gravity

Blue giant companion star

Gas forms a long streamer, travelling faster as it gets closer to the black hole

Billion-tonne (ton) black hole only a million-billionth of a metre (foot) across

Gas is heated to 100 million°C (212 million°F) by the pull of the black hole's gravity

Particles generated by intense gravitational field cause a faint glow

Black hole shrinks and loses mass through Hawking radiation

X-rays emitted by superheated gas as it falls into the black hole

Black hole finally disappears, exploding with a blast of gamma rays

Gas forms a whirling vortex around the hole – the accretion disc

Disc is dark and cold around edges and heated and glowing nearer the centre

MINI BLACK HOLES

Tiny black holes may have been created by the immense forces of the Big Bang. These black holes are the size of atoms but have masses up to billions of tonnes (tons). Stephen Hawking showed that the intense gravity around a mini black hole can cause it to slowly release "Hawking radiation", which drains away its energy and mass. The mini black hole eventually disappears.

INSIDE A BLACK HOLE

BLACK HOLES ARE PRISONS of light, with gravity so strong that they distort space and time and allow nothing to escape. Mathematicians explore black holes using Einstein's Theory of General Relativity. This shows the strange effects of a black hole where its matter has collapsed into a singularity – a tiny point of infinite density.

Sun makes a shallow gravitational well

Steeper gravitational well

A white dwarf, being denser, dents space more noticeably

A neutron star – denser still than a white dwarf – creates a gravitational well with very steep sides

Very steep well

ANATOMY OF A BLACK HOLE
Einstein's Theory of General Relativity sees gravity as a distortion of space. He thought of space as being like a thin, rubber sheet, which dents, or forms a gravitational well, if heavy objects are placed on it. Black holes have this same basic structure. The singularity at the centre is also surrounded by an invisible boundary called the event horizon – nothing can escape from inside here.

A black hole makes such a steep dent that objects enter at the speed of light

Objects may go into orbit around the black hole

Objects approaching a black hole are deflected by steeply curved space

Objects that come too close to the black hole are inevitably drawn in

Once inside the event horizon, the object spirals down the steep sides of the gravitational well

Objects can escape the black hole if they give it a wide berth

Event horizon – once inside it, light cannot escape from the hole

A gravitational well is bottomless, trapping matter and light in the black hole forever

1 As the fall into the black hole begins, the astronaut looks normal and undistorted, with a watch keeping normal time

2 Closer to the black hole, the astronaut's body begins to stretch, turning redder as light struggles upwards against gravity. The watch slows down

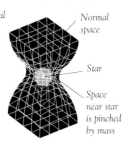

3 Long after the astronaut has been fatally spaghettified and fallen in, a frozen, reddened mirage remains on the event horizon. The watch has stopped

Spaghettification

Objects that fall into a black hole are "spaghettified". A hypothetical astronaut, falling in feet first, feels a stronger pull on their feet than their head as they are stretched apart. Closer to the hole, the astronaut is pulled into a tube. The effect is worse for smaller black holes, because they make steeper gravitational wells. As gravity distorts light and time around the black hole, the astronaut's colleagues see a variety of strange effects as they watch them fall in.

Distorting space and time

These diagrams offer a convenient simplification of space as two-dimensional, like a sheet. In reality, space has three dimensions. According to Einstein's Theory of General Relativity, a massive object like a star distorts space. Time – an extra, fourth dimension, not shown here – is also theoretically affected by strong gravitational fields. As something falls into a black hole, time slows down relative to the object's speed. Eventually, the object reaches the speed of light at the event horizon, and its time completely stops.

A three-dimensional view shows the star's gravity distorting space in a more complex way. Objects that would normally travel in straight lines are forced to follow the curved gridlines

Normal space

Star

Space near star is pinched by mass

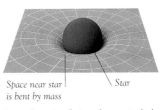

Space near star is bent by mass | Star

A two-dimensional view of a massive body making a dent in space-time. The distortion is shown on gridlines that would lie in a flat plane if the star were absent

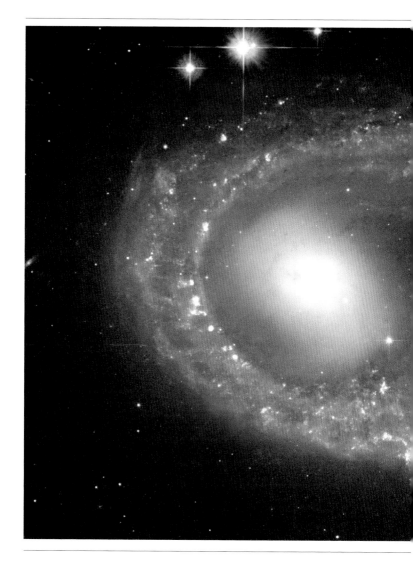

GALAXIES

WHAT IS A GALAXY?

A GALAXY IS AN enormous group of stars. A large galaxy may have billions of stars, a small galaxy only a few hundred thousand. Even the smallest galaxies are so big that it takes light thousands of years to cross them. Galaxies form from vast, spinning clouds of gas. They continue to spin, and come in a number of different shapes.

DISTANT STAR CITY
The Andromeda galaxy is so far away that its light takes 2,500,000 years to travel to Earth. We therefore see it as it was 2,500,000 years ago.

GALAXY TYPES

ELLIPTICAL
These range from ball-shaped to egg-shaped. They contain mainly old stars, and are the most common type.

SPIRAL
These are disc-shaped. Most material is in the spiral arms where new stars are formed. Old stars are in the nucleus.

BARRED-SPIRAL
These are like spiral galaxies, but the nucleus is elongated into a bar. The spiral arms extend from the ends of the bar.

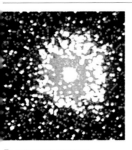

BRIGHTEST LIGHTS
This is an X-ray image of a quasi-stellar object – one of the brightest and remotest objects. The most distant are about 14,000 million light years away. Known as quasars, they are probably the cores of the first galaxies to be formed.

BRIGHT GALAXIES: DATA		
Galaxy	Distance (in light years)	Type
Andromeda (M31)	2,500,000	Sb
M33	2,800,000	Sc
NGC 300	4,200,000	Sc
NGC 55	5,800,000	Sc
NGC 253	8,000,000	Sc
M81	14,000,000	Sb
M82	14,000,000	peculiar
Centaurus A	16,000,000	E (peculiar)
M83	16,000,000	SBc
M101	17,000,000	Sc
M64	18,000,000	Sab
Whirlpool (M51)	27,000,000	Sbc
M104	44,000,000	Sa/b
M87	55,000,000	E0
M100	55,000,000	Sc
M77	62,000,000	Sb
NGC 1316 (Fornax A)	66,000,000	Sa (peculiar)

IRREGULAR
Some of these have a hint of spiral structure, while others do not fit any known pattern. They are the rarest type.

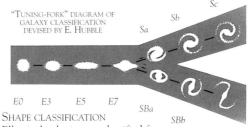

"TUNING-FORK" DIAGRAM OF GALAXY CLASSIFICATION DEVISED BY E. HUBBLE

Sc
Sb
Sa
E0 E3 E5 E7
SBa
SBb
SBc

SHAPE CLASSIFICATION
Elliptical galaxies are classified from E0 (spherical) to E7 (very flattened). Spirals (S) and barred spirals (SB) are graded from a to c, according to the compactness of the central nucleus and the tightness of the arms. Irregular galaxies (Irr) are not shown here, but can be divided into types I (completely irregular) and II (regular galaxies distorted by collisions or violent activity).

177

COLLIDING GALAXIES

GALAXIES SOMETIMES CRASH TOGETHER in a spectacular pile-up, spawning thousands of hot new stars. One sign of a past collision is a starburst – a sudden spurt of star formation in an ordinary-looking galaxy. Colliding galaxies often merge. Eventually, most galaxies will merge with their neighbours, and the Universe will consist of a smaller number of much bigger galaxies.

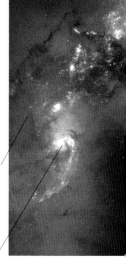

Turmoil in the central regions as giant gas clouds collide

Dust and gas from spiral arms have fallen into the cores of both galaxies, making the stars here appear redder

CARTWHEEL GALAXY

A spectacular example of a direct hit between two galaxies, the Cartwheel Galaxy was once a normal spiral, like the Milky Way. About 300 million years ago, a smaller galaxy sped through its centre. The impact triggered a burst of star formation, producing the ring of young blue stars.

Ring could easily contain the entire Milky Way

Central region, choked with dust, hides giant clusters of young stars

Gas and dust ripple out from a direct hit on the core, creating a starburst

INTERACTING GALAXIES

When galaxies collide, the interaction is complex. Each galaxy is held together only by gravity, and the collision causes a tug of war as each galaxy pulls at the other. In the centre, gas clouds crash together, while at the edge, stars are flung out into space. In galaxies NGC 4038 and 4039, the collision formed a pair of long, curved streamers of stars.

300 MILLION YEARS AGO	200 MILLION YEARS AGO	100 MILLION YEARS AGO	TODAY

GLANCING BLOW

About 300 million years ago, the Whirlpool Galaxy had a near miss with a smaller galaxy. The massive Whirlpool escaped relatively unhurt, but the collision wreaked havoc on the smaller galaxy as the Whirlpool's gravity tore out stars to form a temporary bridge between the two.

False-colour image combines optical and radio observations

Blue regions are gas

WHIRLPOOL GALAXY

The Whirlpool appears to have a smaller galaxy dangling from one spiral arm. This is the galaxy that struck the Whirlpool hundreds of millions of years ago, and now lies some distance beyond it. The gravity of the passing galaxy has stirred up the gas and stars in the Whirlpool.

Green regions are stars

Red reveals strong magnetism

Blue regions are star formation clusters triggered by the collision

The collision has created more than a thousand new star clusters

HUBBLE VIEW OF ANTENNAE

Hot stars, less than 10 million years old, show that the collision is recent

___ *In 5 billion years' time, our galaxy will smash into the Andromeda Galaxy, perhaps forming a system like the Antennae*

STARBURST GALAXY

A starburst galaxy is usually the aftermath of a galactic collision in which the galaxy's gas clouds are squeezed together, triggering a sudden burst of star formation. Spotted in 1983 by the Infrared Astronomical Satellite, starburst galaxies are filled with hot young stars – seen as red spots in this infrared view of M82 (a galaxy in Ursa Major).

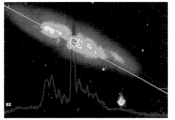

179

GALAXIES

ACTIVE GALAXIES

A SMALL NUMBER of galaxies are different from all the rest, pouring out huge amounts of energy from a tiny region, about the size of the Solar System, at their centres. These so-called active galaxies, which include quasars, radio galaxies, Seyfert galaxies, and blazars, have many features in common.

INSIDE AN ACTIVE GALAXY
An active radio galaxy spouts radio-emitting gas jets from either side. At its heart lies a glowing, doughnut-shaped ring of hot dust and gas. This contains a supermassive black hole, which generates enough power to outshine the Sun a trillion times.

RADIO LOBES
Jets of hot gas are blown out of the galaxy's centre across hundreds of thousands of light years. Where they encounter intergalactic gas clouds, they billow out into huge radio-emitting lobes.

Jet emits radio waves and sometimes visible light

CENTRAL DUST RING
The core of an active galaxy is an intense energy source, hidden by a ring of dust and gas. Dark on the outside, but glowing on the inner edge, the ring absorbs radiation from the core. Jets emerge from either side of its centre.

Huge gas lobe emits radio waves

Core

Inner edge of gas and dust cloud is hot and rotates rapidly

Central region

Galaxy

Energy from the core heats the inside of the ring, making it glow

Outer edge of gas and dust cloud is cool and slow-moving

Jet wavers as it runs into other particles

QUASARS

Quasars are among the most powerful objects in the Universe. They emit radio waves, X-rays, and infrared, as well as light, and they sometimes have visible jets. They are the brilliant cores of remote galaxies, with the dust ring tilted to reveal the radiation emitted by the accretion disc.

A faint galaxy surrounds the brilliant core of the quasar PKS 2349-01

SEYFERT GALAXIES

About one in ten big spiral galaxies has a very bright spot of light at its centre. This is a Seyfert galaxy, and may be a less powerful version of a quasar, with a smaller black hole in its core. Some astronomers think that all large spiral galaxies, including the Milky Way, may become Seyferts at some time.

Seyfert galaxy NGC 1566 lies 50 million light years away and is a dimmer version of a quasar

RADIO GALAXIES

Radio galaxies are among the largest objects in the sky. One or two jets shoot out for thousands of light years from the centre, feeding streams of gas into huge clouds on either side of the galaxy. The central dust ring is seen edge-on, so the core is hidden and the fainter jets become visible.

The blue lines show the intensity of the radio emissions from the radio galaxy 3C 368

BLAZARS

Blazars are active galaxies, similar to quasars. Their brightness varies rapidly by as much as 100 times, showing daily changes. It is believed that their jets are pointed directly towards us, so that we can look into the core, seeing light and other radiation from the accretion disc around the black hole.

This gamma-ray image shows high-energy radiation from the core of the blazar 3C 279

THE MILKY WAY

OUR HOME IN the Universe is the Milky Way – a spiral galaxy with a nucleus of old stars surrounded by a halo of even older stars. All the young stars are located in the spiral arms. The Sun is just one of 200 billion stars that inhabit our galaxy. The Milky Way is so large that it takes light 100,000 years to travel from edge to edge. All the stars that we see at night are in the Milky Way.

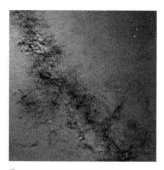

SAGITTARIUS STAR CLOUD
This infrared image shows young stars in Sagittarius, looking towards the Milky Way's centre. Infrared reveals millions of stars that are obscured by dust clouds when viewed in visible light.

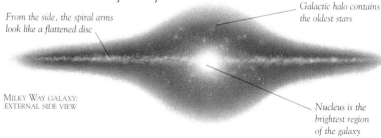

From the side, the spiral arms look like a flattened disc

Galactic halo contains the oldest stars

MILKY WAY GALAXY:
EXTERNAL SIDE VIEW

Nucleus is the brightest region of the galaxy

SIDE-ON SPIRAL
Viewed sideways-on, from a distance of about a million light years, the Milky Way galaxy would look like a giant lens – with flattened edges and a bright central nucleus. Around the nucleus is a roughly spherical halo that contains the oldest stars in the galaxy.

• The Milky Way is now thought to be a barred spiral galaxy.

• Our galaxy rotates. The Sun takes about 220 million years to make one revolution – a period sometimes known as a "cosmic year". Stars in other parts of the galaxy travel at different rates.

THE MILKY WAY AS SEEN FROM EARTH

ABOVE THE SPIRAL
From above, or below, the spiral arms of the Milky Way galaxy would be clearly visible. These contain most of the galaxy's gas and dust, and this is where star-forming regions are found.

Galactic nucleus

Crux-Centaurus Arm

Location of the Solar System

Orion Arm (Local Arm)

Sagittarius Arm

MILKY WAY GALAXY: EXTERNAL OVERHEAD VIEW

185

STRUCTURE OF THE MILKY WAY

THE MILKY WAY STARTED LIFE billions of years ago as a vast, round, gas cloud that collapsed under its own gravity and was flattened by rotation. It contains 200 billion stars, and vast clouds of dust and gas – the material for future stars. In places, the clouds are pierced by glowing nebulas in which stars have just formed.

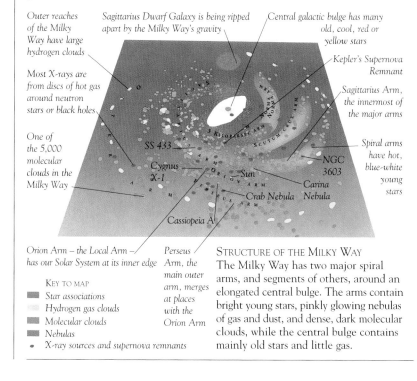

Outer reaches of the Milky Way have large hydrogen clouds

Sagittarius Dwarf Galaxy is being ripped apart by the Milky Way's gravity

Central galactic bulge has many old, cool, red or yellow stars

Most X-rays are from discs of hot gas around neutron stars or black holes

Kepler's Supernova Remnant

Sagittarius Arm, the innermost of the major arms

One of the 5,000 molecular clouds in the Milky Way

Spiral arms have hot, blue-white young stars

SS 433

Cygnus X-1

Sun

NGC 3603

Carina Nebula

Crab Nebula

Cassiopeia A

Orion Arm – the Local Arm – has our Solar System at its inner edge

Perseus Arm, the main outer arm, merges at places with the Orion Arm

KEY TO MAP

- Star associations
- Hydrogen gas clouds
- Molecular clouds
- Nebulas
- X-ray sources and supernova remnants

STRUCTURE OF THE MILKY WAY
The Milky Way has two major spiral arms, and segments of others, around an elongated central bulge. The arms contain bright young stars, pinkly glowing nebulas of gas and dust, and dense, dark molecular clouds, while the central bulge contains mainly old stars and little gas.

Mapping the Galaxy

Astronomers map the galaxy using radio telescopes, which can penetrate the dust clouds that get in the way of optical telescopes. The key to mapping is to find the rotational speed of an object, which is done by measuring small changes in the length of the radio waves given out by the object as it moves. Astronomers know how fast the different parts of the galaxy spin, so they use the object's rotational speed to calculate its distance from the Sun.

This tiny radio telescope, only 1.2 m (4 ft) across, mapped gas clouds in our galaxy from the top of a building in the heart of New York City, USA

Observing the Milky Way

The Milky Way appears especially bright from June to September, when Earth's night-time side is turned towards the denser regions of the galactic centre. Because the galaxy is relatively thin, and because we live inside it, the stars of the Milky Way appear as a band across the night sky. The dark rifts against this band are huge dust clouds that obscure the stars behind them.

Milky Way Data	
Type of galaxy	Spiral (between Sb and SBc)
Luminosity	14 billion solar luminosities
Total mass (including dark matter)	1,000 billion solar masses
Mass in stars	200 billion solar masses
Mass in gas	20 billion solar masses
Mass in dust	200 million solar masses
Diameter	100,000 light years
Thickness of disc	2,000 light years
Thickness of central bulge	6,000 light years
Distance of Sun from centre	25,000 light years
Time for Sun to orbit centre	220 million years
Speed of Sun in orbit	240 kps (149 mps)
Age of oldest star clusters	12 billion years
Number of globular clusters	140 known; total 200 (estimated)

INTERSTELLAR MEDIUM

SPACE IS NOT ENTIRELY empty. Tiny amounts of gas and dust between the stars add up to 10 per cent of a galaxy's mass. This interstellar medium is always churning and evolving, giving birth to stars and absorbing their material when they die.

GALACTIC COMPOSITION
Most of a galaxy's visible mass is in the form of stars. Just 10 per cent is gas and dust – molecular clouds and the warm intercloud medium.

Warm intercloud medium contains hydrogen gas, which glows pink when radiation is absorbed from nearby sources

Invisible cosmic rays are high-energy protons from supernovas

Alnitak is a star in Orion's Belt

HORSEHEAD
NEBULA IN ORION

BETWEEN THE STARS
The interstellar medium is not uniform. Most of it is a "warm" intercloud medium, at about 8,000°C (14,432°F). Within this are bubbles of thin gas, exceeding 1 million°C (1.8 million°F), made by supernovas or young stars. There are also cold clouds of hydrogen atoms. Finally, there are very dark, dense molecular clouds of gas and dust where stars are born.

Dust clouds look blue as dust particles scatter short wavelength light

Horsehead Nebula is 4 light years across and part of a molecular cloud

EFFECTS OF DUST

Cosmic dust particles spin around and impede the passage of light through space. This has a very dramatic effect on how we see the stars. For example, the two nebulas NGC 3603 and NGC 3576 look rather like twins when viewed from Earth, but NGC 3603 is, in fact, by far the most brilliant of the two. However, it appears comparatively faint to us because its brilliant light is dimmed and reddened by dust lying in front of it.

NGC 3576 forms part of the Carina complex of star formation

NGC 3603 is the most massive nebula in the galaxy visible to optical telescopes

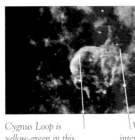

Cygnus Loop is yellow-green in this infrared image

Warm intercloud medium

HOT GAS BUBBLES

The hottest but least dense parts of the interstellar medium are gas bubbles such as the Cygnus Loop, which was created by a supernova more than 20,000 years ago. It is still being heated by the shock waves from the explosion.

Magnetic fields align dust particles and make the interstellar medium behind the Horsehead appear striped

Molecular clouds are thick with dust, which blocks out light from newborn stars

MOLECULAR CLOUDS

With the naked eye, a molecular cloud can be seen in the Cygnus region of the Milky Way. It is the starless gash down the centre – the Cygnus Rift – where a giant molecular cloud blocks out the light from the stars behind.

OUR LOCAL NEIGHBOURHOOD

THE PART OF THE MILKY WAY around the Sun is home to many sensational sights, such as the spectacular star-forming complex in Orion. Our neighbourhood covers 5,000 light years around the Sun. It includes the stars making up all the familiar constellations, such as Taurus, but is mostly filled with the spiral Orion Arm.

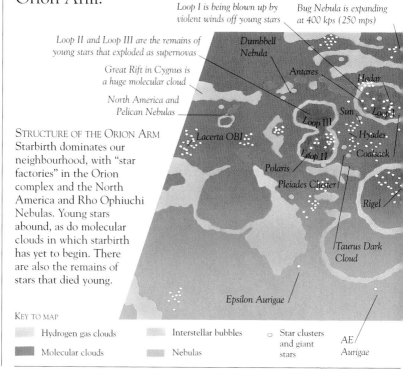

Loop I is being blown up by violent winds off young stars

Bug Nebula is expanding at 400 kps (250 mps)

Loop II and Loop III are the remains of young stars that exploded as supernovas

Great Rift in Cygnus is a huge molecular cloud

North America and Pelican Nebulas

Dumbbell Nebula

Antares

Hadar

Sun

Loop I

Loop III

Hyades

Lacerta OB1

Loop II

Coalsack

Polaris

Rigel

Pleiades Cluster

Taurus Dark Cloud

Epsilon Aurigae

AE Aurigae

STRUCTURE OF THE ORION ARM
Starbirth dominates our neighbourhood, with "star factories" in the Orion complex and the North America and Rho Ophiuchi Nebulas. Young stars abound, as do molecular clouds in which starbirth has yet to begin. There are also the remains of stars that died young.

KEY TO MAP

Hydrogen gas clouds

Molecular clouds

Interstellar bubbles

Nebulas

Star clusters and giant stars

HELIX NEBULA

At 450 light years away, the Helix Nebula is the closest planetary nebula to the Sun, and covers about half the area of the full moon in the sky. Its helix shape is probably the result of a red giant puffing off its outer layers on two separate occasions.

RHO OPHIUCHI COMPLEX

This star-forming complex is the most colourful in the sky, with blue and magenta predominant. The real action, vigorous starbirth, is hidden behind a molecular cloud.

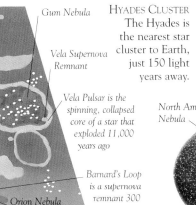

Gum Nebula

Vela Supernova Remnant

Vela Pulsar is the spinning, collapsed core of a star that exploded 11,000 years ago

Barnard's Loop is a supernova remnant 300 light years across

Orion Nebula

Horsehead Nebula

The gas is made to glow by radiation from young stars in the molecular cloud beside it

Monoceros R2 contains a star that is 10,000 times brighter than the Sun

HYADES CLUSTER

The Hyades is the nearest star cluster to Earth, just 150 light years away.

The stars in the Hyades Cluster form a V-shape in the sky

Aldebaran forms the point of the V-shape

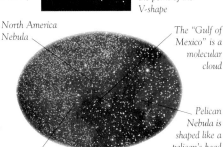

North America Nebula

The "Gulf of Mexico" is a molecular cloud

Pelican Nebula is shaped like a pelican's head

NORTH AMERICA NEBULA

The shape of the North America Nebula amazingly mirrors that of the continent. This and the Pelican Nebula are the visible parts of a vast, glowing nebula 100 light years across – six times bigger than the Orion Nebula.

THE PERSEUS ARM

IN 1951, WILLIAM MORGAN provided proof that the
Milky Way is indeed a spiral galaxy. From the
brightness of the stars in the Cassiopeia, Perseus, and
Cepheus constellations, he realized that they must all
be at about the same distance. He showed that they
lie in a band 5,000–8,000 light years away. This is
the Perseus Arm, the outermost main spiral arm.

*Cassiopeia A is the tangled
wreck of a dead star*

*NGC 7538 is
a dark molecular
cloud hiding a
cluster of new stars*

*IC 1795 is
the biggest star-
forming region*

*NGC 457
contains phi
Cassiopeiae,
a supergiant*

*IC 1805 and
IC 1848
form a
double
cluster*

*Tycho Brahe's
Supernova Remnant
has a collapsed white
dwarf at its centre*

*Chi Persei and
h Persei make up
the Double Cluster*

*In places, the Perseus
Arm nearly merges
with the Orion Arm*

*M36, M37, and
M38 are young
star clusters in
the constellation
of Auriga*

*Plaskett's Star
is actually
two stars
very close
together*

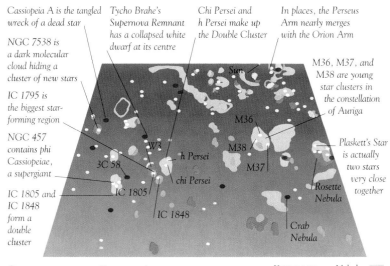

STRUCTURE OF THE PERSEUS ARM
The Perseus Arm is one of the galaxy's main
arms, but instead of wrapping itself around
the galaxy, it is made up of unconnected
patches of young stars and nebulas. It also
contains numerous supernova remnants.

KEY TO MAP   Nebulas
Molecular clouds
Star associations
Hydrogen gas clouds
Clusters and giant stars   ○
Pulsars and supernova remnants   ●

CRAB NEBULA

The gases are spreading outwards at a speed of 1,500 kps (932 mps)

The curving filaments of the nebula look like a crab's pincers

While most supernova remnants are spherical, the Crab Nebula consists of countless long filaments that stretch out across 15 light years of space. The ghostly blue glow inside the mass of filaments is synchrotron radiation produced by very fast-moving electrons. These electrons are generated by a central, rapidly spinning pulsar. The Crab Nebula Pulsar is only 25 km (16 miles) across, and yet its mass is greater than that of the Sun.

CASSIOPEIA A

The brightest radio source that can be observed from Earth is Cassiopeia A – the remains of a star that exploded 300 years ago. A radio telescope view reveals it to be a shell of gases speeding outwards at 6,000 kps (3,728 mps). The bright, colour-coded parts are the dense, hot edges of the shell.

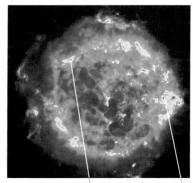

The radio waves come from electrons moving in strong magnetic fields

The yellow and red areas show where the radio waves are most intense

Young stars have already blown a hole as large as the famous Orion Nebula

The Rosette Nebula is found in the constellation of Monoceros

The stars at the centre form the open cluster NGC 2244

ROSETTE NEBULA

Appearing bigger than the full Moon in the sky, the huge Rosette Nebula lies 5,500 light years away. It is gradually growing larger and fainter as the radiation and strong winds, from young stars born at its centre, blow away the gas that helped create them.

THE SAGITTARIUS ARM

LYING BETWEEN THE ORION ARM and the galactic centre, the Sagittarius Arm is one of the Milky Way's two major spiral arms. Although radio waves and infrared radiation can pass through the dust that blocks our view of it, astronomers find that objects are often obscured because they lie along the same line of sight as other, closer objects.

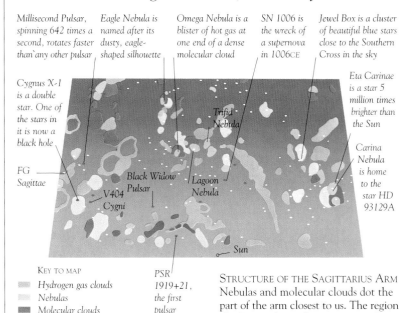

Millisecond Pulsar, spinning 642 times a second, rotates faster than any other pulsar

Eagle Nebula is named after its dusty, eagle-shaped silhouette

Omega Nebula is a blister of hot gas at one end of a dense molecular cloud

SN 1006 is the wreck of a supernova in 1006CE

Jewel Box is a cluster of beautiful blue stars close to the Southern Cross in the sky

Cygnus X-1 is a double star. One of the stars in it is now a black hole

Eta Carinae is a star 5 million times brighter than the Sun

Trifid Nebula

Carina Nebula is home to the star HD 93129A

FG Sagittae

Black Widow Pulsar

Lagoon Nebula

V404 Cygni

Sun

KEY TO MAP
- ▨ Hydrogen gas clouds
- ▨ Nebulas
- ▨ Molecular clouds
- Star associations
- • Pulsars and supernova remnants
- ∘ Star clusters

PSR 1919+21, the first pulsar discovered

STRUCTURE OF THE SAGITTARIUS ARM
Nebulas and molecular clouds dot the part of the arm closest to us. The region also has its share of star corpses, pulsars, and black holes. Closer to the galactic centre, molecular clouds dominate.

BLACK HOLES IN CYGNUS

The Sagittarius Arm has its share of black holes, which astronomers can "weigh" if they are situated in double-star systems. The masses of the two bodies involved dictate how they orbit one another. In V404 Cygni, the black hole is heavier than the star, so the balance point lies almost in the hole and the star swings around the hole. In Cygnus X-1, the star is heavier than the hole, so the balance point lies inside the star and the hole orbits the star.

Companion star

Balance point

V404 CYGNI

Black hole

Black hole

Balance point

Star orbits black hole

Black hole orbits around massive star

CYGNUS X-1

Orbital path

TRIFID AND LAGOON NEBULAS
These two nebulas, more than 5,000 light years away, are among the most striking in the sky. The Trifid Nebula (top) gets its name, which means "divided into three parts", because dark dust lanes split the nebula three ways. The nebula surrounds a compact cluster of stars whose radiation heats the hydrogen inside it until it glows pink. The Lagoon Nebula (bottom) envelops a cluster of stars about 2 million years old, many of which are so massive and bright that they can be seen with the naked eye.

HEART OF THE MILKY WAY

THE CENTRE OF THE MILKY WAY is a bar-shaped bulge of old red and yellow stars, with comparatively little gas. Radio and infrared telescopes have shown jets of gas moving at considerable speed, and areas of strong magnetism. The temperature increases towards the core. This activity is due to recent star formations, and energy from gas falling into a black hole.

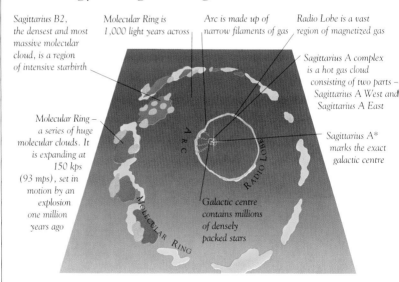

Sagittarius B2, the densest and most massive molecular cloud, is a region of intensive starbirth

Molecular Ring is 1,000 light years across

Arc is made up of narrow filaments of gas

Radio Lobe is a vast region of magnetized gas

Sagittarius A complex is a hot gas cloud consisting of two parts – Sagittarius A West and Sagittarius A East

Molecular Ring – a series of huge molecular clouds. It is expanding at 150 kps (93 mps), set in motion by an explosion one million years ago

Sagittarius A* marks the exact galactic centre

Galactic centre contains millions of densely packed stars

STRUCTURE OF THE GALACTIC CENTRE
The galaxy's biggest and heaviest objects congregate at the centre. At its core is a star cluster, containing many red supergiants, and an intense radio source – Sagittarius A* – which is a massive black hole.

MAGNETIC STRUCTURES

The innermost 100 light years are dominated by the strongest magnetic fields. This is part of the Radio Lobe – a vast region of magnetized gas in the shape of a chimney. Within this region are many unique objects, such as the Mouse.

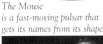

The Mouse is a fast-moving pulsar that gets its names from its shape

The Tail is a cloud of radio-wave-emitting particles 55 light years long

The Arc, which curves like a colossal solar prominence, consists of filaments of gas 150 light years long but only half a light year wide

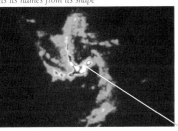

CENTRAL SPIRAL

The central 10 light years consist of three areas: Sagittarius A West, Sagittarius A*, and the central star cluster. The smaller spiral arms of Sagittarius A West are streams of gas falling inwards, while its two main arms are parts of a tilted, spinning disc of hot gas.

Sagittarius A*

CENTRAL STAR CLUSTER

Within Sagittarius A West is the central star cluster, which contains 2.5 million stars. This infrared image shows stars in the innermost 2 light years. Right at the centre is Sagittarius A*, a possible black hole with a mass of 2.5 million Suns. It is not active at present, but it was once. If enough gas exists to "feed" it, it may become active again in the future.

Sagittarius A*

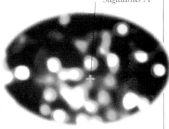

MAGELLANIC CLOUDS

JUST AS EARTH'S GRAVITY holds the Moon in orbit, so the Milky Way Galaxy holds two satellite galaxies – the Large and Small Magellanic Clouds – in orbit around it. These galaxies orbit together on an elliptical path, taking over a billion years to travel once around it.

Tarantula Nebula is the biggest and brightest gas cloud in the LMC

Site of Supernova 1987A

LARGE MAGELLANIC CLOUD
The Milky Way's "little cousin", the Large Magellanic Cloud (LMC) is only one-twentieth the size of our galaxy, but contains the same mix of stars and gas. It is too small to grow spectacular spiral arms, but is more ordered than many smaller galaxies. Lying 160,000 light years away, the LMC is the nearest major galaxy to us.

NGC 419 is a globular cluster of almost a million stars

NGC 2100 is a giant open star cluster only 20 million years old

NGC 346 is a giant nebula surrounding a cluster of massive young stars

SMALL MAGELLANIC CLOUD
Only a quarter the size of the LMC, the Small Magellanic Cloud (SMC) lies 190,000 light years away. Because of its small size, it is being ripped apart by the gravity of the Milky Way. The galaxy contains 2,000 star clusters.

S Doradus is one of the LMC's brightest stars

Central bar of stars is 10,000 light years long

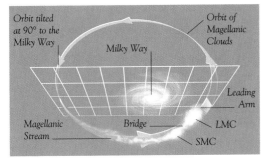

TARANTULA NEBULA

The Tarantula is one of the biggest and brightest of all nebulas. Some 800 light years across, it is 50 times the size of the famous Orion Nebula in our Milky Way. This gas cloud is lit up by hot young stars. The cluster at its centre contains more than a hundred stars, each heavier than 50 Suns.

Faint spiral shape extends from this end of the central straight bar

Orbit tilted at 90° to the Milky Way

Orbit of Magellanic Clouds

Milky Way

Leading Arm

Magellanic Stream

Bridge

LMC

SMC

LMC contains 6,500 star clusters

Dark dust clouds are less common in the LMC than in the Milky Way

MAGELLANIC STREAM

Pulled by the Milky Way's mighty gravity, gas from the Magellanic Clouds has spilt out into space. A pool of gas – the Bridge – envelops both Clouds, while a long gas trail – the Magellanic Stream – has been left along the galaxies' elliptical orbits. Some gas – the Leading Arm – has even splashed ahead of the two galaxies.

SPOTTING THE MAGELLANIC CLOUDS

The Clouds are easily seen from the Southern Hemisphere, and are highest in the sky during the spring. Look south on a moonless night, and they appear as two large hazy patches, like detached pieces of the Milky Way. Binoculars will show the Tarantula Nebula and the brightest clusters.

SMC   LMC

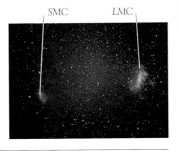

LOCAL GROUP

Elliptical
NGC 205

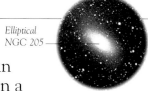

GALAXIES IN THE UNIVERSE are in clusters, and our Milky Way is in a cluster known as the Local Group. This consists of about 30 galaxies spread over about 5 million light years. The Local Group is dominated by three elliptical galaxies, these being the Milky Way, Andromeda (M31), and Triangulum (M33).

ELLIPTICAL GALAXIES
About half the Local Group galaxies are ellipticals, including NGC 205 – one of Andromeda's satellites. Ellipticals are uniform balls of old red stars, with no gas to fuel further starbirth.

M32   NGC 205

ANDROMEDA GALAXY
At 2.5 million light years away, this galaxy is the most distant object visible to the naked eye. It is the largest in the Local Group and, with 400 billion stars, is one of the biggest spirals known. Our galaxy would look much like it from afar.

GALACTIC NEIGHBOURHOOD
The Local Group's galaxies cluster around the massive Andromeda and Milky Way. Their strong gravities allow them to gather smaller satellite galaxies around them. Other, more distant galaxies are also held into the group by gravity. Most of the members of the Local Group are dwarf elliptical and dwarf irregular galaxies.

IC 1613
WLM

Dwarf galaxies are so faint they would be undetectable in a more distant galaxy cluster

Gas-rich
spiral arms

NGC
604

TRIANGULUM GALAXY
Triangulum is a spiral, half the size of the Milky Way, and with one-tenth the stars of Andromeda. It is the third largest member of the Local Group, with many huge, bright nebulas. One of them, NGC 604, is among the biggest regions of starbirth known.

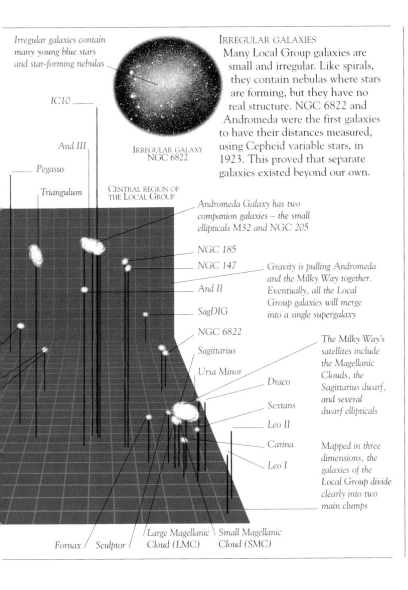

Irregular galaxies contain many young blue stars and star-forming nebulas

IC10

And III

And III

Pegasus

Triangulum

IRREGULAR GALAXY
NGC 6822

CENTRAL REGION OF
THE LOCAL GROUP

IRREGULAR GALAXIES

Many Local Group galaxies are small and irregular. Like spirals, they contain nebulas where stars are forming, but they have no real structure. NGC 6822 and Andromeda were the first galaxies to have their distances measured, using Cepheid variable stars, in 1923. This proved that separate galaxies existed beyond our own.

Andromeda Galaxy has two companion galaxies – the small ellipticals M32 and NGC 205

NGC 185

NGC 147

And II

SagDIG

NGC 6822

Sagittarius

Ursa Minor

Gravity is pulling Andromeda and the Milky Way together. Eventually, all the Local Group galaxies will merge into a single supergalaxy

Draco

Sextans

Leo II

Carina

Leo I

The Milky Way's satellites include the Magellanic Clouds, the Sagittarius dwarf, and several dwarf ellipticals

Mapped in three dimensions, the galaxies of the Local Group divide clearly into two main clumps

Fornax / Sculptor / Large Magellanic Cloud (LMC) \ Small Magellanic Cloud (SMC)

CLUSTERS AND SUPERCLUSTERS

GALAXIES GATHER TOGETHER in pairs, or in clusters containing thousands of galaxies. Clusters grow by merging, and irregularly shaped clusters may have merged more recently than regularly shaped ones. Clusters are grouped into superclusters – the largest structures in space.

NGC 4473
Type E4

VIRGO CLUSTER

The Milky Way is a member of a cluster of about 30 mostly small and faint galaxies known as the Local Group. The nearest large cluster is the Virgo Cluster, which lies 50 million light years away. It is an irregular cluster of more than 2,000 galaxies that has been known for two centuries. Though it is dominated by three giant elliptical galaxies, most of its brighter members are spirals.

NGC 4461
Type Sa

Arp 120
Type Sa

Virgo Cluster is dominated
by spiral galaxies – some
other clusters contain
mainly ellipticals

NGC 4425
Type Sb

CLUSTER EVOLUTION

Clusters form when smaller groups of galaxies merge. This X-ray picture of gas in Abell 2256 shows a bright spot to the right of the centre, caused as another group of galaxies is absorbed into the cluster. In clusters that are no longer swallowing groups, the gas is more evenly spread throughout the cluster.

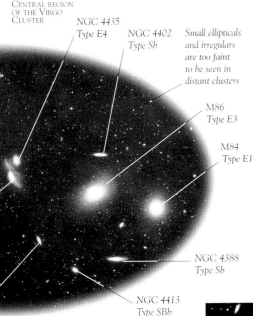

CENTRAL REGION
OF THE VIRGO
CLUSTER

NGC 4435
Type E4

NGC 4402
Type Sb

*Small ellipticals
and irregulars
are too faint
to be seen in
distant clusters*

M86
Type E3

M84
Type E1

NGC 4388
Type Sb

NGC 4413
Type SBb

GIANT ELLIPTICAL GALAXIES

Many clusters have a huge galaxy, perhaps 500,000 light years across, at their centre. These giant galaxies grow by swallowing other galaxies in the cluster. Often they are strong sources of radio waves and X-rays. They have a halo of faint stars and globular clusters around them, and often have more than one central nucleus.

LOCAL SUPERCLUSTER

A supercluster may contain dozens of clusters and be over 100 million light years across. Our Local Group is part of the Local Supercluster, centred on the Virgo Cluster. The Local Group is falling towards the centre of the Supercluster at 250 kps (155 mps).

Virgo
Cluster

Leo
Cluster

Canes Venatici Cluster

Local Group

Crater
Cluster

NGC 4889
Type E4

NGC 4874
Type E0

COMA CLUSTER

The nearest dense, regular cluster to the Milky Way – the Coma Cluster – lies about 300 million light years away. It contains over 3,000 galaxies, mostly elliptical and lenticular. It has two clumps, each centred on a giant elliptical galaxy.

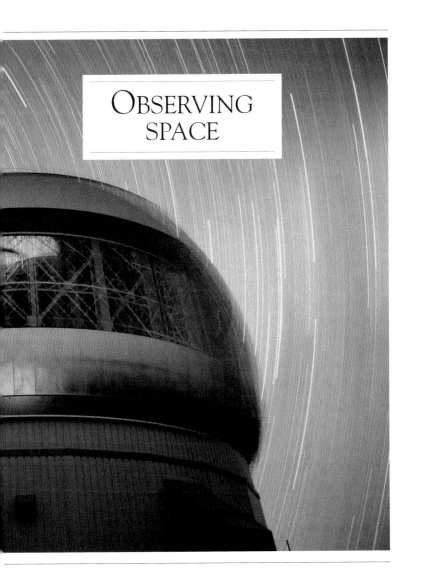

OBSERVING
SPACE

ABOVE OUR HEADS

AS OUR PLANET SPINS on its axis, it is hurtling around the Sun at 107,000 kph (66,700 mph), providing ever-changing views of the Universe. By day the sky is dominated by the Sun. At night the blackness of space is studded with countless stars and galaxies that are an unchanging backdrop.

CIRCULAR STAR TRAILS
Earth's daily rotation causes the stars to appear to circle around the sky. This effect can be captured by a long-exposure photograph.

Stars appear as patterns against the sphere

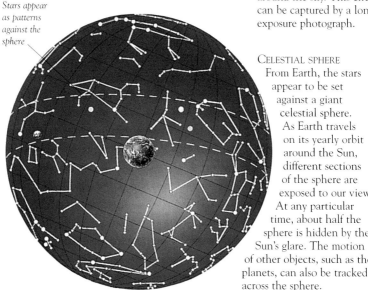

CELESTIAL SPHERE
From Earth, the stars appear to be set against a giant celestial sphere. As Earth travels on its yearly orbit around the Sun, different sections of the sphere are exposed to our view. At any particular time, about half the sphere is hidden by the Sun's glare. The motion of other objects, such as the planets, can also be tracked across the sphere.

GALAXY
All the stars
that we can see in the
sky, including the Sun, are in the Milky Way Galaxy.
This panoramic view of the Milky Way (looking towards
the centre of the Galaxy), was photographed
from Christchurch, New Zealand.

GOOD VIEWING CONDITIONS
Some nights are good for looking
at stars, while others are better
for planets. Brilliantly clear
evenings often have turbulent
air. This spoils views of the
Moon and planets, but is good
for finding faint nebulas.
Windless conditions are more
suited for studying the Moon
and planets, despite the mist
that may form. It is important
to get one's bearings before
observing. The position of the Sun
and Moon can be noted in relation
to nearby objects, such as trees,
that can be identified at night.

STARGAZING

ASTRONOMY CAN BE FUN by day and by night. Most celestial objects can only be seen at night, but others, like the Sun, are bright enough to be seen even when the sky is not dark. Plan carefully what to observe ahead of time – it is frustrating to miss seeing a particular favourite object while diverted by other activities in the sky. Learn how the stars and planets move.

Cover a torch with red cellophane or use a red bicycle lamp

RED-COVERED TORCH

ESSENTIAL EQUIPMENT

Keep a record of what you see. Write down the time, date, location, weather conditions, and instruments used. To look at star maps or to take notes, use a torch covered with red cellophane. The reddish light will not affect night vision.

Organize your notes into categories of objects to be recorded

A notebook with plain sheets is better for drawing

CHECKLIST
- Warm clothing, including waterproof shoes
- Notebook and pen or pencil
- Accurate watch
- Red-covered torch
- Binoculars
- Something to sit on
- Books and star maps
- A small table (useful to put everything on)

Use the card as a mask to stop the Sun shining directly onto the screen

Cut a hole in the centre of the mask the same size as one of the binocular lenses. Tape the mask to the binoculars so that one lens lets light through

Prop up a second piece of card to act as a screen

DAYTIME ASTRONOMY

To observe the Sun for sunspots, or during an eclipse, project its image onto a card, using binoculars or a telescope of less than 100 mm (4 in) and a magnification of less than 30. Aim the instrument at the Sun, turning, tilting, and focusing it until a sharp-edged disc of light appears on the screen.

FINDING OBJECTS

The brighter stars and planets can be seen in daylight with binoculars, but finding them can be difficult. The planets can always be found close to the ecliptic – the Sun's path through the sky. If a bright star is not on a star map, it is probably a planet.

Over the months, the position of Jupiter in the sky changes

LIGHT POLLUTION

City lights cause light pollution that often drowns out the fainter stars. Town dwellers should choose a spot far from lights, and make sure that no lights shine into their eyes. If the Moon is full, even country dwellers will find it difficult to see faint objects.

All the stars and planets rise and set in the night sky

STARGAZING TIPS

At night, it can take up to 30 minutes for the eyes to become properly accustomed to the dark and to get full night vision. Some types of light are particularly bad for night vision, such as fluorescent lights, and TV and computer screens, so try to avoid them before going outside to observe.

• Once outside, use only red light and try to persuade other family members not to switch on any distracting house lights.

• If outside lights are a problem, rig up a temporary light shield, such as a blanket draped over a stepladder.

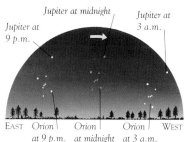

Jupiter at midnight
Jupiter at 3 a.m.
Jupiter at 9 p.m.

EAST Orion Orion Orion WEST
at 9 p.m. at midnight at 3 a.m.

Orion at midnight
Orion at 3 a.m.
Orion at 9 p.m.

WEST Jupiter Jupiter Jupiter EAST
at 3 a.m. at midnight at 9 p.m.

ORION IN NORTHERN SKIES

Earth's rotation makes stars and planets appear to move across the sky at night. The constellation Orion is visible from November to March. It rises in the east where it appears tilted, and sets in the west. It is highest when due south.

ORION IN SOUTHERN SKIES

In the southern hemisphere, Orion is also visible from November to March. It reaches its highest point when due north. It seems to move right to left – the opposite to the motion seen in the northern hemisphere.

211

SPECIAL EFFECTS

FROM EARTH, it is possible to see several "special effects" in the sky. Some of these effects are due to some peculiarities of Earth's magnetic field and atmosphere. Other effects depend on the position of the objects in the Solar System, mainly the Sun, the Moon, and Earth. Meteor showers are an effect produced by space dust burning up in the atmosphere.

AURORA BOREALIS
Charged particles from the Sun, carried by the solar wind, cause dramatic light shows when they enter Earth's atmosphere.

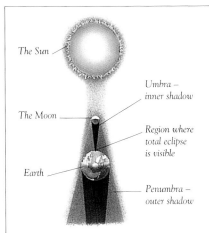

The Sun

Umbra –
inner shadow

The Moon

Region where
total eclipse
is visible

Earth

Penumbra –
outer shadow

ECLIPSE OF THE SUN
Occasionally, the Moon comes into perfect alignment between the Sun and Earth. When this happens, the Moon blocks out the Sun's light causing what is called a solar eclipse. From some parts of Earth's surface, the disc of the Moon appears to completely cover the Sun's face, and there is a brief period of darkness. Although the Moon is a great deal smaller than the Sun, it is able to block the light totally because it is so much nearer to Earth.

HALO AROUND THE MOON

On some winter nights, a halo appears around the Moon, but this has nothing to do with the Moon itself. Sunlight, reflected towards Earth by the Moon, is refracted (bent) by ice crystals high in Earth's atmosphere. This refraction of light creates a circular halo.

METEOR RADIANT

Dust particles from space are seen as meteors when they burn up in the atmosphere. In a meteor shower, which is caused by dust from a comet, all the meteors appear to come from a single point in the sky. This point is known as the radiant of the meteor shower.

OPTICAL TELESCOPES

THE OPTICAL TELESCOPE is one of the main tools of astronomy. Today, little time is spent looking through a telescope eyepiece – modern instruments collect and store visual information electronically. The optical telescope remains an important tool because it gathers basic information.

PALOMAR DOME
The protective dome of the Hale Telescope at the Mount Palomar Observatory, California, USA, shields the telescope from the effects of weather.

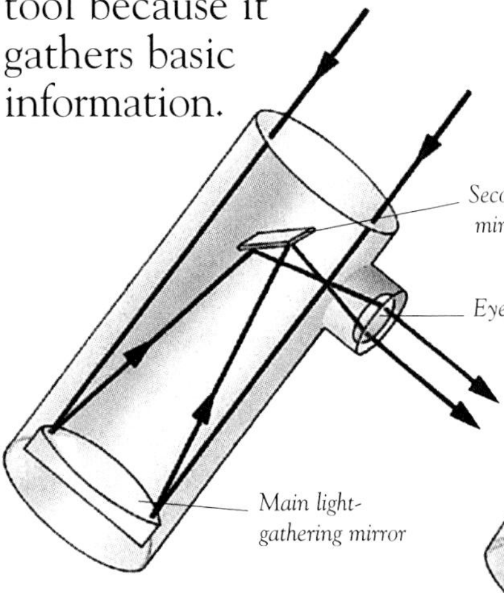

Secondary mirror

Eyepiece

Main light-gathering mirror

Main light-gathering lens

Eyepiece lens

REFLECTOR TELESCOPES
Telescopes use lenses and mirrors to gather light and produce an image. Reflector telescopes, which make use of curved mirrors, are the most useful type for astronomy.

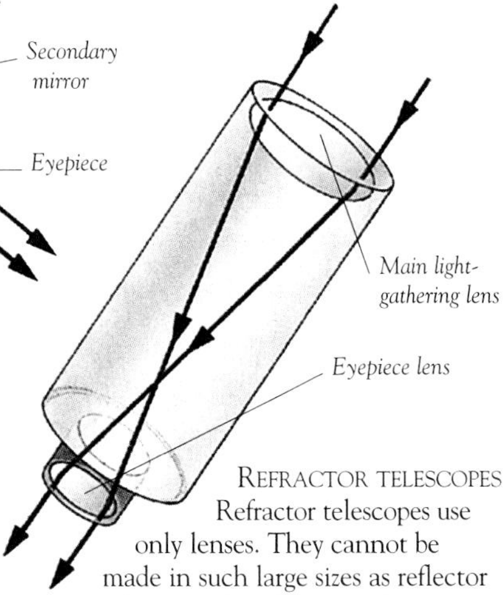

REFRACTOR TELESCOPES
Refractor telescopes use only lenses. They cannot be made in such large sizes as reflector telescopes, but they remain very popular with amateur astronomers.

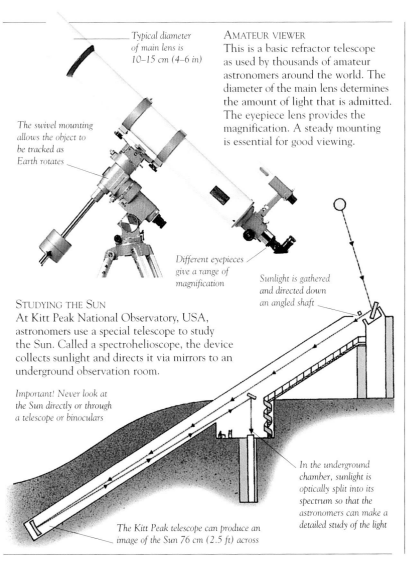

Typical diameter of main lens is 10–15 cm (4–6 in)

AMATEUR VIEWER

This is a basic refractor telescope as used by thousands of amateur astronomers around the world. The diameter of the main lens determines the amount of light that is admitted. The eyepiece lens provides the magnification. A steady mounting is essential for good viewing.

The swivel mounting allows the object to be tracked as Earth rotates

Different eyepieces give a range of magnification

Sunlight is gathered and directed down an angled shaft

STUDYING THE SUN

At Kitt Peak National Observatory, USA, astronomers use a special telescope to study the Sun. Called a spectrohelioscope, the device collects sunlight and directs it via mirrors to an underground observation room.

Important! Never look at the Sun directly or through a telescope or binoculars

In the underground chamber, sunlight is optically split into its spectrum so that the astronomers can make a detailed study of the light

The Kitt Peak telescope can produce an image of the Sun 76 cm (2.5 ft) across

RADIO TELESCOPES

WE HAVE BEEN LISTENING in to the radio energy of the Universe for more than 50 years. Radio telescopes can obtain additional information about familiar objects, as well as seek out new ones. Two major discoveries – quasars and pulsars – were made by radio astronomers.

VERY LARGE ARRAY
A radio telescope consists of a large metal dish. In order to gather more information, radio astronomers sometimes use a number of large dishes linked together. The Very Large Array (VLA) in New Mexico, USA, uses up to 27 linked dishes, each one 25 m (82 ft) across, to collect radio signals from space.

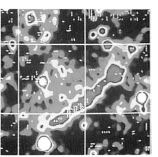

Radio waves

RADIO VISION
Radio telescopes, like ordinary radio sets, can be tuned to a particular wavelength, and the intensity of the radio energy can be measured. Computers are then used to produce "radio-maps" of the sky, such as this image of the bar-shaped radio source known as 1952+28.

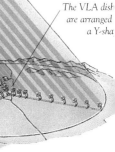

The VLA dish are arranged a Y-sha

LARGEST DISH

The world's largest radio telescope, the 305-m (1,000-ft) Arecibo dish, is built into a natural hollow in the hills of Puerto Rico. The dish is "steered" using Earth's own rotation. Arecibo has also been used to send a radio message out into space.

Simple processing of the Arecibo message produces this visual image, which contains a representation of a human being

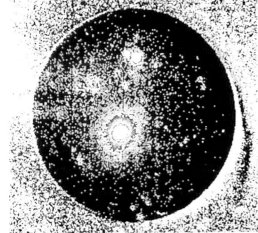

RADIO GALAXIES

Many galaxies that are quite faint visually are very "bright" at radio wavelengths. These are often called radio galaxies, or active galaxies. This optical image of radio galaxy 3C 33 has been colour-coded according to the intensity of light in the visible part of the spectrum – ranging from white (most intense) to blue (the least).

OBSERVATORIES

OPTICAL TELESCOPES are usually installed in
mountain-top observatories, where they suffer
least interference from Earth's atmosphere. Radio
telescopes can be situated almost anywhere,
and are usually located near universities. The
high cost of telescopes using the latest technology
means that observatories are
often shared between
countries.

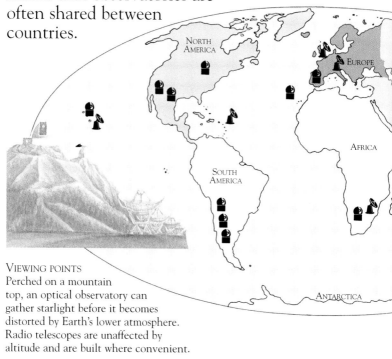

NORTH
AMERICA

EUROPE

AFRICA

SOUTH
AMERICA

ANTARCTICA

VIEWING POINTS
Perched on a mountain
top, an optical observatory can
gather starlight before it becomes
distorted by Earth's lower atmosphere.
Radio telescopes are unaffected by
altitude and are built where convenient.

HIGH AND DRY

The European Southern Observatory is sited on Cerro Paranal, a 2,635-m (8,645-ft) high mountain in Chile's Atacama desert. A dry climate with cloud-free nights and a steady atmosphere makes this remote location ideal for clear viewing of the farthest galaxies, all through the year.

ASIA

AUSTRALIA

MAP KEY

OPTICAL TELESCOPE

RADIO TELESCOPE

OBSERVATORY FACTS

• The oldest existing observatory was built in South Korea in 632CE.

• SOFIA, the flying observatory, will begin operation in late 2006. It is a modified 747 jumbo jet fitted with a 2.5-m (98-in) telescope.

• The 36 elements of the Keck reflector make a larger mirror 10 m (33 ft) across.

• The twin Keck Telescopes are the world's highest, and are situated on Mauna Kea island in Hawaii, about 4,200m (13,796 ft) above sea level.

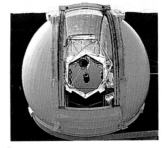

LEAST DISTURBANCE

The Keck Telescopes are situated at the summit of Mauna Kea in Hawaii, an ideal location for an optical telescope. The air is clear and the sky is dark and well removed from city lights.

OBSERVATORY TELESCOPES

LIGHT GATHERED FROM THE SKY is still astronomers' main source of information about the Universe. Apart from the Sun, most celestial bodies are far away and appear relatively dim. A telescope captures as much light as possible – the more light it collects, the more information it provides. There are two types of telescope – reflectors, which capture light using a mirror, and refractors, which use a lens.

USES OF OPTICAL TELESCOPES

Reflectors, such as the twin Gemini telescopes, capture light with a huge curved mirror, and can reflect the image towards any part of the telescope by secondary mirrors. Collecting light with a mirror ensures there is no colour fringing, and as the mirror can be supported at the back, they can now be made 10 m (32 ft) across. Refractors capture light with a lens, which focuses the image onto a photographic plate or electronic light detector.

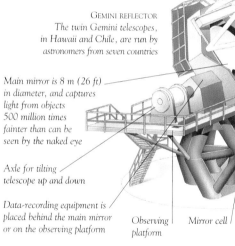

GEMINI REFLECTOR
The twin Gemini telescopes, in Hawaii and Chile, are run by astronomers from seven countries

Main mirror is 8 m (26 ft) in diameter, and captures light from objects 500 million times fainter than can be seen by the naked eye

Axle for tilting telescope up and down

Data-recording equipment is placed behind the main mirror or on the observing platform

Observing platform

Mirror cell

MIRRORS

Telescope mirrors are made of low-expansion glass ceramic and are coated with a film of aluminium. It takes over a year to polish them, keeping them smooth to avoid blurring. The Gemini Telescope mirror is accurate to 1/20th of the wavelength it is reflecting.

The telescope can be pointed to any part of the sky, and can then track the chosen object as it moves across the sky. Long exposures produce the best data for analysis

Secondary mirror

Open frame lessens weight

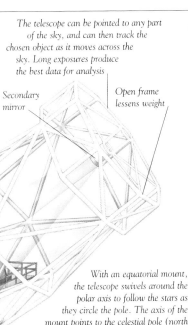

LIGHT PATH IN REFLECTOR

Incoming light from objects in space is collected by the main mirror

Convex secondary mirror

Concave main mirror

Light is reflected from the main mirror towards the secondary mirror

Light is focused onto a battery of instruments waiting to record the data

Light reflected from secondary mirror passes through hole in the main mirror

With an equatorial mount, the telescope swivels around the polar axis to follow the stars as they circle the pole. The axis of the mount points to the celestial pole (north or south, depending on the hemisphere)

Whole telescope mounting swings around horizontally

North-south position is fixed for viewing a particular star

Telescope swings around polar axis at a steady rate

Polar axis points at the pole

Telescope tilts up and down

MOUNTINGS

A telescope's mounting is important because it supports its weight, and swings it around as Earth spins on its axis in order to keep objects being observed in view. The two main types of mounting are equatorial and altazimuth. The altazimuth is the mainstay of today's professional telescopes. Continuous computer control allows giant telescopes such as Gemini to follow the paths of objects as they move across the sky.

Telescope swings around horizontally

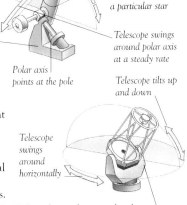

With an altazimuth mount, the telescope has to be driven up and down (in "altitude") and be swung around (in "azimuth") to follow a star

221

NEW DESIGNS

THE BIGGER THE MIRROR in a telescope, the more light it can collect and the more detail that can be seen. But mirrors more than 8 m (26 ft) in diameter have limitations. One is the atmosphere – even a huge mirror will have its vision blurred by moving pockets of air. The other is size, as bigger mirrors are more difficult to transport and handle. The latest ground-based telescopes use ingenious solutions to get around these limitations.

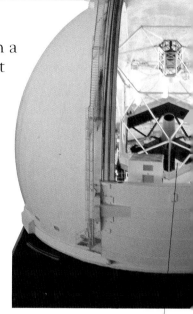

Keck mirror has a total light-collecting area 17 times greater than the Hubble Space Telescope and can see farther, though not as clearly, as Hubble

ACTIVE OPTICS

The first segmented mirror was built in 1992 on the Keck 1 Telescope. It uses active optics systems to counteract distortions caused by the weight of the mirrors or the wind. A computer adjusts each mirror segment twice every second to an accuracy that is a thousand times finer than a human hair. As a result, the 36 segments behave as a single unchanging sheet of glass.

KECK TELESCOPES

These two telescopes are situated on the 4,200-m (13,796-ft) summit of Mauna Kea in Hawaii, high above the clouds and water vapour of the lower atmosphere. Their mirrors measure 10 m (33 ft) across. A single mirror this size would bend under its own weight, so every mirror is made of 36 six-sided segments, which weigh 400 kg (882 lb) each.

VERY LARGE TELESCOPE

The European Southern Observatory's Very Large Telescope (VLT) in Chile is the biggest in the world. It consists of four 8.2-m (27-ft) telescopes linked together – each a billion times more powerful than the naked eye. The telescopes can scoop up as much light as a single mirror 16.4 m (54 ft) across.

Domes protect the Keck Telescope, which weighs 298 tonnes (293 tons) and stands eight storeys tall

Swivelling mirror gathers light

Small mirror reflects light into aluminium tubes

Fixed telescope mirror focuses light

OPTICAL SYNTHESIS

The Cambridge Optical Aperture Synthesis Telescope (COAST) is made up of five small telescopes, each with a mirror. Radio astronomy techniques are used to combine light from the telescopes, giving improved resolution.

ADAPTIVE OPTICS

In adaptive optics, a powerful laser creates an artificial star high in the atmosphere, in the same direction as the star under observation. A computer works out the distortion of its light as it travels through the atmosphere. It then shapes a constantly moving flexible mirror to focus the light back into a point, sharpening the images the telescope is seeing.

UNUSUAL TELESCOPES

OUR KNOWLEDGE OF THE distant Universe comes from studying radiation – light, radio waves, infrared, ultraviolet, X-rays, and gamma rays. Cosmic rays and neutrinos are more exotic messengers. Some messengers, such as dark matter and gravitational waves, have been predicted but are still undiscovered.

VIOLENT BEGINNINGS

Mighty explosions erupt in space due to stars dying as supernovas, neutron stars colliding, and superhot gas being sucked into black holes. These explosions generate radiation – light, radio waves, gamma rays, plus other more exotic particles and waves, which carry unique information about these events.

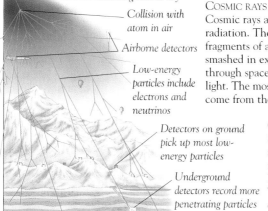

Incoming cosmic ray

Collision with atom in air

Airborne detectors

Low-energy particles include electrons and neutrinos

Detectors on ground pick up most low-energy particles

Underground detectors record more penetrating particles

COSMIC RAYS

Cosmic rays are not radiation. They are fragments of atoms, smashed in explosions, that whizz through space at almost the speed of light. The most energetic cosmic rays come from the centres of quasars.

COSMIC AIR SHOWER

Several low-energy particles are created when a cosmic ray collides with atoms in Earth's upper atmosphere. These particles rain down on Earth over a wide area.

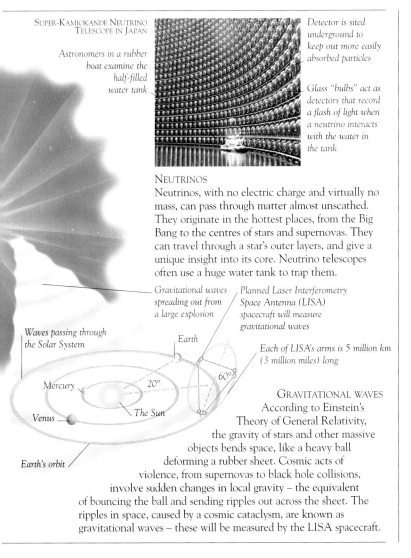

SUPER-KAMIOKANDE NEUTRINO
TELESCOPE IN JAPAN

*Astronomers in a rubber
boat examine the
half-filled
water tank*

*Detector is sited
underground to
keep out more easily
absorbed particles*

*Glass "bulbs" act as
detectors that record
a flash of light when
a neutrino interacts
with the water in
the tank*

NEUTRINOS

Neutrinos, with no electric charge and virtually no mass, can pass through matter almost unscathed. They originate in the hottest places, from the Big Bang to the centres of stars and supernovas. They can travel through a star's outer layers, and give a unique insight into its core. Neutrino telescopes often use a huge water tank to trap them.

*Gravitational waves
spreading out from
a large explosion*

*Planned Laser Interferometry
Space Antenna (LISA)
spacecraft will measure
gravitational waves*

*Waves passing through
the Solar System*

Earth

*Each of LISA's arms is 5 million km
(3 million miles) long*

Mercury

20°

60°

Venus

The Sun

Earth's orbit

GRAVITATIONAL WAVES

According to Einstein's Theory of General Relativity, the gravity of stars and other massive objects bends space, like a heavy ball deforming a rubber sheet. Cosmic acts of violence, from supernovas to black hole collisions, involve sudden changes in local gravity – the equivalent of bouncing the ball and sending ripples out across the sheet. The ripples in space, caused by a cosmic cataclysm, are known as gravitational waves – these will be measured by the LISA spacecraft.

ANALYSING LIGHT

PROFESSIONAL ASTRONOMERS rarely look directly through telescopes. Instead, sensitive electronic cameras build up an image over minutes or even hours if the object is very faint. Spectographs split up the light, and computers analyse the results. Photographic plates are now rarely used.

LIGHT-SENSITIVE CHIPS

Pictures of galaxies are built from a grid of squares, or pixels (picture elements). They are taken with electronic cameras built around a light-sensitive computer chip called a charge-coupled device (CCD). CCDs are more sensitive than photographic plates.

Spider mount

CCD from a big telescope, containing 524,288 pixels on a surface the size of a postage stamp

CHARGE-COUPLED DEVICE (CCD)

A CCD is a light-sensitive silicon chip, with a surface divided into thousands or millions of pixels. Light falling on a pixel builds up an electric charge, which is read by circuits built into the chip and fed into a computer, where it is stored as part of a digital image.

SEEING IN COLOUR

A CCD sees in black and white. To obtain full-colour images, the same view is taken several times with different filters and the images are combined. All astronomers use the same colour filters – green, blue, and red – making comparison of images taken by different telescopes easier.

Rotating disc of filters

Light from telescope

The CCD is exposed three times, once through each filter

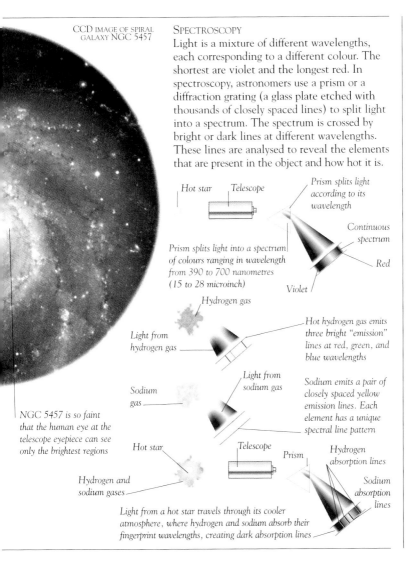

CCD IMAGE OF SPIRAL
GALAXY NGC 5457

SPECTROSCOPY

Light is a mixture of different wavelengths, each corresponding to a different colour. The shortest are violet and the longest red. In spectroscopy, astronomers use a prism or a diffraction grating (a glass plate etched with thousands of closely spaced lines) to split light into a spectrum. The spectrum is crossed by bright or dark lines at different wavelengths. These lines are analysed to reveal the elements that are present in the object and how hot it is.

Hot star   Telescope

Prism splits light according to its wavelength

Continuous spectrum

Red

Prism splits light into a spectrum of colours ranging in wavelength from 390 to 700 nanometres (15 to 28 microinch)

Violet

Hydrogen gas

Hot hydrogen gas emits three bright "emission" lines at red, green, and blue wavelengths

Light from hydrogen gas

Light from sodium gas

Sodium gas

Sodium emits a pair of closely spaced yellow emission lines. Each element has a unique spectral line pattern

NGC 5457 is so faint that the human eye at the telescope eyepiece can see only the brightest regions

Hot star   Telescope   Prism

Hydrogen absorption lines

Sodium absorption lines

Hydrogen and sodium gases

Light from a hot star travels through its cooler atmosphere, where hydrogen and sodium absorb their fingerprint wavelengths, creating dark absorption lines

INFORMATION FROM SPACE

GATHERING AND STUDYING starlight is one
way that we learn about the Universe.
Visible light is only a small part of the
electromagnetic spectrum, which
covers all forms of radiation.
By studying different types of
radiation, we learn about the
visible and the invisible
parts of the Universe.

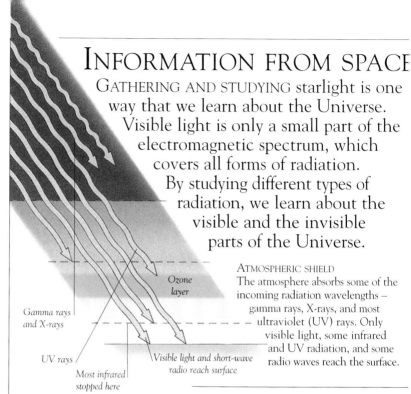

Ozone
layer

Gamma rays
and X-rays

UV rays

Most infrared
stopped here

Visible light and short-wave
radio reach surface

ATMOSPHERIC SHIELD
The atmosphere absorbs some of the
incoming radiation wavelengths –
gamma rays, X-rays, and most
ultraviolet (UV) rays. Only
visible light, some infrared
and UV radiation, and some
radio waves reach the surface.

INFORMATION SPECTRUM
Electromagnetic radiation travels
through space as waves of varying
length (the distance between
wave crests). Gamma rays have
the shortest wavelength, then
X-rays, and so on through the
spectrum to the longest radio
waves. Visible light, which is all
that we can see naturally, occupies
a very narrow portion (less than
0.00001 per cent) of the spectrum.

10^{-13} M
0.0000000000001 METRES

X-RAYS

GAMMA RAYS

228

CRAB NEBULA IN INFRARED LIGHT

The Crab Nebula – the remnant of a supernova explosion seen in 1054CE – emits a wide range of radiation wavelengths. When viewed in infrared light, the nebula looks like a huge cloud. The red areas represent the cooler parts of the nebula.

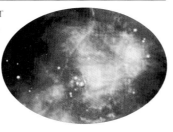

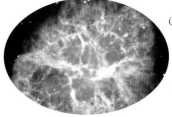

CRAB NEBULA IN VISIBLE LIGHT

In visible light, vast filaments of hot gas can be seen spreading out into space after the explosion. The blue glow comes from fast-moving particles accelerated by the strong magnetic field of the inner nebula.

CRAB NEBULA UNDER X-RAY

An X-ray image reveals the source of the magnetism – a rapidly spinning pulsar at the heart of the nebula. The pulsar is surrounded by high-energy particles that spiral around the pulsar's magnetic field lines.

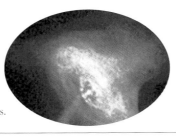

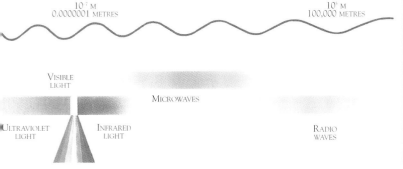

10^{-7} M
0.0000001 METRES

10^{5} M
100,000 METRES

VISIBLE
LIGHT

MICROWAVES

ULTRAVIOLET
LIGHT

INFRARED
LIGHT

RADIO
WAVES

IMAGES OF SPACE

MUCH OF THE information that astronomers obtain through their instruments is presented as visual images. Conventional and electronic cameras are used to record these images. The information is usually stored on computers that can process images to improve the picture and bring out details.

PIXELATED VIEW
Electronic cameras make images with a grid of tiny square picture-elements (pixels). This view of a dim and distant star cluster was obtained with a ground-based telescope. The individual pixels are clearly visible, although it takes a trained eye to identify the image as a star cluster

MARTIAN CHEMICAL PHOTOMAP
This image of the Martian surface was produced from data collected by a device called a neutron spectrometer aboard the Mars Odyssey probe. It is colour-coded to show concentrations of hydrogen in the soil. Deep blue areas contain the most hydrogen, and red areas the least. In the deep blue regions near the poles, the hydrogen is mostly combined with oxygen in the form of water-ice.

Soil near the poles may be up to 50 per cent water-ice

ADDING FALSE COLOUR

Astronomers have several techniques for analysing the information contained in images. One of the most important is adding false colour to the image. Saturn has a fairly muted appearance in ordinary photographs. This image has been colour-coded to emphasize the banding of the planet's upper atmosphere.

COLOURING THE SUN

This false-colour ultraviolet image from the TRACE spacecraft shows plasma exploding off the Sun's surface and travelling through the solar atmosphere along loops of the Sun's magnetic field. The colours represent different temperatures. The red regions are the hottest, at 15 million°C (27 million°F).

COMBINING SERIES OF IMAGES

Images of space are often obtained through a series of coloured filters. The object is photographed through each filter in turn, and the resulting images are then combined to give a much fuller picture than with any single ordinary photograph.

This series was taken with the Hubble Space Telescope, and shows Pluto and its moon, Charon.

INFRARED ASTRONOMY

IF OUR EYES WERE SENSITIVE to infrared radiation, the
night sky would be filled with glowing cosmic clouds
and scattered galaxies ablaze with newborn stars.
Everything in the Universe cooler than about
3,000°C (5,400°F) emits most of their energy in the
infrared, which can travel through interstellar dust.

By using infrared
telescopes, we can
reveal information
invisible to the
optical telescope.

INFRARED WAVELENGTHS
As its name suggests, infrared
lies just beyond the red end of
the visible spectrum. It covers
a much wider part of the
electromagnetic spectrum than
visible light: from 700 nm
(28 µin) to 1 mm (0.04 in),
where radio waves begin.
Astronomers divide infrared into
four bands: near, mid-, and far
infrared, and submillimetre
waves. Observing infrared
radiation is always a struggle
within Earth's atmosphere, where
carbon dioxide and water vapour
absorb infrared. Some of the
shorter and longer wavelengths,
however, do reach mountain tops.

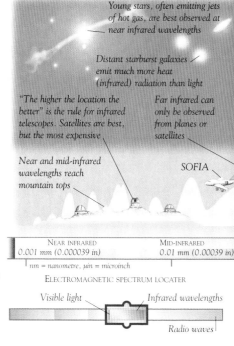

*Young stars, often emitting jets
of hot gas, are best observed at
near infrared wavelengths*

*Distant starburst galaxies
emit much more heat
(infrared) radiation than light*

*"The higher the location the
better" is the rule for infrared
telescopes. Satellites are best,
but the most expensive*

*Far infrared can
only be observed
from planes or
satellites*

*Near and mid-infrared
wavelengths reach
mountain tops*

SOFIA

NEAR INFRARED	MID-INFRARED
0.001 mm (0.000039 in)	0.01 mm (0.00039 in)

nm = nanometre, µin = microinch

ELECTROMAGNETIC SPECTRUM LOCATER

Visible light   *Infrared wavelengths*

Radio waves

Liquid helium in an infrared camera cools it to –270°C (–454°F)

EARTH-BASED TELESCOPES

Infrared telescopes resemble optical telescopes. In fact, the latest big reflectors are designed to observe both infrared and visible light. An infrared camera, however, must have a cooling system so that any heat it gives off does not overwhelm the faint infrared from space.

The constellation of Orion is dominated at optical wavelengths by seven stars making the Hunter's outline

Immense, cool dust clouds dominate the same region in this image captured by the Infrared Astronomical Satellite (IRAS)

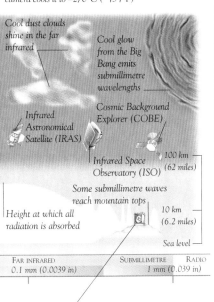

Cool dust clouds shine in the far infrared

Cool glow from the Big Bang emits submillimetre wavelengths

Infrared Astronomical Satellite (IRAS)

Cosmic Background Explorer (COBE)

Infrared Space Observatory (ISO)

100 km (62 miles)

Some submillimetre waves reach mountain tops

Height at which all radiation is absorbed

10 km (6.2 miles)

Sea level

FAR INFRARED	SUBMILLIMETRE	RADIO
0.1 mm (0.0039 in)	1 mm (0.039 in)	

Submillimetre telescopes are like small, high-precision radio telescopes

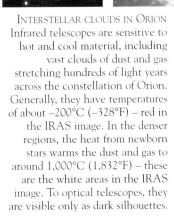

INTERSTELLAR CLOUDS IN ORION
Infrared telescopes are sensitive to hot and cool material, including vast clouds of dust and gas stretching hundreds of light years across the constellation of Orion. Generally, they have temperatures of about –200°C (–328°F) – red in the IRAS image. In the denser regions, the heat from newborn stars warms the dust and gas to around 1,000°C (1,832°F) – these are the white areas in the IRAS image. To optical telescopes, they are visible only as dark silhouettes.

235

ULTRAVIOLET ASTRONOMY

A STAR HOTTER than 10,000°C (18,032°F) shines brightest at ultraviolet wavelengths, and can be tracked with ultraviolet radiation. Ultraviolet can also reveal what is in the hot gas clouds between the stars. Earth's ozone layer protects us from the Sun's ultraviolet radiation, and this makes observation difficult. Hydrogen in space absorbs extreme ultraviolet wavelengths and acts as a fog, hiding most of the distant Universe.

Hot gas streams around massive black holes produce extreme ultraviolet radiation

Rosat satellite carried an extreme ultraviolet telescope to seek out very hot stars and gas

The Sun's chromosphere is hotter than the surface and shines at ultraviolet wavelengths

Solar and Heliospheric Observatory (SOHO) observes fine details in the Sun's atmosphere

_____ Height where all ultraviolet is absorbed

Ozone layer _____

EXTREME ULTRAVIOLET		ULTRAVIOL
50 nm (1.9 μin)	100 nm (3.9 μin)	150 nm (5.9 μ

nm = nanometre, μin = microinch

Visible light

X-rays | Ultraviolet wavelengths

ELECTROMAGNETIC SPECTRUM LOCATER

ULTRAVIOLET WAVELENGTHS

Ultraviolet radiation has shorter wavelengths than visible light and stretches from the violet end of the visible spectrum (390 nm or 15 μin) down to the start of the X-ray region (10 nm or 0.4 μin). Wavelengths between 10 and 91 nm (0.4 and 3.6 μin) are called extreme ultraviolet. Oxygen and nitrogen atoms at high altitudes block the shorter ultraviolet wavelengths, and the ozone layer blocks the remainder, so telescopes must fly above Earth's atmosphere.

GLOWING GASES IN SOLAR ATMOSPHERE
A colour-coded extreme ultraviolet image of the
Sun reveals a thin, patchy shell of glowing gas
around a black globe. The Sun's visible surface
appears dark, while the chromosphere shines
brightly. The temperature and density of gas varies
with changes in the Sun's magnetic field.

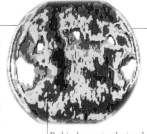

Red is the gas producing the
faintest radiation in ultraviolet,
and white is the brightest

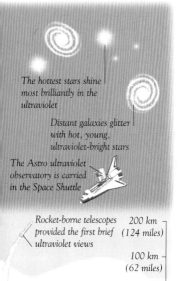

The hottest stars shine
most brilliantly in the
ultraviolet

Distant galaxies glitter
with hot, young,
ultraviolet-bright stars

The Astro ultraviolet
observatory is carried
in the Space Shuttle

Rocket-borne telescopes   200 km
provided the first brief   (124 miles)
ultraviolet views

                          100 km
                          (62 miles)

                          Sea level

Hot gas in
central core

Individual
massive stars

HOT STARS IN GALAXIES
Spiral galaxies appear most spectacular in
the ultraviolet, which reveals the hottest
stars. This is a view of galaxy M81, which
lies 12 million light years away in Ursa
Major. The bright spots are clusters of
massive stars that will quickly burn out.

ULTRAVIOLET
(7.8 µin)   250 nm (9.8 µin)   300 nm (11.8 µin)

STARBURST GALAXY
An ultraviolet image of M94 shows a
different structure than an optical image.
Instead of the central bulge of cool old
stars, there is a giant ring of hot young stars
formed within the past 10 million years.

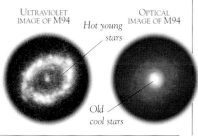

ULTRAVIOLET
IMAGE OF M94

Hot young
stars

OPTICAL
IMAGE OF M94

Old
cool stars

237

X-RAY ASTRONOMY

AT X-RAY WAVELENGTHS, the sky is filled with large glowing clouds of gas and strange fluctuating X-ray stars. X-rays are very short wavelength, high-energy radiation, given out by objects that are hotter than 1 million°C (1.8 million°F). Supernova remnants and the gas around pulsars and black holes, where the temperatures may reach 100 million°C (180 million°F) or more, are powerful X-ray sources.

X-RAY SPECTRUM

X-rays are high-energy electromagnetic radiation with wavelengths between 0.01 and 10 nanometres (3.9 x 10⁻³ and 3.9 x 10⁻¹ microinches), much shorter than visible light. The shortest X-rays carry the most energy. X-rays may be extremely penetrating on Earth – doctors use them to show the body's interior – but the upper atmosphere absorbs all the X-rays from space. So X-ray detectors must be carried beyond the atmosphere on rockets or satellites.

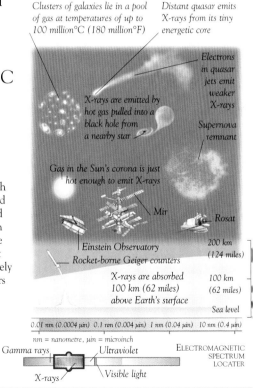

Clusters of galaxies lie in a pool of gas at temperatures of up to 100 million°C (180 million°F)

Distant quasar emits X-rays from its tiny energetic core

Electrons in quasar jets emit weaker X-rays

X-rays are emitted by hot gas pulled into a black hole from a nearby star

Supernova remnant

Gas in the Sun's corona is just hot enough to emit X-rays

Mir

Rosat

Einstein Observatory

Rocket-borne Geiger counters

200 km (124 miles)

X-rays are absorbed 100 km (62 miles) above Earth's surface

100 km (62 miles)

Sea level

0.01 nm (0.0004 μin) 0.1 nm (0.004 μin) 1 nm (0.04 μin) 10 nm (0.4 μin)

nm = nanometre, μin = microinch

Gamma rays

Ultraviolet

ELECTROMAGNETIC SPECTRUM LOCATER

X-rays

Visible light

X-RAY TELESCOPES

X-rays are very difficult to focus because they are absorbed by traditional curved mirrors. They can be reflected only if they hit a metal surface at a very shallow angle, grazing it like a bullet ricocheting off a wall. X-ray telescopes use highly polished tapering metal cylinders, called grazing incidence mirrors, to focus radiation.

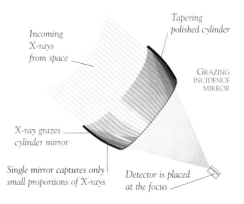

Incoming X-rays from space

Tapering polished cylinder

GRAZING INCIDENCE MIRROR

X-ray grazes cylinder mirror

Single mirror captures only small proportions of X-rays

Detector is placed at the focus

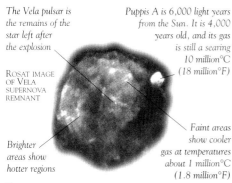

The Vela pulsar is the remains of the star left after the explosion

ROSAT IMAGE OF VELA SUPERNOVA REMNANT

Brighter areas show hotter regions

Puppis A is 6,000 light years from the Sun. It is 4,000 years old, and its gas is still a searing 10 million°C (18 million°F)

Faint areas show cooler gas at temperatures about 1 million°C (1.8 million°F)

SUPERNOVA REMNANTS

About 11,000 years ago a supernova exploded in the constellation Vela, 1,500 light years from Earth. It may have been very bright once, but all that remains is a hot bubble of gas, 140 light years across. Optical telescopes can barely detect it, but Rosat's sensitive X-ray telescope revealed the gas, which is still 8 million°C (14 million°F) in places. It also detected a smaller, more distant supernova remnant, Puppis A.

ROSAT VIEWS THE MOON

In this view, the right side of the Moon is illuminated by the Sun's X-rays. The dark side is silhouetted against the scattered dots of an X-ray background that comes from distant galaxies. Each dot is an individual X-ray hit. (The bright dots on the dark side are electronic noise in the X-ray detector.)

GAMMA-RAY ASTRONOMY

GAMMA RAYS REVEAL the most violent corners of the Universe, including pulsars, quasars, and black holes. They are radiation with the shortest wavelengths and highest energies of all. Gamma rays are created by radioactive atoms in space, by particles colliding at almost the speed of light, and by matter and antimatter annihilating each other.

GAMMA-RAY SPECTRUM
Even the longest gamma rays, bordering on X-rays, have wavelengths that are smaller than an atom. There is no lower limit to gamma-ray wavelengths – the shortest ever detected is a million billion times shorter than ordinary light. Such short-wavelength gamma rays are uncommon, because objects with the energy to create them are extremely rare in the Universe. All gamma rays from space are absorbed by Earth's atmosphere.

CERENKOV DETECTOR
Gamma rays never reach Earth, but a Cerenkov detector can detect them. It looks out for flashes of light in Earth's atmosphere, caused by gamma rays colliding with gas atoms.

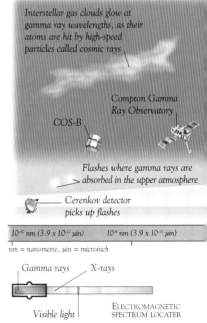

Interstellar gas clouds glow at gamma ray wavelengths, as their atoms are hit by high-speed particles called cosmic rays

Compton Gamma Ray Observatory

COS-B

Flashes where gamma rays are absorbed in the upper atmosphere

Cerenkov detector picks up flashes

10^{-6} nm (3.9 x 10^{-12} µin) 10^{-8} nm (3.9 x 10^{-10} µin)

nm = nanometre, µin = microinch

Gamma rays   X-rays

Visible light

ELECTROMAGNETIC SPECTRUM LOCATER

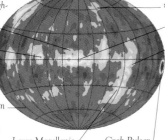

Clouds of gas in the Milky Way, bombarded by high-speed electrons

Cygnus X-1 – gas swirling around a black hole

The whole sky map from the Compton satellite. Red shows the strongest gamma-ray sources, while yellow and green show less intense regions

Large Magellanic Cloud contains many pulsars and black holes

Crab Pulsar flashes 30 times a second

Quasar 3C 279 – a distant galaxy with a massive central black hole

Centre of the Milky Way Galaxy

Vela Pulsar flashes 13 times a second

SKY IN GAMMA RAYS

The sky looks very different when viewed at gamma-ray wavelengths. We see none of the usual stars and constellations. Instead, huge glowing clouds of gas stretch across the view. Among them are bright points, flashing on and off. Some are pulsars, with a regular period to their flashing. Others, called gamma-ray bursters, flare brilliantly for just a few seconds, outshining everything else in the gamma-ray sky.

High-speed electrons from a spinning neutron star generate pulses of gamma rays

A gamma-ray burster may be a neutron star collision or a hypernova – a spinning black hole within an exploding star

Gamma rays can smash through the matter in space, travelling for billions of light years

Altitude at which gamma rays are absorbed by the atmosphere

Balloon gamma-ray telescope

100 km (62 miles)

Sea level

nm $(3.9 \times 10^{-8}$ μin) | 10^{-4} nm $(3.9 \times 10^{-6}$ μin) | 10^{-2} nm $(3.9 \times 10^{-4}$ μin)

CODED MASKS

When exposed to a gamma-ray source, a coded mask detector casts a shadow where no gamma rays are detected. The position of this shadow can pinpoint the position of the gamma-ray source.

CODED MASK GAMMA-RAY DETECTOR

Gamma rays from space

Cross-shaped mask absorbs gamma rays

Shadow cast by mask

No sparks in shadow

Gamma rays trigger sparks

EXPLORING SPACE

TELESCOPES IN SPACE

BY PLACING THEIR TELESCOPES in orbit above Earth's atmosphere, astronomers get a much better view. They can see farther and can collect information from wavelengths that are absorbed by the atmosphere. Information and images gathered in orbit are transmitted back to Earth for study and analysis.

ORBITING TELESCOPE
Two astronauts from the Space Shuttle Columbia make repairs to the Hubble Space Telescope in 2002.

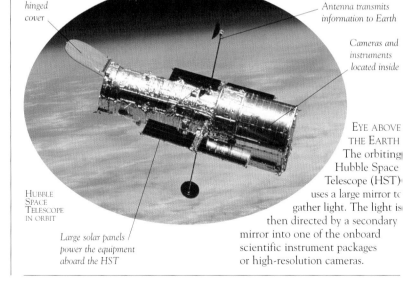

Protective hinged cover

Antenna transmits information to Earth

Cameras and instruments located inside

HUBBLE SPACE TELESCOPE IN ORBIT

Large solar panels power the equipment aboard the HST

EYE ABOVE THE EARTH
The orbiting Hubble Space Telescope (HST) uses a large mirror to gather light. The light is then directed by a secondary mirror into one of the onboard scientific instrument packages or high-resolution cameras.

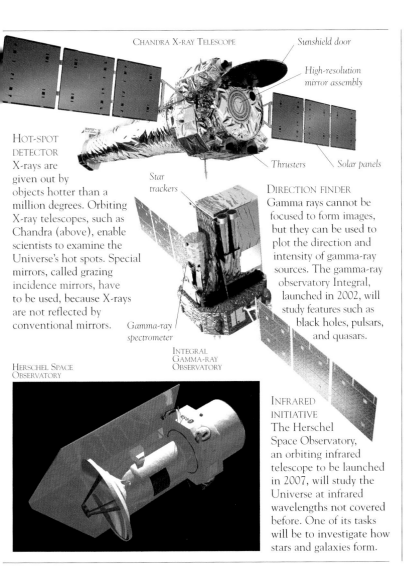

CHANDRA X-RAY TELESCOPE

Sunshield door

*High-resolution
mirror assembly*

HOT-SPOT
DETECTOR
X-rays are
given out by
objects hotter than a
million degrees. Orbiting
X-ray telescopes, such as
Chandra (above), enable
scientists to examine the
Universe's hot spots. Special
mirrors, called grazing
incidence mirrors, have
to be used, because X-rays
are not reflected by
conventional mirrors.

*Star
trackers*

Thrusters   *Solar panels*

*Gamma-ray
spectrometer*

DIRECTION FINDER
Gamma rays cannot be
focused to form images,
but they can be used to
plot the direction and
intensity of gamma-ray
sources. The gamma-ray
observatory Integral,
launched in 2002, will
study features such as
black holes, pulsars,
and quasars.

INTEGRAL
GAMMA-RAY
OBSERVATORY

HERSCHEL SPACE
OBSERVATORY

INFRARED
INITIATIVE
The Herschel
Space Observatory,
an orbiting infrared
telescope to be launched
in 2007, will study the
Universe at infrared
wavelengths not covered
before. One of its tasks
will be to investigate how
stars and galaxies form.

ROCKETS

SATELLITES, SPACE PROBES, and astronauts are lifted into space by rockets. There are two main types: the conventional tall, thin rocket made from several stages stacked on top of each other, and the newer Space Shuttle design, which lifts off with the aid of massive booster rockets. When it returns from space, the Shuttle lands like an aircraft.

LIFT-OFF
A Soyuz-Fregat rocket blasts off from its launch-pad. Its engines burn thousands of litre (gallons) of fuel per second.

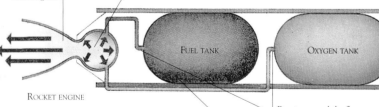

Nozzle shapes the stream of hot exhaust gases

Liquid fuel and oxygen are combined in the combustion chamber

FUEL TANK

OXYGEN TANK

ROCKET ENGINE

Pumps control the flow of fuel and oxygen to the combustion chamber

Fuel and oxygen stored in reinforced pressurized tanks

ROCKET POWER
A rocket is propelled upwards by hot exhaust gases streaming from nozzles at the tail. These gases are the result of burning a mixture of liquid oxygen and fuel (such as liquid hydrogen) inside a combustion chamber. Carrying its own oxygen supply enables a rocket engine to function in the airless vacuum of space.

ESCAPE VELOCITY

A rocket, or any other object, is held on Earth's surface by the force of gravity. To escape the effects of Earth's gravity and enter space, a rocket needs to achieve a speed of 40,000 kph (25,000 mph) – this is the "escape velocity" of planet Earth. On the Moon, where the force of gravity is only one sixth as powerful as on Earth, the escape velocity is lower – only about 8,600 kph (5,300 mph).

Payload –
satellite or
space probe

Third
stage
rocket
engines

ARIANE: A TYPICAL
THREE-STAGE
LAUNCH VEHICLE

Second
stage
rocket
engines

External booster
rockets assist first
stage engines at
liftoff

First
stage
rocket
engines

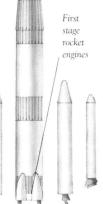

REUSABLE SPACECRAFT

A streaming exhaust trail marks the beginning of another Space Shuttle mission. Unlike conventional rockets, which can be used only once, the Shuttle is reusable. The massive booster rockets are jettisoned two minutes after launch and recovered. The Shuttle's own engines carry it on into orbit, and small thruster rockets steer it as it travels around Earth.

ROCKET FUELS

COMPARED TO WHEN the space age began, rockets are now far more reliable as rocket scientists have learnt the best way to make, combine, and supply the propellant, or fuel. The fuels carried by rockets need oxidants to burn and release energy. Fuel and oxidants can be solid or liquid.

SPACE SHUTTLE FUEL
At liftoff, nearly 90 per cent of the Space Shuttle's weight is propellant – both solid and liquid. Liquid hydrogen and liquid oxygen are carried, separate to one another, in the external tank. About 470 kg (1,036 lb) of fuel is delivered to each of the three main engines every second. The 83-tonne (81.5-ton) boosters carry 504 tonnes (496 tons) of fuel each.

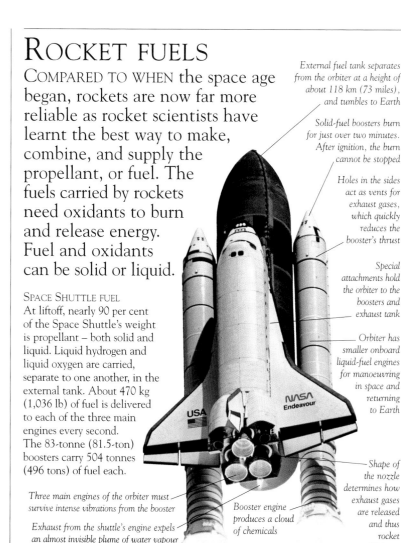

External fuel tank separates from the orbiter at a height of about 118 km (73 miles), and tumbles to Earth

Solid-fuel boosters burn for just over two minutes. After ignition, the burn cannot be stopped

Holes in the sides act as vents for exhaust gases, which quickly reduces the booster's thrust

Special attachments hold the orbiter to the boosters and exhaust tank

Orbiter has smaller onboard liquid-fuel engines for manoeuvring in space and returning to Earth

Shape of the nozzle determines how exhaust gases are released and thus rocket efficiency

Three main engines of the orbiter must survive intense vibrations from the booster

Booster engine produces a cloud of chemicals

Exhaust from the shuttle's engine expels an almost invisible plume of water vapour

SOLID ROCKET FUEL

The propellant in solid-fuel rockets is shaped into pellets, which contain an oxidant, a fuel, and substances to prevent them decomposing in storage. The way the propellant is packed into the casing determines whether the surface will burn at a constant rate (neutral burn), providing an even thrust; whether it will increase gradually, causing thrust to increase (progressive burn); or whether it will decrease, causing thrust to decrease gradually (regressive burn).

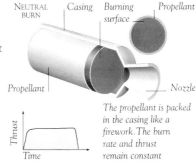

NEUTRAL BURN · Casing · Burning surface · Propellant · Propellant · Nozzle

The propellant is packed in the casing like a firework. The burn rate and thrust remain constant

Thrust / Time

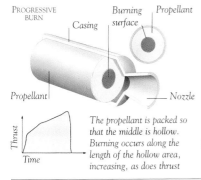

PROGRESSIVE BURN · Burning surface · Propellant · Casing · Propellant · Nozzle

Thrust / Time

The propellant is packed so that the middle is hollow. Burning occurs along the length of the hollow area, increasing, as does thrust

REGRESSIVE BURN · Casing · Burning surface · Propellant · Propellant · Nozzle

Thrust / Time

The propellant is loosely packed in a rod-like casing. Burning occurs along its length. Thrust decreases as the rod shrinks

LIQUID ROCKET FUEL

Liquid propellants produce more thrust per second than solid propellants. Liquid oxygen boils at –183°C (–297°F), cold enough to crack metal or shatter rubber, while liquid hydrogen boils at –253°C (–423°F). Though difficult to handle, these make an efficient propellant.

Liquid oxygen and liquid hydrogen mix and burn in the combustion chamber, propelling the rocket

SPACE LAUNCHERS

RELIABILITY, COST, AND TECHNICAL capability are the important factors in determining which air-launch rocket should place a spacecraft in orbit. Heavy-lift launchers send space probes on interplanetary journeys or put satellites into high geostationary orbit. Smaller air launch rockets are used to place small payloads in low-Earth orbit.

Proton launches large satellites, such as the Asiasat HSG-1, which beams television and telephone signals to Asia and the Pacific

HEAVY-LIFT ROCKETS
The Russian Proton rocket and Europe's Ariane 5 can be thought of as rockets with muscle. They can place 20 tonnes (19 tons) – the equivalent of 20 cars – into low-Earth orbit. For such launches, Proton has three stages. There is also a four-stage version for launching spacecraft on interplanetary journeys.

AIR-LAUNCH ROCKETS
L1011 Stargazer aircraft carry the Pegasus rocket to an altitude of 12.2 km (7.5 miles), releasing it above the open ocean. Thereafter, three rocket stages place a payload of up to 500 kg (1,105 lb) in orbit.

WORKHORSE OF ROCKETRY

The Delta family have launched satellites since 1960 and Delta II since 1989. Delta II can launch 1.8 tonnes (1.75 tons) into a transfer orbit for geostationary orbit. Delta II's reliability led to the Delta family being called the "workhorse" of rocketry. Delta III, the latest addition, can place 8 tonnes (7.8 tons) in low-Earth orbit, or 4 tonnes (3.9 tons) in a geostationary orbit (*see* p 262).

Delta rockets ferry large satellites, such as the Thor III communications satellite, to orbit

Long March rockets have carried small satellites, like the Asia-Pacific Mobile Telecommunications system, to orbit

ROCKET CHALLENGERS

Spacecraft are complicated. A tiny mistake can destroy a multimillion dollar mission. Nearly all orders for launchers go to companies (usually in the United States, Russia, Europe, or Japan) with the most experience of manufacturing space technology. Other countries launch their own rockets, but find it hard to sell them to others. China is now trying to sell its rockets abroad.

LAUNCH CENTRES

LAUNCH CENTRES ARE the gateways to space. They can be small sites, or vast, expensive complexes sprawling over many hectares. Larger spaceports have many launchpads. Before the launch, engineers assemble the launch vehicle in multistorey buildings. Then giant platforms lumber to the pad carrying the assembled launcher. Scattered around the site are the control room from which mission specialists oversee the final countdown, huge tanks for the propellant, weather stations to check conditions on the day of launch, and tracking stations to monitor the ascent to space.

KENNEDY SPACE CENTER
The 56,600-hectare (139,862-acre) Kennedy Space Center at Cape Canaveral is NASA's launch site for the Space Shuttle. The 4.5-km (2.8-mile) runway is checked for stray animals before a landing.

The Alcantara launch centre in Brazil is the newest one in the world

Vandenberg •

• Kennedy

Equator

Kourou •

Alcanta

KOUROU SPACE CENTRE

Kourou is used by Arianespace and the European Space Agency to launch satellites. It is close to the equator and therefore favourable for placing satellites into the geostationary orbit directly above the equator.

BAIKONUR COSMODROME

Baikonur, in Kazakhstan, is the world's largest space centre and one of the oldest. The very first satellite, Sputnik, was launched from Baikonur in 1957.

LAUNCH LOCATIONS

Several factors influence the choice of a launch site. It has to be away from populated areas, yet it must be accessible because of the heavy equipment needed for a launch. The United States and Europe have sites located in coastal areas, launching over oceans. Geography is also important – launches to the east are preferred as they benefit from Earth's eastward rotation, as are those near the Equator, where rotation is greatest.

Plesetsk near the Arctic Circle launches to polar orbit

China's launch site for civil satellites is in the Gobi Desert

Kagoshima and Tanegashima launch only at limited times to protect Japan's fishing industry

Plesetsk

Kapustin Yar

Baikonur

Jiuquan

Kagoshima

Xichang

Tanegashima

Sriharikota

San Marco

Equator

BLAST OFF
The USA's Space Shuttle awaits launch at Cape Canaveral, Florida

COUNTDOWN

Communications satellite being prepared for Ariane 5

THE FINAL PART of every launch campaign begins when all the separate components arrive at the launch centre to be assembled into the launch vehicle. During this final countdown, engineers make the site ready for launch, and personnel are evacuated from the area in preparation for liftoff.

MISSION CONTROL

The Jupiter control room in Kourou, French Guiana, directs the Ariane 5 liftoff. Three teams monitor the status of the launcher, the payload, and the tracking stations that will follow its ascent, while weather and safety teams work elsewhere.

PAYLOAD INTEGRATION

Satellites are mounted on the launcher in the final assembly building eight days before liftoff. The satellite is linked via Ariane 5 to the Jupiter control room so that the payload can be monitored.

The leader of the tracking team monitors the launcher's path with radar

Mission controllers monitor launch support equipment

Four computers are reserved for senior personnel from the French and European Space Agencies, the satellite owner, and Arianespace

Director of operations (DDO) authorizes the final countdown

Leader of the launch team filters information about launcher status to DDO

Screen displays the trajectory of launch

Telecoms link with stations that track the launcher's ascent

Payload team ensures that the tracking stations receive signals once the satellite is in orbit

Deputy leader of the launch team acts as backup to DDO

TO THE LAUNCHPAD

An 870-tonne (856-ton) launch table supports the launcher during assembly. The day before liftoff, a truck tows the launcher and table along rail tracks to the launchpad. Propellant is piped into the launcher at the pad.

ON THE LAUNCHPAD

There are three trenches at the launch area through which flames from the boosters and main engine escape during liftoff. A tower supplies water to reduce noise and to cool the trenches and launch table, in order to avoid damage to the launcher and its payload.

LIFTOFF

Six hours before liftoff, the launch area is prepared. The flight program is loaded into the two onboard computers, and then initiated to check radio links between launcher and ground. Five hours before launch, the main stage tanks are filled with propellant. Six minutes before liftoff, the synchronized sequence leading to liftoff begins.

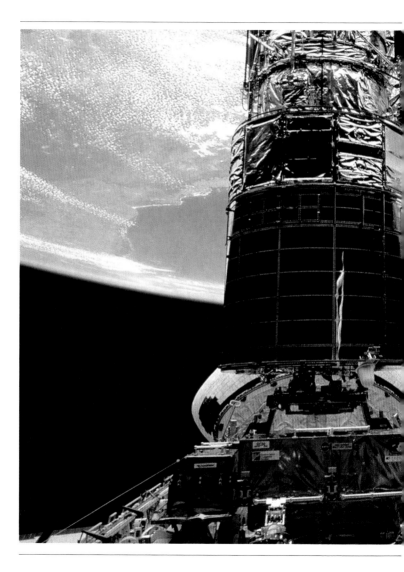

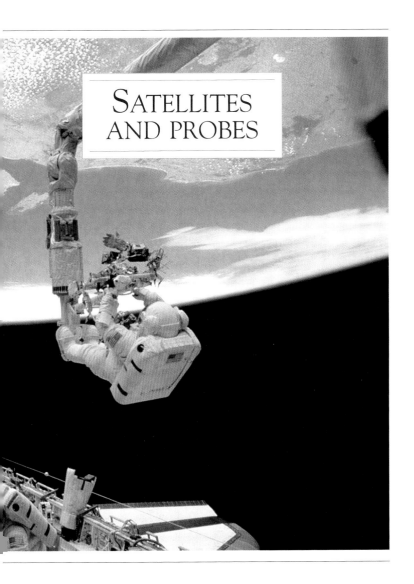

SATELLITES
AND PROBES

HUBBLE SPACE TELESCOPE

THE ULTIMATE TELESCOPE for astronomers seeking pin-sharp views of the depths of the Universe, the Hubble Space Telescope was launched in 1990 after decades of planning. It is an unmanned observatory in orbit far above the clouds and atmospheric haze that block the view of Earth-based telescopes.

HOW HUBBLE WORKS

Hubble is a reflecting telescope much like those on Earth. In space, however, it must operate without mains electricity, a mounting to swivel it around, or cables linking it to control computers. Instead, it has solar panels to provide power, reaction wheels for pointing, and radio antennas for communicating with Earth.

Reaction wheels point Hubble at targets in space

Tape recorders

Wide Field and Planetary Camera (WF/PC)

Space Telescope Imaging Spectrograph splits light into its constituent wavelengths

COSTAR replacement optics, correct Hubble's defective mirror

Position occupied by COSTAR

Faint Object Camera is very sensitive, but its view is more restricted than the WF/PC

Fine guidance sensors lock onto bright stars, keeping the telescope steady and the images sharp

Near-Infrared Camera and Multi-Object Spectrometer with three infrared detectors

Main mirror, 2.4 m (8 ft) in diameter, collects and focuses light

TDRS ground station in New Mexico relays signals to and from Hubble and the Goddard Space Flight Centre —

HUBBLE DATA	
Launched	25 April 1990
Main mirror	2.4-m (7.9-ft) diameter
Secondary mirror	0.34-m (1.1-ft) diameter
Length	13.1 m (43 ft)
Diameter	4.3 m (14.1 ft)
Solar panels	12.1 x 2.4 m (39.7 x 7.9 ft)
Mass	11.6 tonnes (11.4 tons)
Height of orbit	610 km (379 miles)
Period of orbit	95 minutes
Speed	27,700 kph (17,213 mph)
Intended lifetime	15 years +
Cost (at launch)	£844 million ($1.5 billion)

Tracking and Data Relay Satellite (TDRS) – a go-between for Hubble's radio messages. From its high orbit, it keeps both Hubble and ground control in sight

Sunshade protected the telescope at launch, and helps to prevent bright sunlight spoiling images

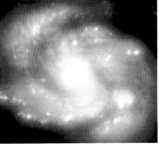

Signals to and from TDRS and Earth

High-gain antenna receives commands from Earth, and returns Hubble pictures as TV signals

Magnetometer senses Hubble's movement through Earth's magnetic field

ADVANTAGES OF HUBBLE

Telescopes viewing the Universe from Earth must look upwards through our turbulent atmosphere, which constantly shifts and distorts the light from stars and galaxies – rather like looking through the water in a busy swimming pool. That's why stars seem to twinkle. From its perch above the atmosphere, Hubble has a clear view of objects in the Universe, from planets to quasars billions of light years away.

Handrail for astronauts

Secondary mirror, supported within the telescope tube

Light is reflected from the main to the secondary mirror, and then to the cameras and detectors behind the main mirror

Solar arrays convert sunlight into electricity

Second high-gain antenna

Computers coordinate onboard systems

DEFECTIVE MIRROR

The first pictures received from Hubble were out of focus, though still better than any ground-based telescope. NASA realized that the mirror was 0.002 mm (0.00008 in) too shallow at the outer edge.

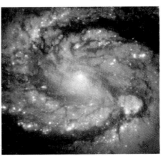

HUBBLE'S IMAGE OF GALAXY M100

SATELLITES AND ORBITS

ANYTHING IN ORBIT around another object is called a satellite. The Moon is a natural satellite of Earth. Since 1957, hundreds of artificial satellites of all shapes and sizes have been launched into orbit around Earth. They occupy different types of orbit, depending on what they are designed to do. Satellites must remain stable so that their instruments always point in the right directions.

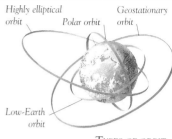

Highly elliptical orbit   Polar orbit   Geostationary orbit

Low-Earth orbit

TYPES OF ORBIT
Most satellites are launched into one of four main orbits. A nearly circular low-Earth orbit is about 250 km (155 miles) above Earth. Polar orbits are often 800 km (500 miles) high. A highly elliptical orbit has a far lower altitude when it is at its closest to Earth (its perigee) than at its most distant (its apogee). A geostationary orbit is 36,000 km (22,320 miles) above the equator.

TELEMETRY, TRACKING, AND COMMAND
Telemetry allows people on the ground to receive measurements from satellites in orbit. These measurements, sent as radio signals, include information that allows operators to pinpoint the satellite's position so that they can track it, and send command signals to change its orbit.

Ground antenna sends and receives signals to and from the satellites

Antenna for telemetry
and command

Antenna feed
radiates radio
signals that
reflect off the dish

Antenna
dish does
not spin

Equipment is
designed to fit
into the satellite's
cylindrical shape

If sensors detect
a wobble in the
satellite, thrusters
correct spin and
restore stability

Outer panels slip
down in orbit to
uncover solar
panels beneath.
This increases the
power available to
the satellite

Solar cell panels

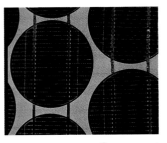

SOLAR CELLS

Solar cells produce electrical power when light falls on them. On satellites, the cells are arranged into solar panels, sometimes called arrays. They provide a satellite with the electrical power to do its job and to keep both the satellite and its payload in orbit.

Space Shuttle astronaut
retrieves the Westar
satellite to bring it back
to Earth for repair

SPIN STABILIZATION

Things that spin are naturally stable. A spinning top remains stable if it is spun fast enough. In the early days of satellites, designers decided to exploit this principle. The result is spin-stabilized satellites. These are often cylindrical in shape, and make about one revolution every second. The antenna dish must always point to Earth, so it does not spin. Designers must take care that the dish does not destabilize and unbalance the satellite.

HOUSEKEEPING DATA

Information about a satellite's health is called housekeeping data. This data alerts ground control when something is wrong – if the satellite is becoming unstable, for instance. Ground-based operators can often send a command to solve the problem, or even organize a rescue mission.

263

COMMUNICATIONS SATELLITES

TELEPHONE CALLS, TELEVISION BROADCASTS, and the
Internet can all be transmitted by communications
satellites. Many are in geostationary orbit (GEO), bu
so great is the demand for communications that this
orbit has become crowded. Now, satellites are being
launched into low-Earth orbit (below GEO).

GEOSTATIONARY SATELLITES
Satellites in GEO above the Equator
appear stationary because at this altitude,
they take the same time to complete one
orbit as Earth takes to spin on its axis.

*Three satellites, spaced evenly
apart in GEO, can view the
entire planet, except the poles*

*Telephone calls are now
possible between aircraft
and ground*

EARTH STATIONS
The antennas and other equipment needed on
the ground to transmit signals to and from
satellites are known as the Earth station.
These can be housed in large buildings
and their antennas act as a gateway
through which, for example,
thousands of telephone calls
are transmitted. Earth
stations can also
be small units,
designed to
fit on ships
or planes.

*Antennas
transmit and
receive signals,
and are the
key to an Earth
station's operation*

SATELLITE
FOOTPRINT
Radio waves
from a satellite fall
on Earth with a
pattern – the satellite
footprint. Antennas
within it can transmit
signals to and from
the satellite.

*A satellite footprint might
cover a whole continent
or one small country*

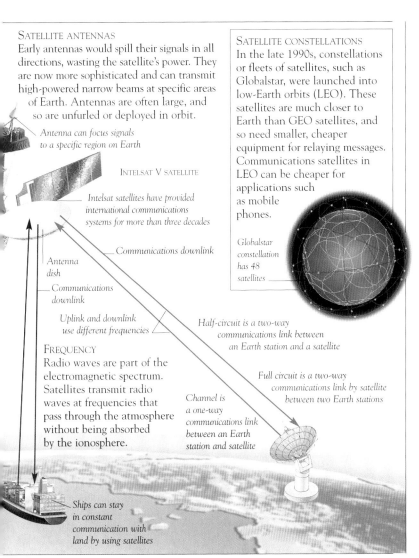

SATELLITE ANTENNAS

Early antennas would spill their signals in all directions, wasting the satellite's power. They are now more sophisticated and can transmit high-powered narrow beams at specific areas of Earth. Antennas are often large, and so are unfurled or deployed in orbit.

Antenna can focus signals to a specific region on Earth

INTELSAT V SATELLITE

Intelsat satellites have provided international communications systems for more than three decades

Communications downlink

Antenna dish

Communications downlink

Uplink and downlink use different frequencies

FREQUENCY

Radio waves are part of the electromagnetic spectrum. Satellites transmit radio waves at frequencies that pass through the atmosphere without being absorbed by the ionosphere.

SATELLITE CONSTELLATIONS

In the late 1990s, constellations or fleets of satellites, such as Globalstar, were launched into low-Earth orbits (LEO). These satellites are much closer to Earth than GEO satellites, and so need smaller, cheaper equipment for relaying messages. Communications satellites in LEO can be cheaper for applications such as mobile phones.

Globalstar constellation has 48 satellites

Half-circuit is a two-way communications link between an Earth station and a satellite

Full circuit is a two-way communications link by satellite between two Earth stations

Channel is a one-way communications link between an Earth station and satellite

Ships can stay in constant communication with land by using satellites

265

NAVIGATION SATELLITES

SATELLITES CAN BE USED in navigation to establish an exact position on Earth. They transmit radio waves that can be detected even if it is cloudy. As a result, navigation is now possible in any weather. The Global Positioning System (GPS) is the most reliable and accurate navigation system ever.

HOW GPS WORKS

GPS consists of 24 satellites as well as equipment on the ground. The satellites broadcast their positions and the time as given by their accurate atomic clocks. They are spaced in orbits so that a receiver anywhere on Earth can always receive signals from at least four satellites, and they remain at an altitude of 20,200 km (12,552 miles). The GPS receiver knows precisely when the signal was sent and when it arrived, and so can calculate the distance between itself and each of the satellites. With this information, it works out its own position, including altitude. Each satellite is designed to last for seven and a half years.

GLONASS

The Global Orbiting Navigation Satellite System (GLONASS), owned by Russia, allows users to work out their positions to between 20 and 100 m (66 and 328 ft). Special techniques permit greater precision, if needed. These satellites give worldwide coverage. The European Space Agency is improving coverage of Europe by building equipment designed to receive signals from both GLONASS and GPS.

Antennas

Thrusters keep the satellite orientated correctly towards Earth

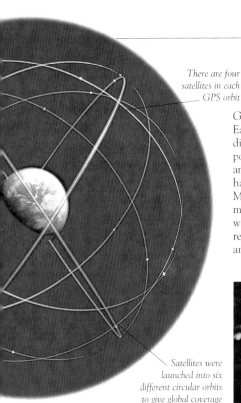

There are four satellites in each GPS orbit

GPS receivers can be as small as mobile phones

GPS RECEIVERS

Early receivers displayed the user's position as latitude and longitude, which had to be plotted on a map. Modern ones display a map marking the user's position to within a few metres (feet). The receivers also calculate speed and direction of travel.

IN-CAR NAVIGATION ROUTE MAP

Satellites were launched into six different circular orbits to give global coverage

ATOMIC CLOCKS

Atomic clocks keep time accurately. They are used on GPS satellites to keep time to within one second every 300,000 years, enabling accurate time signals to be transmitted.

CAESIUM ATOMIC CLOCK

CAR NAVIGATION

Several car manufacturers now install GPS receivers to aid route planning. Companies that own a large fleet of vehicles may also use GPS to keep track of them. Some emergency vehicles use GPS signals to quickly find the fastest route to the scene of an emergency.

267

METEOROLOGY SATELLITES

METEOROLOGY SATELLITES RECORD images to make weather forecasts, show cloud cover, and monitor hurricanes across oceans. They carry instruments to take readings, which are converted to temperatures, pressures, and humidities. These, together with information from sources such as weather buoys, balloons, and ships, help forecasters make predictions.

HURRICANE FRAN IN 1996

HURRICANE FORECASTING

Before weather satellites existed, hurricanes would develop unseen over oceans and strike land with very little warning, sometimes killing thousands of people. Hurricanes are extreme tropical storms, with wind speeds over 120 kph (75 mph). In tropical storms, winds circle a calm eye of low air pressure. Now weather satellites constantly monitor the oceans for possible tropical storms.

Hurricane eye

SCANNING THE GLOBE
Geostationary satellites scan the region beneath them every 30 minutes. If a tropical storm develops, they scan in more detail every 15 minutes. The satellites also measure temperature.

HURRICANE
FLORENCE IN 1994

268

HOMING IN

As a tropical storm becomes a hurricane and nears land, the US Air Force sends its Weather Squadron – the Hurricane Hunters – into the storm to take further measurements.

Meteosat satellites collate weather data over Europe and Africa and relay it to computing and forecasting centres around Europe

METEOSAT SATELLITE

Meteosat's instruments record both images and temperatures in the atmosphere

SATELLITES AND COMPUTING

Computers are essential for scientists to turn satellite measurements into the temperatures, pressures, humidities, and wind speeds needed for a weather report. The computers also combine data from radar, ships, buoys, planes, and satellites to give timely and accurate forecasts.

WEATHER ORBITS

Weather satellites occupy both geostationary and polar orbits. Geostationary satellites, such as GOES, stay above the same place on the equator and record changes continually. They have a wide view, except of the northern regions. Polar orbit satellites, such as NOAA 10, do not have a constant view of the same region, but can see the poles and more detail than is possible from geostationary orbit.

NOAA 10 orbits Earth in 100 minutes. It is over the same place once every 12 hours

NOAA 10 SATELLITE

GOES satellites are positioned in geostationary orbit to observe the USA and either the Atlantic or Pacific Ocean

GOES SATELLITE

Scale exaggerated for clarity

The geostationary orbit is 36,000 km (22,320 miles) above Earth

The polar orbit is typically 900 km (560 miles) above Earth, passing over the poles

HURRICANE NEARING JAPAN

PREDICTING LANDFALL

For each year during the past 20 years, satellites have contributed to improvements of between 0.5 and 1 per cent in the accuracy of hurricane forecasts. The place where a hurricane will meet land – known as landfall – can now be predicted to within 160 km (99 miles).

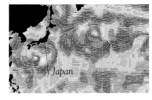

Japan

269

EARTH RESOURCES SATELLITES

SATELLITES THAT HELP SCIENTISTS to study Earth's surface are called Earth resources satellites. Their instruments analyse light and radiation reflected and emitted from surface features. Satellites pass regularly over the globe, allowing scientists to map how an area changes over time.

THEMATIC MAPPER

Different types of radiation have different wavelengths. The thematic mapper – an instrument aboard Landsat satellites – measures the intensity of radiation in seven different wavelength bands as they cover more than two-thirds of the globe. By assigning different colours to each band, scientists can build up a map of an area.

Thematic mapper

LANDSAT 4 SATELLITE

WHAT THE MAPPER REVEALS

Each of a thematic mapper's bands reveals something different. Band five, for example, detects the range of infrared wavelengths that shows moisture content in vegetation. If the intensity is low, the crops might be on the verge of failing.

OCEAN SURVEILLANCE

To understand Earth and its climate, we need to know what happens in and above its oceans as they cover more than two-thirds of the globe. ERS-1 was one of the first satellites for ocean surveillance.

Infrared instrument measured sea-surface and cloud temperature

MONITORING CROPS IN CALIFORNIA, USA

ERS-1 carried instruments to measure infrared and microwave radiation, which are the wavelength bands that give the most information about ocean and atmospheric conditions

Radar worked with two types of antennas to give a microwave image of the ocean and coastal areas and to show the winds on the ocean's surface

MULTISPECTRAL SCANNER

Antennas monitored the choppiness of the ocean

Antennas collected data for a microwave image of the ocean and coastal areas

Radar altimeter recorded wave height and the shape of the ocean surface to help deduce wind speed

SPECTRAL RESOLUTION
The multispectral scanner (MSS) on Landsat 1 was the first satellite instrument to record radiation intensity in different wavelength bands. It uses a range of wavelengths to gather information about different aspects of Earth's surface.

DEFORESTATION
A Landsat image shows forests in the Ivory Coast in Africa. The colours identify different types of surface: red is forest and pale blue is soil, while brown indicates crops. Successive images taken over months or years showed the red areas decreasing as trees were cut down.

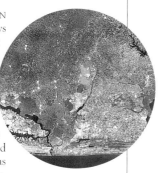

MINERAL DEPOSITS IN CHILE

FALSE COLOURS
People cannot see infrared so scientists give each wavelength band an identifying colour. Maps that use this are called false colour images. In this image, volcanic soil is brown, vegetation is red, water is blue, and mineral deposits are white.

SPACE DEBRIS

ANYTHING IN ORBIT that has no use is called space debris. This includes discarded rockets and obsolete satellites, or fragments of destroyed ones, that could stay in orbit for hundreds of years. Space nations are trying to reduce "space junk", which accounts for 90 per cent of all objects orbiting Earth.

HAZARDS IN SPACE
There are an estimated 8,500 items of space debris bigger than 10 cm (3.9 in) in orbit around Earth. The rubbish is created at many stages of a space operation, such as during separation when the nose cone is discarded once a satellite is in orbit. Space junk accumulates most quickly in those orbits that are used most often. Satellites and debris could collide at speeds of up to 40,000 kph (24,855 mph), causing serious damage.

Each yellow dot is a piece of space junk orbiting Earth

Most space debris is in low-Earth orbit

TRACKING DEBRIS
The worldwide radar network of the North American Aerospace Defense Command (NORAD) monitors objects in orbit. Items as small as a tennis ball are routinely detected in low-Earth orbit, while 1-m (3.2-ft) objects can be observed in geostationary orbit. Computers use this information to predict the likelihood of a collision with spacecraft.

DEBRIS ORBITING
EARTH

*Debris in geostationary
orbit is marked as a loop
around Earth*

MEEP MODULE ON MIR

DAMAGE CONTROL

The best form of damage control is not to be hit in the first place, so the International Space Station (ISS) is designed to move out of the path of large chunks of debris. Experiments such as the Mir environmental effects payload (MEEP) provide data on the risks that the ISS faces.

PROTECTION

One way to protect sensitive areas of a spacecraft is to wrap it in layers of lightweight ceramic fibre. Each layer disperses the energy of a particle, which disintegrates before it hits the spacecraft wall. These ceramic bumpers are used on the ISS to prevent the type of damage recorded in hypervelocity test chambers.

INTERNATIONAL SPACE STATION

APOLLO 12 AFTER SPLASHDOWN FROM ORBIT

RE-ENTRY

Satellites return to Earth slowly. Friction with the air heats them when they re-enter Earth's atmosphere. Some disintegrate, while others survive and hit the ground or sea. Today, owners have to control the end of their satellite's life so that it is removed from orbit and does not remain as debris.

FLY-BYS AND ORBITERS

LIFTED INTO SPACE by rockets, space probes are computer-controlled robots packed with scientific instruments. Probes are sent to fly by a planet, or even orbit around it, sending data and images back to Earth. After they have completed their planned missions, some probes continue on into space.

VOLCANIC DISCOVERY
The probe Voyager I obtained this image of Io, which shows the first active volcano seen outside Earth.

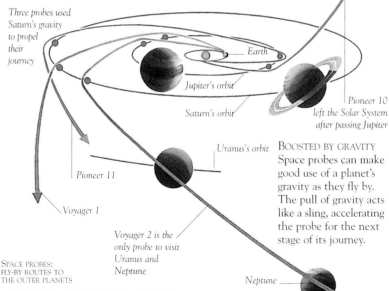

Three probes used Saturn's gravity to propel their journey

Earth

Jupiter's orbit

Saturn's orbit

Pioneer 10 left the Solar System after passing Jupiter

Uranus's orbit

Pioneer 11

Voyager 1

Voyager 2 is the only probe to visit Uranus and Neptune

Neptune

SPACE PROBES: FLY-BY ROUTES TO THE OUTER PLANETS

BOOSTED BY GRAVITY
Space probes can make good use of a planet's gravity as they fly by. The pull of gravity acts like a sling, accelerating the probe for the next stage of its journey.

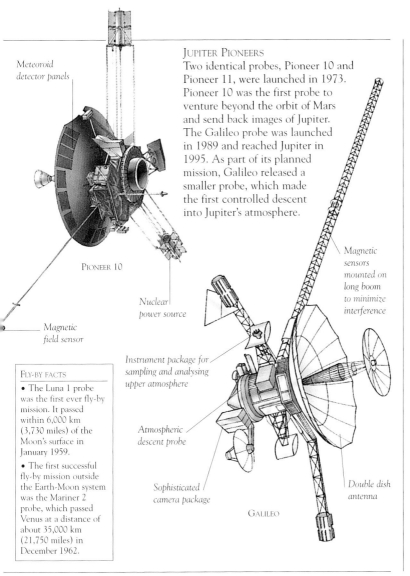

Meteoroid detector panels

JUPITER PIONEERS

Two identical probes, Pioneer 10 and Pioneer 11, were launched in 1973. Pioneer 10 was the first probe to venture beyond the orbit of Mars and send back images of Jupiter. The Galileo probe was launched in 1989 and reached Jupiter in 1995. As part of its planned mission, Galileo released a smaller probe, which made the first controlled descent into Jupiter's atmosphere.

Magnetic sensors mounted on long boom to minimize interference

PIONEER 10

Nuclear power source

Magnetic field sensor

FLY-BY FACTS

• The Luna 1 probe was the first ever fly-by mission. It passed within 6,000 km (3,730 miles) of the Moon's surface in January 1959.

• The first successful fly-by mission outside the Earth-Moon system was the Mariner 2 probe, which passed Venus at a distance of about 35,000 km (21,750 miles) in December 1962.

Instrument package for sampling and analysing upper atmosphere

Atmospheric descent probe

Sophisticated camera package

Double dish antenna

GALILEO

LANDERS

SPACE PROBES SENT to orbit a planet can release a second craft to land on the surface. The lander, a scientific robot, carries out its pre-programmed tasks and then relays the data it has obtained back to Earth. Only six piloted spacecraft have made landings, during the Apollo Moon programme.

COMING IN TO LAND
This dramatic photograph of the Hadley Rille valley was taken from the piloted Apollo 15 lander during its low-altitude descent to the Moon's surface.

IS THERE LIFE ON MARS?
Two Viking orbiters released a lander each onto Mars. In total about 3,000 photographic images were sent back to Earth. The landers also tested the Martian soil to check for any sign of life – none was found. In 2004, Spirit and Opportunity, two expedition rovers, landed on Mars and have sent back useful data and images.

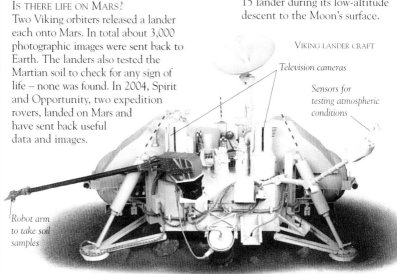

VIKING LANDER CRAFT

Television cameras

Sensors for testing atmospheric conditions

Robot arm to take soil samples

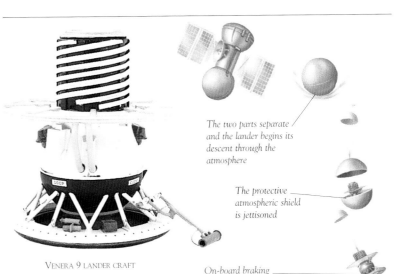

VENERA 9 LANDER CRAFT

The two parts separate
and the lander begins its
descent through the
atmosphere

The protective
atmospheric shield
is jettisoned

On-board braking
engines begin to slow
Venera 9

LANDER FACTS

• The first successful
lander was Luna 9,
which soft-landed on
the Moon in 1966.

• Venera 7 became the
first lander to transmit
data from the surface of
Venus in 1970.

• The Viking landers
analysed Mars's soil and
found that it contained
the following chemical
elements:

silica	14%
iron	18%
aluminium	2.7%
titanium	0.9%
potassium	0.3%

HOT LANDING

A series of Venera space
probes was sent to Venus.
Each consisted of two parts,
one of which descended to
the surface. Conditions on
Venus – very high temperature
and pressure – meant that
the landers could function
for only a few minutes.

Parachutes
further slow
the descent

Venera 9 obtains
and transmits
several images
before failing

PROBES TO THE PLANETS

ONCE THE FIRST ROCKETS had reached space, scientists and astronomers began to use space probes – car-sized robot craft launched by rockets to a predetermined target, which they investigate using their on-board instruments. Probes have given us close-ups of moons, comets, asteroids, and all but one of the planets, and have taught us much about the Solar System.

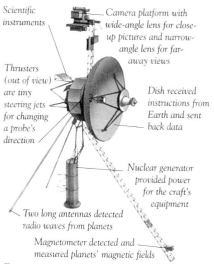

Scientific instruments

Camera platform with wide-angle lens for close-up pictures and narrow-angle lens for far-away views

Thrusters (out of view) are tiny steering jets for changing a probe's direction

Dish received instructions from Earth and sent back data

Nuclear generator provided power for the craft's equipment

Two long antennas detected radio waves from planets

Magnetometer detected and measured planets' magnetic fields

FLY-BY PROBES

These probes survey the target as they fly past, often at distances of several thousand kilometres (miles). The most successful were Voyagers 1 and 2, which investigated Jupiter, Saturn, Uranus, and Neptune between 1979 and 1989.

ORBITERS AND LANDERS
Orbiters travel to the target, move into orbit around it, and then survey it. Landers, like the Pathfinder, which landed on Mars in 1997, land on a target and survey it. Probes may be combinations of orbiter and lander, like the Viking probes.

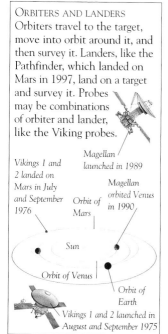

Vikings 1 and 2 landed on Mars in July and September 1976

Magellan launched in 1989

Magellan orbited Venus in 1990

Orbit of Mars

Sun

Orbit of Venus

Orbit of Earth

Vikings 1 and 2 launched in August and September 1975

EQUIPMENT AND EXPERIMENTS

A probe may receive instructions from Earth or may follow a mission programmed into its on-board computers. It may be powered by electricity generated by solar panels or a nuclear generator. On board are control systems that operate the probe and its scientific equipment. The Huygens lander, part of the Cassini orbiter, landed on Titan – Saturn's largest moon – in January 2005 to investigate its surface and atmosphere.

Antenna dish allows probes to stay in touch with Earth

Cassini reached Saturn in 2004 and will orbit the ringed planet and its moons for 4 years

Huygens was released to investigate Titan

Surface science package, with separate experiments

Experiment platform with equipment to test Titan's surface and atmosphere

This instrument was the first part of Huygens to touch Titan's surface

Heat-resistant shield stops Huygens from burning up in Titan's atmosphere

Device to test water's depth had Huygens landed in an ocean

Instruments to measure the density, composition, and temperature of Titan's atmosphere and surface

KEY SPACE PROBES				
Probe	**Type**	**Target**	**Encounter**	**Achievements**
Pioneer 10	Fly-by	Jupiter	1973	First to cross Asteroid Belt; took close-ups of Jupiter
Mariner 10	Fly-by	Mercury	1974–75	Only probe to Mercury
Venera 9	Orbiter / lander	Venus	1975	First views of Venusian surface
Vikings 1 and 2	Orbiter / lander	Mars	1976	Photographed surface; searched for life
Giotto	Fly-by	Comet Halley	1986	First view of the nucleus of a comet
Voyagers 1 and 2	Fly-by	Jupiter	1979	Details of all four
		Saturn	1980–81	planetary systems;
		Uranus	1986	Voyager 2 was first probe
		Neptune	1989	to Uranus and Neptune
Galileo	Fly-by / orbiter	Gaspra	1991	First fly-by of an asteroid;
		Jupiter	1995	first orbit of Jupiter
Cassini	Fly-by / lander	Saturn	2004	Detailed views of Saturn; launched the Huygens probe to Titan

279

SEARCH FOR LIFE ON MARS

SPECULATIONS THAT LIFE EXISTS on Mars have been rife since the late 18th century, fuelled by various theories. Hopes of finding life on the Red Planet received a setback in July 1965, when the Mariner 4 probe sent back images of its barren surface. Even so, life may have existed or may still exist today in places not yet explored.

EVIDENCE OF A WATERY PAST

Life as known on Earth needs water. Although liquid water cannot exist on Mars in today's frozen conditions, surface features, such as the channels detected by probes, suggest that water must once have flowed on the planet. A huge block-strewn area – the chaotic region – may have formed when water locked in the ground escaped rapidly, fracturing the surface.

The Martian surface probably had water 3 billion years ago

ORIGINS OF THE WATER

Liquid water was widespread on Mars in its early days. Intense meteorite bombardment and volcanic activity kept the planet warm, even at its great distance from the Sun. Life may have started then. Today, most of the water is locked up as ice in the soil. Pure sheets of ice occur at the poles.

Mangala Vallis dried river bed photographed by the Viking Orbiter

Primitive life may have existed in channels billions of years ago

Lowell's 1905 map shows canals that do not match the channels actually observed on Mars

Channels criss-cross the border between Mars's northern lowlands and southern highlands

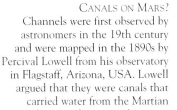

CANALS ON MARS?

Channels were first observed by astronomers in the 19th century and were mapped in the 1890s by Percival Lowell from his observatory in Flagstaff, Arizona, USA. Lowell argued that they were canals that carried water from the Martian poles to arid equatorial regions, and converged at oases. The channels later proved to be an optical illusion.

Channel was formed when huge volumes of groundwater were released on to the Martian surface

The Martian meteorite ALH84001 (magnified 100,000 times) contains tubes that might be fossils of bacterium-like organisms

METEORITE INVESTIGATION

The most intriguing, but inconclusive, evidence of life on Mars comes from an ancient Martian meteorite known as ALH84001, which landed on Antarctica about 13,000 years ago. It contains organic chemicals that could be evidence of life and tiny structures that could have been made by living organisms.

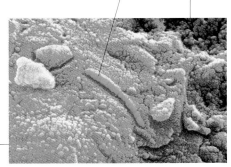

MISSIONS TO MARS

SINCE 1996, A STREAM of robotic spacecraft has left
Earth for Mars. These space probes aim to find out
how geology and climate combine to tell the story
of the planet, and whether primitive life may
have existed there in the past.
These probes will pave the
way for human exploration,
or even colonization, of Mars.

*Antenna relays signals
back to Earth*

*Cameras can detect
surface features just
1.5 m (5 ft) across*

*Solar panels
supply power*

EXPLORING THE SURFACE

NASA's Pathfinder spacecraft landed on Mars on 4 July 1997. It
deployed a small rover (Sojourner) and made measurements of
conditions on Mars. The rover explored the Martian
surface and analysed rocks and soil. Communications
ended in September 1997. Since then, two much
improved landers – Spirit and Opportunity –
touched down, providing amazing results.

PATHFINDER
MARTIAN
PANORAMA

*This panoramic image is a
mosaic of many individual
pictures sent back by Pathfinder*

*Distribution of rocks on the
surface indicates that large bodies
of water once flowed on Mars*

PROBES TO MARS			
Name	Year of arrival	Country	Type of probe
Mariner 4	1965	USA	Fly-by
Mars 3	1971	Russia	Orbiter and lander
Viking 1	1976	USA	Orbiter and lander
Viking 2	1976	USA	Orbiter and lander
Global Surveyor	1997	USA	Orbiter
Pathfinder	1997	USA	Lander and rover
Mars Express	2003	Europe	Orbiter
Nozomi	2004	Japan	Orbiter
Exploration Rover	2004	USA	Lander

Hazy clouds of water-ice are sometimes observed

GLOBAL SURVEYOR

In September 1997, Global Surveyor reached Mars and spent 18 months slowing down into a low orbit just 350 km (217 miles) above the surface. It carried cameras and spectrometers designed to map the planet in detail, and study its weather patterns and chemical composition.

HOSTILE TO LIFE

There is no liquid water on Mars since it is too cold most of the time. The oxygen is not breathable, and the surface is scoured by violent winds carrying dust particles. There is also no ozone in the upper atmosphere to protect life from damaging ultraviolet radiation.

The depth of the Sojourner Rover's tracks showed that the soil is fine and powder-like

The Rover samples a rock nicknamed "Yogi"

Pathfinder found that Martian airborne dust is magnetic

SPACE TRAVEL

FLYING TO SPACE

AT ONE TIME, people considered satellites and spaceflight to be science fiction. But some scientists and engineers did believe in technology that could launch satellites and people into space. In 1957, those believing in space exploration were proved right.

4 OCTOBER 1957 — SPACE AGE DAWNS

Fascination, excitement, and fear dominated people's emotions when they learnt that the Soviet Union had launched the first ever artificial satellite, named Sputnik. The satellite transmitted a tracking signal for 21 days.

RECOVERY

Sputnik 5 carried two dogs – they became the first creatures to survive the weightlessness of space and the forces of re-entry.

20 AUGUST 1960

12 APRIL 1961

FIRST PERSON IN SPACE

Yuri Gagarin, the first person in space, flew in a spherical Vostok spaceship, seated in an ejector seat on rails. His successful flight followed two Soviet space programme disasters.

US CREWED SPACE PROGRAMME

The US crewed space programme began with Alan Shepard reaching an altitude of 180 km (112 miles) and returning to Earth. His suborbital flight was part of the Mercury programme.

5 MAY 1961

25 MAY 1961

LUNAR CHALLENGE

President John F. Kennedy boosted America's space ambitions by launching the Apollo lunar exploration programme. The Apollo programme was one of the most technically complex projects of the 20th century.

SPACEWALK

Soviet cosmonaut Alexei Leonov made the first spacewalk from the Voskhod 2 spacecraft. During the spacewalk, which lasted 20 minutes, his spacesuit expanded, so he had to struggle to close the airlock's outer hatch on re-entry.

18 MARCH 1965

24 APRIL 1967

SOYUZ SPACECRAFT

Soviet cosmonaut Vladimir Komorov became the first person to die in space when he was killed aboard his Soyuz 1 spacecraft. Four months earlier three American astronauts had died in a fire on the launchpad while testing Apollo 1. All four were victims of the race to be first to land on the Moon.

15–24 JULY 1975

20 JULY 1969

MOON LANDING

Neil Armstrong, Commander of US Apollo 11, marked the arrival of people on the Moon. Armstrong and Buzz Aldrin guided Eagle, the lunar module, to the surface while Michael Collins remained in control of the command module. Armstrong and Aldrin spent 22 hours on the surface, collecting rock and dust samples.

APOLLO-SOYUZ LINK

In the midst of the Cold War, the United States and the Soviet Union achieved one cooperative space mission – the Apollo-Soyuz rendezvous. The crews manoeuvred their craft together and docked. For a few days they worked on scientific experiments in each other's spacecraft, and then completed their missions independently.

SPACE SHUTTLE

THE FIRST TEST FLIGHT of the Space Transportation System (STS) – the Space Shuttle – was in 1981. The Shuttle is an orbiter with three main engines, an external tank, and two solid rocket boosters. Cargo is carried in the orbiter's payload bay. After each mission, the orbiter returns to Earth. The STS launches satellites and space probes and is used for construction and repairs in space.

Payload bay

Flight deck where commander and pilot sit

SHUTTLE ORBITER

An orbiter is a space plane. It can carry seven crew members and stay in orbit for at least 10 days. The orbiters' cabins have three decks – the flight deck, a mid-deck, and a lower deck that houses life-support equipment.

SHUTTLE ORBITER

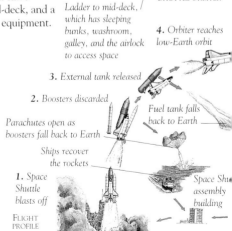

Ladder to mid-deck, which has sleeping bunks, washroom, galley, and the airlock to access space

4. Orbiter reaches low-Earth orbit

3. External tank released

2. Boosters discarded

Fuel tank falls back to Earth

Parachutes open as boosters fall back to Earth

Ships recover the rockets

1. Space Shuttle blasts off

Space Shuttle assembly building

FLIGHT PROFILE

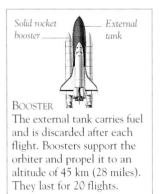

Solid rocket booster

External tank

BOOSTER

The external tank carries fuel and is discarded after each flight. Boosters support the orbiter and propel it to an altitude of 45 km (28 miles). They last for 20 flights.

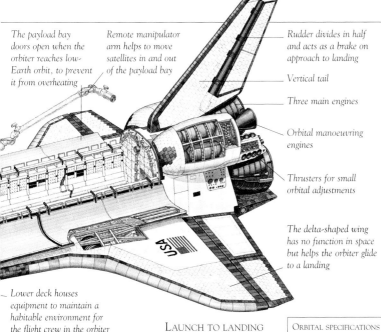

The payload bay doors open when the orbiter reaches low-Earth orbit, to prevent it from overheating

Remote manipulator arm helps to move satellites in and out of the payload bay

Rudder divides in half and acts as a brake on approach to landing

Vertical tail

Three main engines

Orbital manoeuvring engines

Thrusters for small orbital adjustments

The delta-shaped wing has no function in space but helps the orbiter glide to a landing

Lower deck houses equipment to maintain a habitable environment for the flight crew in the orbiter

5. Orbiter stays in space for 10–16 days

6. Orbiter positions itself ready to return to Earth

7. Orbiter re-enters Earth's atmosphere

8. Orbiter gets ready for high-speed glide onto runway

9. Orbiter glides in to land on runway

LAUNCH TO LANDING
The three main engines start at 0.12-second intervals, followed by the solid rocket boosters. Bolts holding down the STS are released for liftoff. The orbital manoeuvring system (OMS) places the orbiter into the correct orbit once the boosters and tank are discarded. One hour before landing, the OMS and thrusters position the orbiter for re-entry.

ORBITAL SPECIFICATIONS
- Orbiter length: 37 m (122 ft)
- Orbiter height: 17 m (57 ft)
- Wingspan: 30 m (98 ft)
- Payload bay: 18 x 5 m (60 x 15 ft)
- Orbit speed: 28,800 kph (17,896 mph)
- Withstands temperatures up to 1,500°C (2,732°F)
- Altitude in orbit between 185 and 1,000 km (115 and 621 miles)
- Mission duration between 10 and 16 days

289

WORKING IN SPACE

ASTRONAUTS NOW WORK in space on a regular basis. Many experiments take place aboard orbiting laboratories, while satellites can be launched, retrieved, and repaired while circling Earth.

WORKING ON THE MOON
In this picture, Buzz Aldrin (the second person to walk on the Moon) is seen setting up one of the scientific experiment packages that the Apollo 11 crew left behind on the lunar surface.

Antenna

Television camera

Steering control

Equipment storage rack

LUNAR ROVING VEHICLE (LRV)

Wire-mesh wheels

MOON BUGGY
Crew members of the Apollo 15, 16, and 17 missions made effective use of the LRV. This "moon-buggy" enabled them to travel significant distances across the lunar surface, collecting samples over a wide area.

SPACE SCIENCE
Orbiting laboratories allow scientists to carry out experiments in conditions where gravity's influence is negligible. This scientist is testing how fuel burns in a weightless environment.

SPACE STATION

Assembled in space by astronauts aided by tools, cranes, and a robotic arm, the International Space Station (ISS) is a collaboration between 16 countries. Pressurized living modules for up to seven astronauts are linked to laboratories and work stations. Astronauts live and work on the ISS for up to six months at a time.

Some 4,000 sq m (43,000 sq ft) of solar panels provide power to the ISS

RUNNING REPAIRS

Attached securely to the Space Shuttle's robotic arm – the Remote Manipulator System – astronauts can carry out repairs to satellites, telescopes, and the International Space Station in safety.

The Space Shuttle's robotic arm (at foot of picture) manoeuvres the astronaut into the correct position to carry out a particular task

LIVING IN SPACE

ENGINEERS DESIGN SPACE STATIONS so that astronauts can live in the hostile environment of space, where there is no oxygen, no soil in which to grow food, no water, and no air pressure. Life support systems on board provide oxygen and filter the carbon dioxide people breathe out. The air on board is pressurized to levels close to those on Earth, and the temperature is maintained at comfortable levels. Crews must also be supplied with food and water.

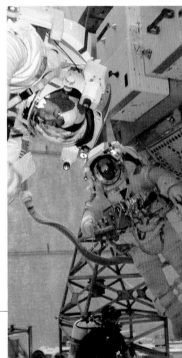

BUOYANCY TANK TRAINING

Astronauts train in weightless environments on Earth, simulated in enormous "neutral buoyancy" water tanks. A full-scale mock-up of an orbiter's payload bay and airlock can be placed in the deep water tanks, allowing trainees wearing pressurized spacesuits to practise space walks for extended periods. Such tanks are also used to design, test, and develop spacecraft and crew equipment.

PERSONAL HYGIENE

On the Space Shuttle, astronauts take sponge baths, and male astronauts shave with foam or not at all, as whiskers tend to escape and get into the eyes if an electric razor is used.

Astronaut shaving on board the Space Shuttle

SPACE FOOD

Food on the Shuttle must be lightweight as it is ferried from Earth. Bits of food may float away, so chunks are sometimes covered in edible gelatin to prevent crumbs. Usually, however, food is dried and water added to it when needed. The Space Shuttle produces some of its own water.

SPACE MENU

Breakfast	Fruit or cereal, beef pasty or scrambled eggs, cocoa, fruit drink
Lunch	Turkey pasta or hot dogs, bread, bananas or almond crunch bar, fruit drink
Dinner	Soup or fruit cocktail, rice pilaff or steak, broccoli au gratin, pudding, fruit drink

SPACE TOILET

On the Space Shuttle, restraints hold astronauts in place and a vacuum ensures a good seal between body and toilet seat. Solid waste is dried, treated for bacteria, and stored, while urine and waste water are stored and periodically dumped.

Handhold

Seat

Operating handle

Control panel

Control to shut off vacuum

Foot restraint

SAFE SLEEP

Waist straps prevent astronauts from floating about when asleep. The Sun rises and sets every hour and a half in near-Earth orbit, so eyeshades are used. Earmuffs may also be used if crew members are working nearby.

Waist strap

Special straps attach the astronaut to the walkway

KEEPING FIT

The body does not have to work as hard in space, because there is so little gravity, so muscles tend to waste away. To prevent this, space crews follow exercise plans, and space stations carry equipment such as exercise bikes.

Using a moving walkway is one way an astronaut can keep fit

293

SPACE WALK
An astronaut's space suit keeps the body at atmospheric pressure and shields it from harmful radiation.

SCIENCE IN SPACE

THE FORCE OF GRAVITY cannot be changed on Earth, so scientists go into orbit to carry out gravity experiments. In orbit, they experience weightlessness, or microgravity, which helps them to study the effects of gravity on biological and physical processes.

SPACELAB

The European Space Agency designed the Spacelab space station to be carried in the payload bay of the Space Shuttle. It was made up of two pressurized laboratories for microgravity experiments, and three unpressurized laboratories, or external pallets, for experiments that needed exposure to space. Launched first in 1983, the last Spacelab mission flew in 1997.

INSIDE SPACELAB

The crew slept in the Shuttle orbiter and floated through the access tunnel to work in Spacelab's pressurized modules. Experiments were contained in specially designed units, called racks.

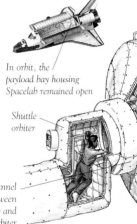

In orbit, the payload bay housing Spacelab remained open

Shuttle orbiter

Access tunnel between Spacelab and orbiter

SPACELAB

Skylab was used by three teams of astronauts between May 1973 and February 1974

SKYLAB

Skylab, the first US space station, was launched in 1973. It studied how people behave if they live in space for long periods of time, and also investigated solar flares.

BIORACK AND ANTHRORACK

The Spacelab carried a Biorack, which had incubators for samples of cells and microorganisms in order to study how microgravity affected their behaviour. Anthrorack carried equipment to examine the effect of microgravity on the human body.

EXTERNAL PALLET

Some instruments for observing Earth or radiation in space need to be exposed to space. These were fitted to external pallets. Control equipment was normally housed in the pressurized module. If Spacelab was in a pallet-only mode, then this was put in a cylindrical container at the front of the first pallet.

Single external pallet

Pressurized modules were 4 m (14 ft) wide

Spacelab was designed to look as though it had a roof, a floor, and walls

Footholds helped to keep the astronauts upright while they worked

SPACE STATIONS		
Name	Nationality	Launch year
Salyut 1	Soviet Union	1971
Skylab	USA	1973
Spacelab	Europe	1983
Mir	Russia	1986
International Space Station	International	1998

INTERNATIONAL MICROGRAVITY LAB

Spacelab flew two international microgravity laboratory missions. Projects included studying the effect of microgravity on the nervous system, and on the development of shrimp eggs, lentil seedlings, and bacteria.

BIOLOGY IN MICROGRAVITY

In 1996, Shannon Lucid, a NASA astronaut, put eggs into Mir's incubator, and each day removed one to stop development. These were compared with eggs on Earth to find out what influences the way fertilized eggs develop.

INTERNATIONAL SPACE STATION

THE UNITED STATES AND RUSSIA launched the first parts of the International Space Station (ISS) in 1998. Brazil, Canada, the European Space Agency, and Japan have also contributed elements. It carries a permanent crew, and completion is scheduled for 2006. Astronauts carry out a wide-ranging programme of research while on board.

STATION ELEMENTS

The International Space Station is made up of more than 100 elements contributed by various countries, including connecting nodes, solar panels, habitation and unpressurized modules, laboratories, a core module, and robotic arms.

The ISS is the size of a football pitch

Thermal panels to control temperature

Interior of the European laboratory

LABORATORIES

The ISS has a research complex with laboratories supplied by the USA, Russia, Europe, and Japan. Here, scientists investigate materials and fluids in microgravity, as well as life sciences and technology development. Japan provided an external platform for experiments that require prolonged exposure to space.

There are 4,000 sq m (43,056 sq ft) of solar panels on the ISS

Solar panels convert the Sun's energy into electricity for powering the station

INTERNATIONAL SPACE STATION

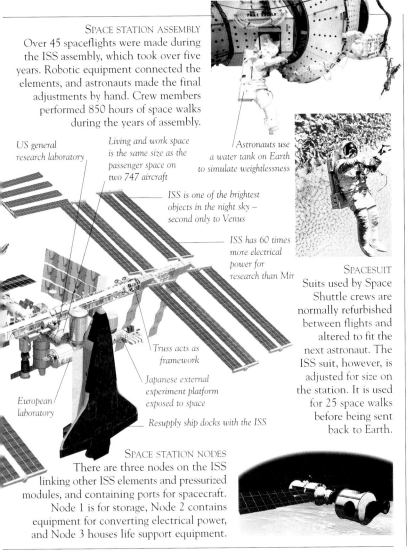

SPACE TRAVEL

SPACE STATION ASSEMBLY

Over 45 spaceflights were made during the ISS assembly, which took over five years. Robotic equipment connected the elements, and astronauts made the final adjustments by hand. Crew members performed 850 hours of space walks during the years of assembly.

US general research laboratory

Living and work space is the same size as the passenger space on two 747 aircraft

Astronauts use a water tank on Earth to simulate weightlessness

ISS is one of the brightest objects in the night sky – second only to Venus

ISS has 60 times more electrical power for research than Mir

Truss acts as framework

Japanese external experiment platform exposed to space

European laboratory

Resupply ship docks with the ISS

SPACESUIT

Suits used by Space Shuttle crews are normally refurbished between flights and altered to fit the next astronaut. The ISS suit, however, is adjusted for size on the station. It is used for 25 space walks before being sent back to Earth.

SPACE STATION NODES

There are three nodes on the ISS linking other ISS elements and pressurized modules, and containing ports for spacecraft. Node 1 is for storage, Node 2 contains equipment for converting electrical power, and Node 3 houses life support equipment.

299

SPACE MISSIONS I

THE SPACE AGE began in 1957 with the launch of the first satellite. Four years later Yuri Gagarin became the world's first astronaut. The next 20 years saw a surge of interest in space exploration.

FIRST SPACE VEHICLE
A model of Vostok I, the craft in which Yuri Gagarin made his historic first orbit of Earth on 12 April 1961.

CONTROLLED LANDING
The probe Luna 9 was the first to make a successful soft landing on the Moon in February 1966. Luna 9 sent back the first panoramic images taken from the surface of the Moon.

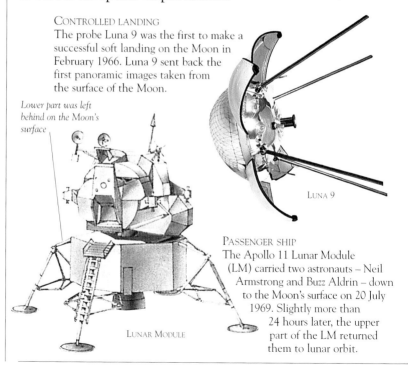

Lower part was left behind on the Moon's surface

LUNA 9

PASSENGER SHIP
The Apollo 11 Lunar Module (LM) carried two astronauts – Neil Armstrong and Buzz Aldrin – down to the Moon's surface on 20 July 1969. Slightly more than 24 hours later, the upper part of the LM returned them to lunar orbit.

LUNAR MODULE

ROBOT MOON ROVER
Two Lunokhod robot vehicles
were sent to the Moon in the
early 1970s. Equipped with
television cameras that
enabled them to be driven
from a control room on Earth,
the two vehicles travelled a
total of 47.5 km (29.5 miles)
across the Moon.

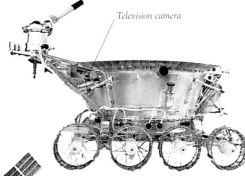

Television camera

LUNOKHOD I

SCIENTIFIC PLATFORM
Launched in 1973, the Skylab
orbiting laboratory and observatory
gave astronauts the opportunity to
work in space for weeks at a time.
Skylab also enabled scientists to
study the workings of Earth's
atmosphere and climate systems
from the viewpoint of space.

*Apollo
Telescope
Mount*

SKYLAB

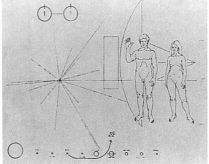

MESSAGE TO THE STARS
The two Pioneer probes each
carry a gold-covered plaque that
shows a visual representation of
human beings, as well as simple
directions for locating the Solar
System and planet Earth.

SPACE MISSIONS II

WORKING IN ORBIT became much easier with the introduction of the Space Shuttle in 1981. Probes have now visited all but one of the outer planets, and further exploration is under way.

The Shuttle has a mechanical arm which can be used to launch or retrieve satellites

The external fuel tank breaks away at a height of 110 km (68 miles)

The booster rockets operate for about two minutes and are jettisoned at a height of 45 km (28 miles)

The Shuttle can lift-off with eight crew and up to 29 tonnes (28 tons) of cargo

INCREASING COMMUNICATIONS
The communications satellite Intelsat was launched by astronauts on the 49th Space Shuttle mission in May 1992. Improved communications is just one of the benefits of space technology now enjoyed by the general public.

ENDURANCE RECORD

Russian astronauts (cosmonauts) have spent increasingly long periods of time in space. The present record of 438 consecutive days was achieved aboard the space station Mir during 1994–95. The picture shows a cosmonaut on the rigorous exercise programme devised to keep the crew fit during long periods of weightlessness. Mir burned up when it re-entered Earth's atmosphere in 2001, after 15 years in orbit.

ROSETTA PROBE

COMET-CHASER

The Rosetta orbiter/lander (right) will attempt to rendezvous with a comet. The lander will detach from the orbiter and descend to the comet's nucleus. Having anchored itself to the surface, it will transmit data to the orbiter, for relaying back to Earth. Scientists hope that Rosetta will shed light on how comets form.

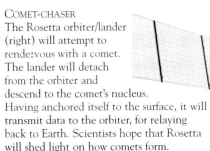

CASSINI-HUYGENS PROBE

Launched in 1997, Cassini reached Saturn in 2004 and will now spend four years studying the planet and its moons. On arrival, it released the mini-probe Huygens, which touched down on Titan, the largest of Saturn's many moons.

SPACEPLANES

GETTING INTO SPACE IS expensive. It typically costs more than £10,000 ($17,300) for every 1 kg (2.2 lb) of payload carried. Huge sums of money are wasted when a multistage rocket is used to reach orbit, as much of the spacecraft is simply lost. Using vehicles that reach orbit in one stage – single-stage-to-orbit (SSTO) spacecraft – might be a way around the problem in the future.

CLIPPER GRAHAM (DC-XA)
A test vehicle for future spaceplane technologies, Clipper Graham was a subsonic aircraft. However, it crashed in 1996 after four flights.

DC-XA was made from advanced, lightweight composite materials

CLIPPER GRAHAM (DC-XA)

VENTURESTAR (X-33)
NASA's VentureStar, or X-33, has a distinctive wedge shape – a "lifting body" design – which helps it to fly. It takes off vertically but glides to a landing. It was a prototype for an SSTO spaceplane. These may take over the role of the Space Shuttle in the future, but NASA is currently looking at simply improving the "old generation" shuttle designs.

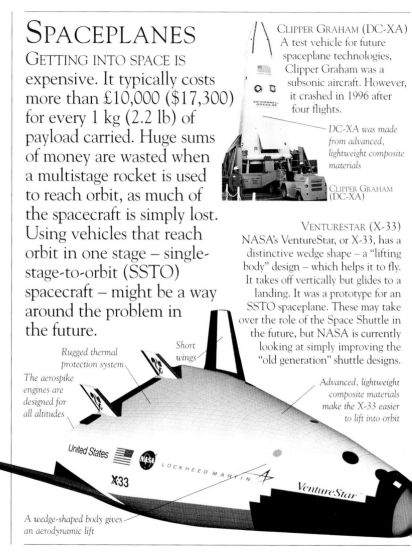

Rugged thermal protection system

Short wings

The aerospike engines are designed for all altitudes

Advanced, lightweight composite materials make the X-33 easier to lift into orbit

United States

X-33

LOCKHEED MARTIN

VentureStar

A wedge-shaped body gives an aerodynamic lift

X-34 is designed for wheeled landing

TEST FLIGHT OF X-34

X-34 technology is a bridge between DC-XA and VentureStar (X-33)

X-34 PROTOTYPE

The X-34 tested the lightweight materials, thermal protection, and landing systems needed for SSTO. It was designed to be launched from the air, beneath an aeroplane. Unfortunately X-33 and X-34 were ultimately disaster-prone and abandoned. A new type of rocket is needed, but progress is slow.

ROTON

A radical but ultimately unsuccessful idea, developed to make rockets light enough for SSTO launches, was to design them without the heavy equipment that pumps propellant. In the Roton rocket, a motor on the launchpad would spin its engine to throw propellant into the combustion chambers. For stability during re-entry, and a soft landing, rotor blades similar to a helicopter's would be deployed.

AEROSPIKE ENGINE

Peak performance is possible all the way to orbit with an aerospike engine. The conventional bell-shaped nozzle is turned inside out to give an inner solid surface. The "outer" surface is simply air pressure and, as air pressure decreases with altitude, the nozzle shape changes as the rocket ascends.

SPACE TOURISM

Access to space may become cheaper and easier with SSTO spacecraft, and many people's dreams of travelling to space may then be realized. One space tourism idea is a hotel in a 1,200 km (746 mile) orbit. A tether 1,000 km (621 miles) long would connect the hotel to a space dock 250 km (155 miles) above Earth. People would travel to the dock in reusable suborbital planes, and take a lift to the hotel.

INTERPLANETARY TRAVEL

SPACE SCIENTISTS ARE experimenting with new technologies for interplanetary travel, for growing crops in space, and for living long periods with limited resources. This will help interplanetary travellers to be self-sufficient.

DEEP SPACE 1

The first of a new series of small NASA spacecraft, known as deep space probes, Deep Space 1 was launched in 1998. It tested risky technologies, such as more efficient solar cells and ion drives.

INTERPLANETARY SPACE PROBES

These probes are initially put into orbit around Earth. Rocket boosters are then fired to put them into a new solar orbit, which is carefully plotted to cross the orbit of the target planet.

ION DRIVE

Spacecraft with ion drives can reach 10 times the speed of conventional spacecraft. Ion-loaded gas is pulled towards a charged grid and expelled at high speed, pushing the spacecraft in the opposite direction.

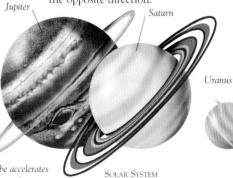

Jupiter

Saturn

Uranus

Sun Venus Mars

Mercury Earth

To reach Mercury and Venus, a probe accelerates away from Earth, opposite to Earth's motion.

SOLAR SYSTEM

SELF-SUFFICIENCY AND PSYCHOLOGY IN SPACE

Future space colonies need to be self-sufficient, growing their own food and recycling the atmosphere as well as plant, animal, and human waste. Such total recycling is very difficult to achieve. If space colonies are to succeed, psychologists need to understand more about how people in small groups interact when completely isolated.

BIOSPHERE II, ARIZONA

In 1991–93, eight people tried to live in a self-contained artificial environment as part of the Biosphere II project in Arizona, USA

Mung beans were successfully grown in space by cosmonauts on Mir

SPACE AGRICULTURE

Scientists on the Mir space station made a modest attempt to grow plants. Successful space colonies will have to cultivate plants for food and to produce oxygen to breathe.

Neptune

Pluto

Once a probe approaches a planet, planetary gravity attracts it. Boosters can then be fired to manoeuvre the probe into orbit.

To reach Mars and the planets beyond, a probe accelerates away from Earth in the same direction as Earth's orbit around the Sun.

With a crew of six, it could take 30 tonnes (29 tons) of fuel to lift off from Mars

CREATING FUEL ON MARS

One idea to help Mars colonists make fuel is to export a fuel-manufacturing plant from Earth, which could use carbon dioxide from Mars's atmosphere and hydrogen shipped from Earth, to make water and methane.

FUTURISTIC STARSHIPS

THE SOLAR SYSTEM'S NEAREST NEIGHBOUR, the Alpha Centauri star system, is about 40 trillion km (25 trillion miles) away from Earth. Using the fastest current technology, it would take spacecraft 10,000 years to get there. Light would take four years. For interstellar exploration such as that aboard *Star Trek's* USS Enterprise, a spaceship would need to travel faster than light. No-one yet knows whether this would be possible.

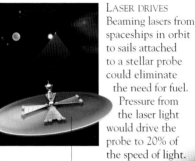

LASER DRIVES
Beaming lasers from spaceships in orbit to sails attached to a stellar probe could eliminate the need for fuel. Pressure from the laser light would drive the probe to 20% of the speed of light.

American scientist Robert Forward's proposed laser-driven stellar probe

LIMITS OF CONVENTIONAL ROCKETS
The Voyager spacecraft, travelling at 60,000 kph (37,300 mph), would take around 80,000 years to reach Alpha Centauri. Travelling there and back again is therefore impossible due to the limitations of current technology.

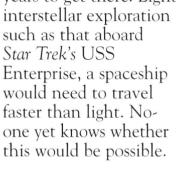

Solar System and Alpha Centauri are 4.3 light years apart in the Orion Arm, 25,000 light years from the centre of the Milky Way

MILKY WAY

Forward's arrangement of nested solar sails

ARTIST'S IMPRESSION
OF ANTIMATTER
SPACECRAFT

ANTIMATTER ENGINES

Antimatter exists and releases huge
amounts of energy when it collides
with matter. Indeed, matter-
antimatter engines may one
day power spaceships –
but not at speeds
faster than light.

*Andromeda galaxy
is 2.5 million
light years away
from Earth*

The TV series Star Trek *made antimatter engines
famous. In* Star Trek, *they power the warp drive
that propels the Enterprise faster than light*

WARP DRIVE

In 1915, Einstein published
his Theory of General
Relativity, which deals with how
space and time are distorted or
"warped" near massive objects. *Star Trek*
writers first coined the phrase "warp
drive" for travelling faster than light,
though antimatter engines could not
have done so. Nevertheless, *Star Trek*
inspired Mexican physicist Miguel
Alcubierre to investigate whether it
might be possible to build a warp drive.

NEGATIVE MASS

A warp drive would need negative mass
to expand space behind a starship, and
equal amounts of positive mass to
contract space in front of it. Quantum
physics suggests that negative mass
might exist, but no-one knows.

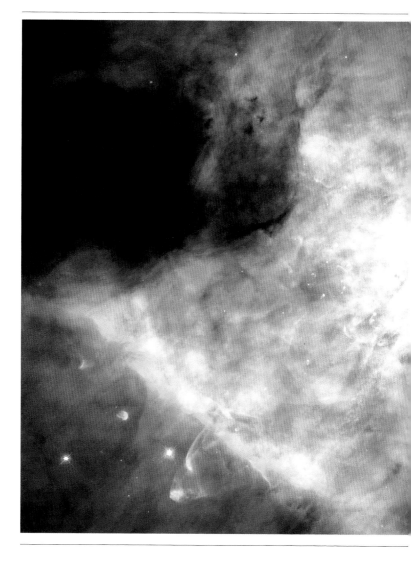

REFERENCE

THE NORTHERN SKY

THE MAP ON THE RIGHT shows the main stars that lie north of the celestial equator. The stars seen on a particular night by people living in the northern hemisphere depend on the observer's latitude, the time of year, and the time of night. The stars near the centre of the sky-map are called circumpolar and can be seen throughout the year. Polaris (the North Star) appears to remain directly over the North Pole.

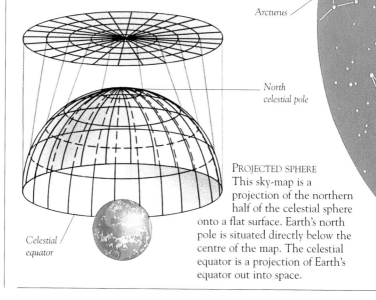

Arcturus

North celestial pole

PROJECTED SPHERE
This sky-map is a projection of the northern half of the celestial sphere onto a flat surface. Earth's north pole is situated directly below the centre of the map. The celestial equator is a projection of Earth's equator out into space.

Celestial equator

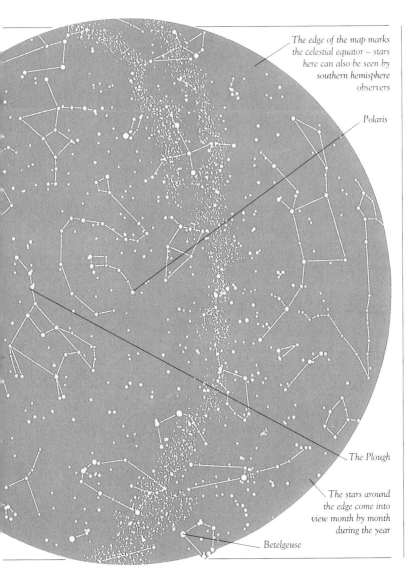

The edge of the map marks the celestial equator – stars here can also be seen by southern hemisphere observers

Polaris

The Plough

The stars around the edge come into view month by month during the year

Betelgeuse

THE SOUTHERN SKY

THE MAP ON THE RIGHT shows the main stars that lie south of the celestial equator. The stars seen on a particular night by people living in the southern hemisphere depend on the observer's latitude, the time of year, and the time of night. The stars near the centre of the sky-map are called circumpolar and can be seen all year round. Alpha Centauri, one of the nearest stars to the Sun, is a southern hemisphere star.

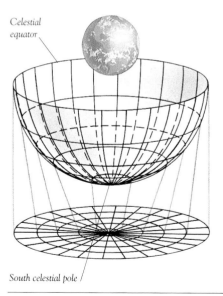

Celestial equator

Alpha Centauri

Antares

South celestial pole

PROJECTED SPHERE
This sky-map is a projection of the southern half of the celestial sphere onto a flat surface. Earth's south pole is situated directly below the centre of the map. The celestial equator is a projection of Earth's equator out into space.

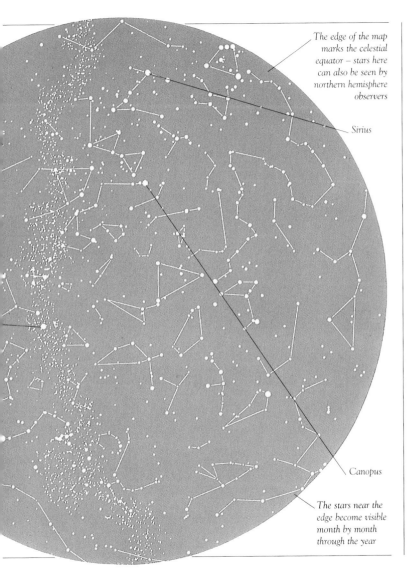

The edge of the map marks the celestial equator – stars here can also be seen by northern hemisphere observers

Sirius

Canopus

The stars near the edge become visible month by month through the year

CONSTELLATIONS GUIDE

There are 88 internationally agreed constellations and all have Latin names, listed here alphabetically. They provide a useful map of the night sky and help astronomers describe the positions of planets, stars, and other objects in the Cosmos. You can only see a fraction of the constellations each night. The constellations you will see depend on the time of night, the time of year, and your location. The maps under each constellation will help you work out which constellations are visible where you live.

KEY TO CONSTELLATION VISIBILITY CHARTS

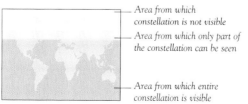

Area from which constellation is not visible

Area from which only part of the constellation can be seen

Area from which entire constellation is visible

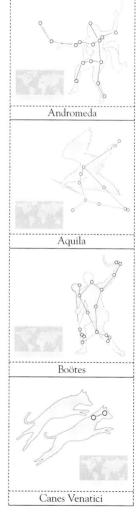

Andromeda

Aquila

Boötes

Canes Venatici

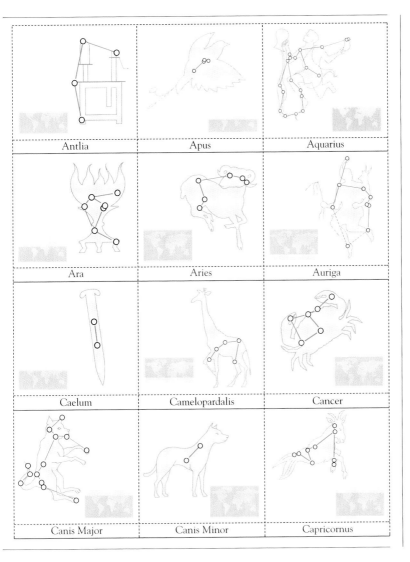

Antlia	Apus	Aquarius
Ara	Aries	Auriga
Caelum	Camelopardalis	Cancer
Canis Major	Canis Minor	Capricornus

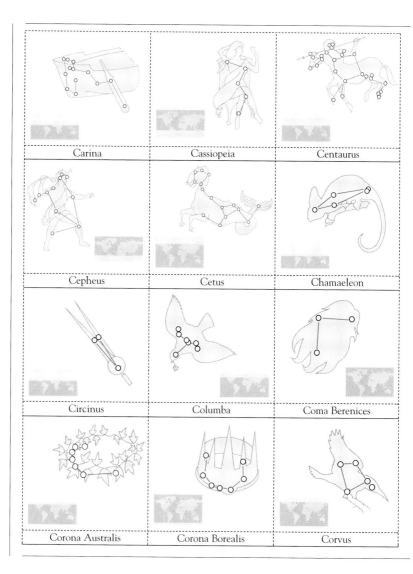

Carina	Cassiopeia	Centaurus
Cepheus	Cetus	Chamaeleon
Circinus	Columba	Coma Berenices
Corona Australis	Corona Borealis	Corvus

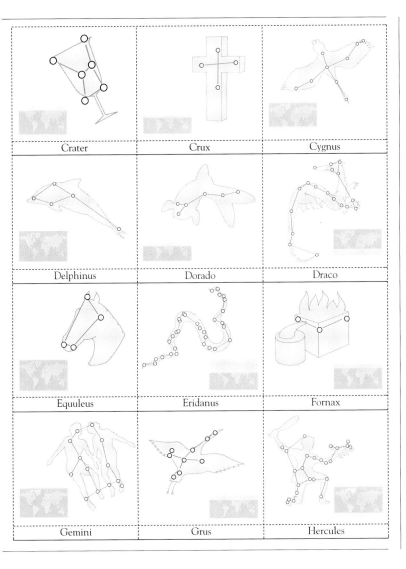

Crater	Crux	Cygnus
Delphinus	Dorado	Draco
Equuleus	Eridanus	Fornax
Gemini	Grus	Hercules

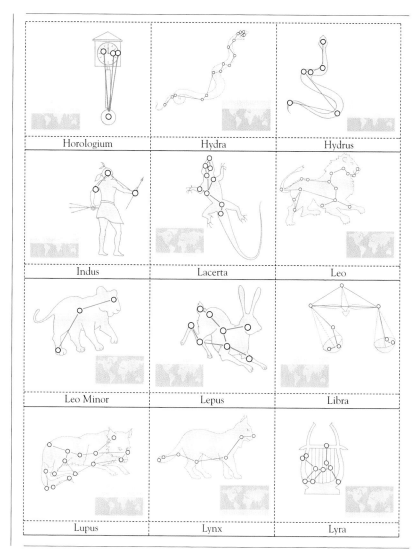

Horologium	Hydra	Hydrus
Indus	Lacerta	Leo
Leo Minor	Lepus	Libra
Lupus	Lynx	Lyra

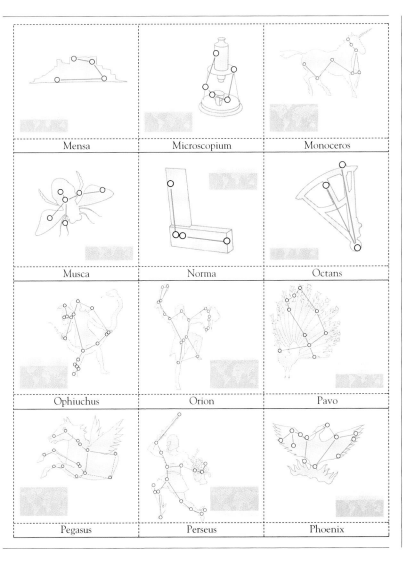

Mensa	Microscopium	Monoceros
Musca	Norma	Octans
Ophiuchus	Orion	Pavo
Pegasus	Perseus	Phoenix

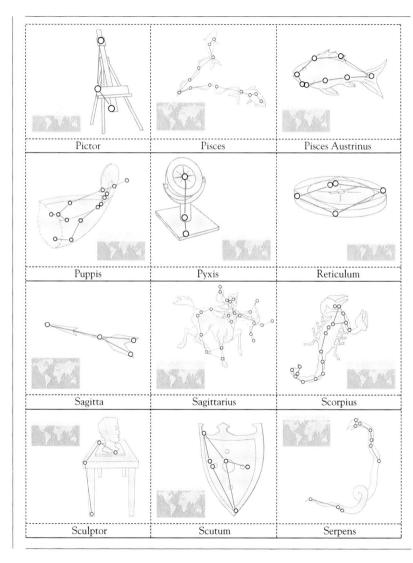

Pictor	Pisces	Pisces Austrinus
Puppis	Pyxis	Reticulum
Sagitta	Sagittarius	Scorpius
Sculptor	Scutum	Serpens

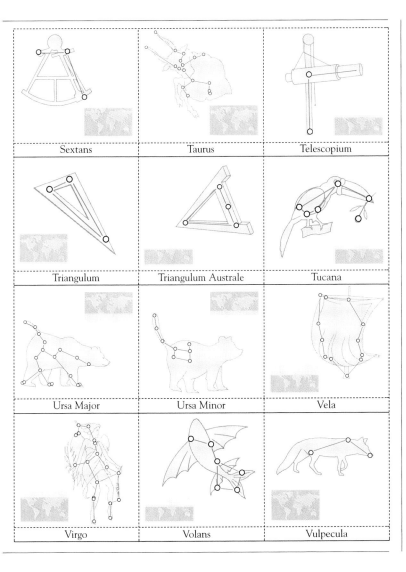

Sextans	Taurus	Telescopium
Triangulum	Triangulum Australe	Tucana
Ursa Major	Ursa Minor	Vela
Virgo	Volans	Vulpecula

ANDROMEDA

DEPICTING A GREEK PRINCESS who was rescued by Perseus, Andromeda contains the nearest major galaxy to us, M31 – the Andromeda Galaxy – which is the most distant object visible to the naked eye.

ANDROMEDA GALAXY

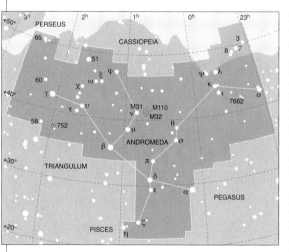

M31 (THE ANDROMEDA GALAXY) ⊙ ♠ ⤢ A spiral galaxy, similar to the Milky Way but larger. On a clear night, it can be seen by the naked eye as an elongated smudge. A large telescope is needed to see its spiral arms.

NGC 752 ♠ An open cluster, visible through binoculars, consisting of faint stars spread over an area of sky wider than the full Moon. It lies about 1,300 light years away.

NGC 7662 ⤢ A planetary nebula, about 4,000 light years away. It looks small but prominent through a telescope, like a blue-green star of 9th magnitude.

GAMMA (γ) ANDROMEDAE ⤢ A double star that appears as a single star to the naked eye. A small telescope will reveal an orange-coloured primary giant star, with a blue companion of 5th magnitude.

OBSERVATION SYMBOLS

- ⊙ Naked eye
- ♠ Binoculars
- ⤢ Telescope
- ♟ Not observable with amateur equipment

STAR MAGNITUDE KEY

● –1 ● 0 ● 1 ● 2 ● 3 • 4 • 5 • 6

DEEP-SKY OBJECTS

- ◌ Galaxy
- ⊛ Globular cluster
- ⁝⁝ Open cluster
- ☐ Diffuse nebula
- ◯ Planetary nebula
- △ X-ray and radio sources

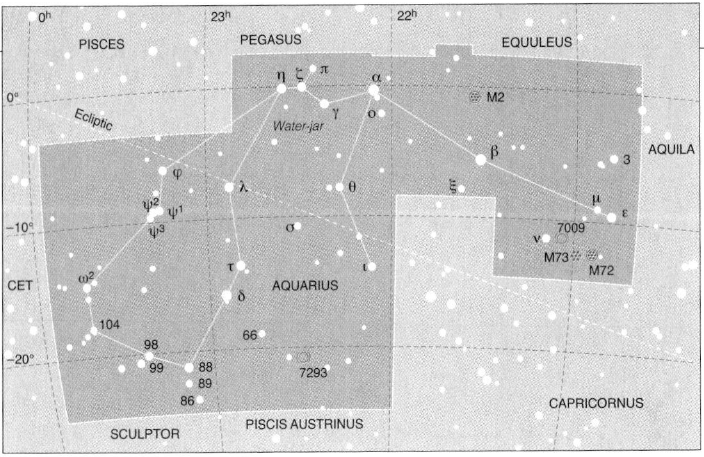

KEY ON PAGE 324

AQUARIUS

THIS CONSTELLATION REPRESENTS a youth pouring water from a jar. The "Water-jar" is represented by a Y-shaped group of four stars, Gamma (γ), Zeta (ζ), Eta (η), and Pi (π) Aquarii. The stream of water flows into the mouth of a large fish, represented by the Piscis Austrinus constellation to the south.

THE HELIX NEBULA

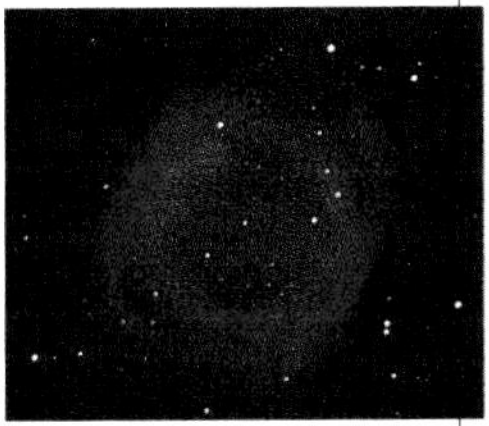

NGC 7293 (THE HELIX NEBULA) Possibly the closest planetary nebula to Earth (only about 300 light years away), and over a third the diameter of the full Moon. Its light is spread over a wide area, making it difficult to spot. It can be seen through binoculars or a wide-field telescope as a pale grey patch.

M2 A globular cluster, resembling a fuzzy star, too faint to be seen with the naked eye but easy to see with binoculars or a small telescope.

NGC 7009 (The Saturn Nebula) A planetary nebula. When seen through a telescope with an aperture of 200 mm (8 in) or more, it appears to have appendages that resemble the rings of Saturn, hence its popular name.

ZETA (ζ) AQUARII A close binary of white, 4th-magnitude stars that orbit each other every 760 years or so. They can be separated using a high magnification 75-mm (3-in) telescope.

CARINA

THIS LARGE CONSTELLATION contains Canopus, the second brightest star. In Greek times, it was part of Argo Navis, a larger constellation, representing the Argonauts' ship, but was made separate in the 18th century. It represents the ship's keel, with Canopus as the rudder. The other parts of the ship – Vela (the sails) and Puppis (the stern) – lie to the north.

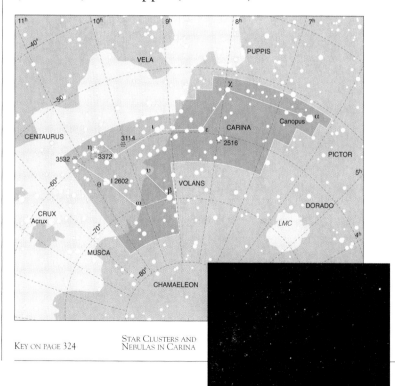

KEY ON PAGE 324

STAR CLUSTERS AND NEBULAS IN CARINA

IC 2602 (The Southern Pleiades)

ETA (η) CARINAE

A remarkable variable star. Currently it is of 5th magnitude, but it has been much brighter in the past, most noticeably in the 19th century, when it flared up to nearly –1. Eta Carinae is thought to be either a supergiant with a mass of 100 Suns – one of the most massive stars known – or possibly a massive binary. Through a telescope, it appears as a hazy orange ellipse, because of matter thrown off in its last outburst. Its distance is estimated at over 8,000 light years, and it lies within the extensive nebula NGC 3372.

NGC 3372 (THE ETA CARINAE NEBULA)

A large, bright, diffuse nebula, four times the apparent width of the full Moon, surrounding the star Eta (η) Carinae. The nebula is visible to the naked eye against the Milky Way and is best seen with binoculars. A V-shaped lane of dark dust runs through it. Near Eta Carinae itself, telescopes show a dark and bulbous cloud of dust called the Keyhole Nebula.

IC 2602 (THE SOUTHERN PLEIADES)

A large and prominent open cluster, containing eight stars brighter than magnitude 6. The brightest member is Theta (θ) Carinae, a blue-white star of magnitude 2.7. The cluster appears twice the size of the full Moon and lies about 500 light years away.

NGC 3532

A bright and dense open cluster, elliptical in shape. It is visible to the naked eye and is a glorious sight through binoculars, being nearly twice the apparent diameter of the full Moon at its widest. It is 1,300 light years away.

NGC 2516

An open cluster, visible to the naked eye. Using binoculars, it is possible to pick out its individual stars, the brightest being a 5th-magnitude red giant, scattered over an area of sky the size of the full Moon. It is about 1,300 light years away.

NGC 3114

An open cluster, visible to the naked eye and appearing about the same size as the disc of the full Moon. Its individual stars can be seen through binoculars. It lies nearly 3,000 light years away.

ALPHA (α) CARINAE (CANOPUS)

The second brightest star in the sky, at magnitude –0.6. It is a white supergiant, 14,000 times more luminous than the Sun, lying 310 light years away.

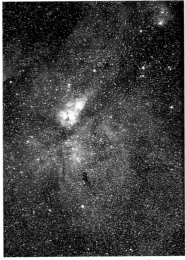

NGC 3372 (The Eta Carinae Nebula)

CENTAURUS

A LARGE CONSTELLATION in the southern Milky Way, Centaurus depicts a centaur, the mythical beast with the legs of a horse and the upper body of a man. Its brightest star, Alpha (α) Centauri, is the third brightest in the sky.

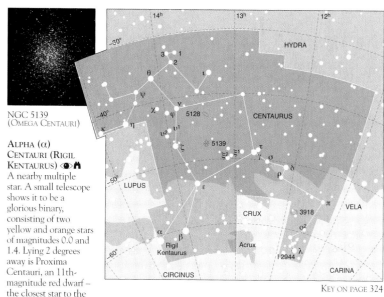

NGC 5139
(OMEGA CENTAURI)

KEY ON PAGE 324

ALPHA (α) CENTAURI (RIGIL KENTAURUS) ◉ ♠

A nearby multiple star. A small telescope shows it to be a glorious binary, consisting of two yellow and orange stars of magnitudes 0.0 and 1.4. Lying 2 degrees away is Proxima Centauri, an 11th-magnitude red dwarf – the closest star to the Sun, being 4.2 light years away, but 0.2 light years closer to us than the two brighter members of the Alpha Centauri system.

NGC 5139 (OMEGA (Ω) CENTAURI) ◉ ♠ ⋨

The largest, brightest globular cluster in the sky, NGC 5139 is about 17,000 light years away. Seen with the naked eye or binoculars, it appears as a hazy 4th-magnitude patch larger than the full Moon. A small telescope shows its main stars.

NGC 5128 (CENTAURUS A) ⋨

An unusual galaxy. With a small telescope, it looks like an elliptical galaxy, but larger apertures show that it is bisected by a dark dust lane due to a merger with another galaxy. It is a strong radio source.

328

CRUX

THE SMALLEST CONSTELLATION, yet Crux forms one
of the most famous star patterns. For the Greeks,
it formed part of the hind legs of Centaurus, the
centaur. It lies in a brilliant region of the Milky Way,
and its longer axis points to the south celestial pole.

USING CRUX TO LOCATE
THE SOUTH CELESTIAL POLE

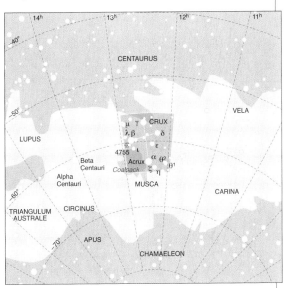

KEY ON PAGE 324

SOUTH CELESTIAL POLE
◉⋔⊁ The pole lies at
the intersection of two
imaginary lines – one
between Alpha (α) and
Gamma (γ) Crucis (top of
picture), the other is at
right angles to a line
joining Alpha (α) and
Beta (β) Centauri (bottom
of picture).

NGC 4755 (THE JEWEL BOX, THE KAPPA
(κ) CRUCIS CLUSTER) ◉⋔⊁ An open
cluster visible to the naked eye as a bright knot
between Beta (β) Crucis and the Coalsack. It is,
in fact, far more distant than either of them, lying
7,600 light years away. Most of its stars are blue-
white supergiants, such as Kappa (κ) Crucis,
although near its centre there is a prominent
red supergiant of 8th magnitude.

THE COALSACK ◉⋔ A prominent, dark,
wedge-shaped nebula 600 light years away that
blots out the light from the stars in the Milky
Way behind it. It has no NGC reference number.

329

CYGNUS

THIS CONSTELLATION DEPICTS the swan into which, according to Greek myth, the god Zeus transformed himself. The swan's beak is marked by Beta (β) Cygni and its tail by Alpha (α) Cygni, named Deneb (from the Arabic meaning "tail"). Deneb forms one corner of the Summer Triangle, with Vega (in Lyra) and Altair (in Aquila) marking the other two. Identifiable by its cross-shape, Cygnus is sometimes called the Northern Cross.

CYGNUS (INSET: ALBIREO)

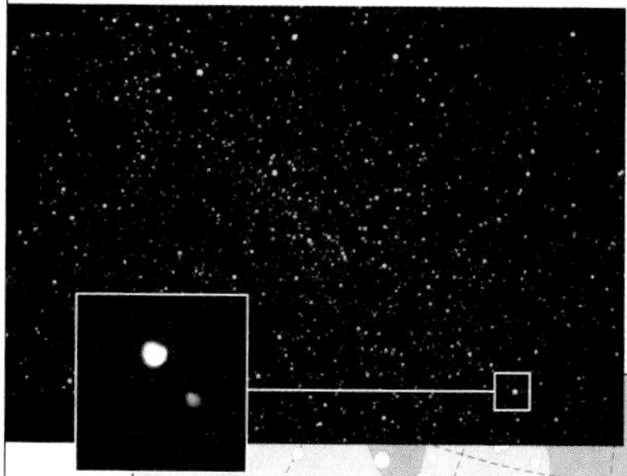

KEY ON PAGE 324

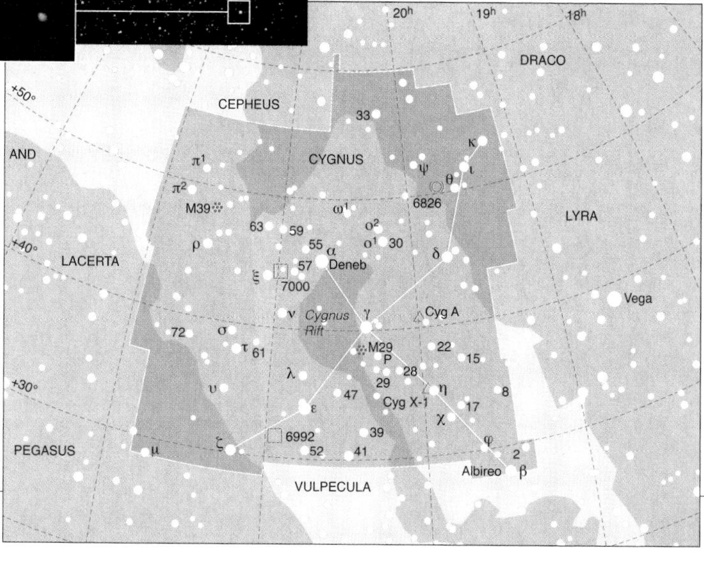

330

NGC 6992 (THE VEIL NEBULA) �☆

Part of a large, complex nebula called the Cygnus Loop, which is the remains of a star that exploded as a supernova perhaps 50,000 years ago. In clear skies, the Veil Nebula section can be seen with binoculars or a small telescope, but the whole nebula is best seen on photographs.

NGC 7000 (THE NORTH AMERICA NEBULA) �☆

A large nebula, visible under dark skies with binoculars or a wide-field telescope, extending for up to four Moon diameters. It is best seen on long-exposure photographs, where it takes the shape of the continent of North America.

BETA (β) CYGNI (ALBIREO) �☆

A beautiful double star. The two stars, magnitudes 3.1 and 5.1, can be divided with powerful binoculars. They are easy to separate with a telescope, which shows a contrast of orange and blue-green. Both stars lie 380 light years away, but it is not known if they form a true binary.

M39 �☆

An open cluster, just visible to the naked eye under good conditions. Binoculars or a small telescope show its brightest stars. It lies nearly 900 light years away.

61 CYGNI ☆

An attractive double star. The two components, of magnitudes 5.2 and 6.1,

NGC 7000 (THE NORTH AMERICA NEBULA)

can be seen separately through a small telescope or even powerful binoculars. Both are orange dwarfs, smaller and fainter than the Sun, and are easily visible because they are only 11.4 light years away.

OMICRON-1 (o¹) CYGNI (31 CYGNI) �☆

An orange-coloured giant, magnitude 3.8, which has a wide 5th-magnitude, bluish companion (30 Cygni), ideal for binocular observation. A closer bluish star of 7th magnitude is also visible with binoculars or a small telescope.

NGC 6826 (THE BLINKING PLANETARY) ☆

A planetary nebula visible with a small telescope as a bluish disc similar in size to the disc of Jupiter. Looking alternately at it and to one side gives the impression that it is blinking on and off.

CHI (χ) CYGNI ◉ â

A pulsating red giant, one of the Mira class of variable stars, that ranges in brightness between 3rd and 14th magnitudes every 13 months or so.

ALPHA (α) CYGNI (DENEB) ◉

The brightest star in Cygnus, at magnitude 1.3. It is a luminous blue-white supergiant lying more than 3,000 light years away, which makes it the most distant star of all first-magnitude stars.

CYGNUS A ▦

A peculiar galaxy, thought to be two distant galaxies in collision. A large telescope is needed to see it, as it is of 15th magnitude. It is also a strong radio source.

NGC 6992 (THE VEIL NEBULA)

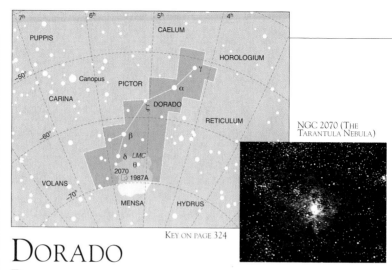

NGC 2070 (The Tarantula Nebula)

KEY ON PAGE 324

DORADO

DORADO, A SOUTHERN CONSTELLATION, was introduced in the 16th century by two Dutch navigators. It represents the goldfish of tropical seas, or a swordfish. It is significant for astronomers as it contains the bulk of the Large Magellanic Cloud – our nearest neighbouring galaxy. Its brightest star is Alpha (α) Doradus of magnitude 3.3.

THE LARGE MAGELLANIC CLOUD (LMC) ◑🔭✦ A small galaxy, a satellite of our own, lying 170,000 light years away. It is somewhat elongated in shape. It has about one-tenth the mass of our galaxy and a true diameter of 20,000 light years. It is usually classified as an irregular galaxy, but there are traces of a barred spiral structure. Scanning it with binoculars or a small telescope brings many star clusters and glowing nebulas into view.

NGC 2070 (THE TARANTULA NEBULA) ◑🔭✦ A bright nebula in the LMC, visible to the naked eye. It appears about the same size as the full Moon, but its true diameter is about 800 light years. The nebula is a star-forming region, and binoculars or a small telescope reveal a star cluster – 30 Doradus – at its centre.

BETA (β) DORADUS ◑ A bright Cepheid variable, ranging between magnitudes 3.5 and 4.1 every 9.8 days. It is a yellow-white supergiant and lies about 1,000 light years away.

SUPERNOVA 1987A ♛ The brightest supernova visible from Earth since 1604. In 1987, it reached magnitude 2.8 in the LMC.

DRACO

THIS EXTENSIVE CONSTELLATION represents a dragon that was slain by Hercules. In the northern sky, Hercules is represented with one foot on the dragon's head. Draco's brightest star is Gamma (γ) Draconis, a red giant about 150 light years away. With the stars Beta (β), Nu (ν), and Xi (ξ) Draconis, it forms the head of the dragon.

KEY ON PAGE 324

MU (μ) DRACONIS ⊀
A double star, each star of 6th magnitude. The stars are 88 light years away and orbit each other every 670 years.

NU (ν) DRACONIS 🔭⊀
A wide, double star with twin white 5th-magnitude components that are almost identical in colour and brightness. Both stars lie 100 light years away.

PSI (ψ) DRACONIS 🔭⊀
A double star. The two components, of magnitudes 4.6 and 5.8, may be divided with powerful binoculars.

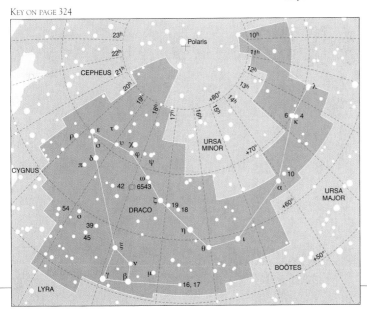

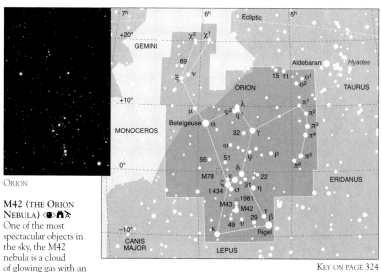

ORION

ORION IS THE MOST magnificent constellation. It represents a hunter with his dogs (marked by Canis Major and Canis Minor) at his heels. In Greek mythology, Orion was killed by a scorpion sting, and his position in the sky is such that he sets as the scorpion (the constellation Scorpius) rises. Orion's most celebrated feature is the M42 nebula.

ORION

KEY ON PAGE 324

M42 (THE ORION NEBULA) ⟨◉⟩ ♙ ⋨

One of the most spectacular objects in the sky, the M42 nebula is a cloud of glowing gas with an apparent diameter over twice that of the full Moon. Visible to the naked eye, it becomes larger and more complex when viewed with binoculars and telescopes of increasing aperture. It is 1,500 light years away and is lit up by the stars of the Trapezium that lie within it.

NGC 1981 ♙ A large, scattered open cluster visible with binoculars, its brightest stars being of 6th magnitude. The cluster appears to the north of the Orion Nebula and lies at about the same distance as it from Earth – approximately 1,400 light years.

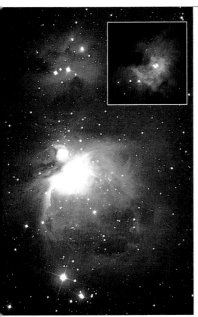

M42 (ORION NEBULA) WITH THE TRAPEZIUM INSET

THETA-1 (θ¹) ORIONIS (THE TRAPEZIUM)
A multiple star, located at the heart of the
Orion Nebula. A small telescope shows it
to be a quadruple star, with components of
magnitudes 5.1, 6.7, 6.7, and 8.0 arranged
in a trapezium shape.

ALPHA (α) ORIONIS (BETELGEUSE)
A red supergiant star of variable brightness,
ranging from about magnitude 0 to 1.3 every
6 years or so. It lies 430 light years away.
The name Betelgeuse is derived from an
Arabic term that incorporates a reference
to an armpit, although the star actually lies on
the hunter's shoulder.

BETA (β) ORIONIS (RIGEL) A blue supergiant of magnitude 0.2, the brightest star in the
constellation, and the seventh brightest in the
sky. It is 770 light years away. The name Rigel
means "left leg", which is the part of the
hunter's body that the star represents.

THETA-2 (θ²) ORIONIS A double star. The
two stars, magnitudes 5.0 and 6.4, are divisible
through binoculars. Theta-2 also forms a wide,
bright double with Theta-1 Orionis when
viewed through binoculars.

IOTA (ι) ORIONIS A double star. The two
components, of magnitudes 2.8 and 7.0, can be
split with a small telescope. Binoculars show
another double nearby – Struve 747 – which
consists of stars of magnitudes 4.8 and 5.7.

SIGMA (σ) ORIONIS A remarkable multiple
star. The main star, of magnitude 3.8, has two
7th-magnitude companions to one side, and a
9th-magnitude companion on the other. A
faint triple star, called Struve 761, should
be visible in the same telescopic field of view.

THE HORSEHEAD NEBULA A dark nebula,
shaped like a chess knight, seen silhouetted
against a strip of brighter nebulosity that
extends south from Zeta (ζ) Orionis.
However, it is too faint to be viewed without
a large telescope, and its shape is most easily
seen on a long-exposure photograph.

THE HORSEHEAD NEBULA

SAGITTARIUS

THIS CONSTELLATION OF THE ZODIAC lies between Scorpius and Capricornus. It depicts Crotus, the inventor of archery, aiming his bow at a scorpion, represented by Scorpius. The Sun passes through Sagittarius from 18 December to 19 January.

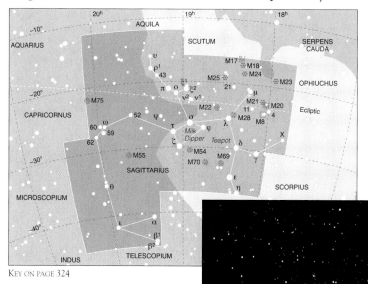

KEY ON PAGE 324

THE TEAPOT ◉ A group of eight stars: Gamma (γ), Epsilon (η), Delta (δ), Lambda (λ), Phi (φ), Zeta (ζ), Sigma (σ), and Tau (τ) Sagittarii. Together, they form the outline of a teapot, with a pointed lid and a large spout. The stars Lambda (λ), Phi (φ), Zeta (ζ), Sigma (σ), and Tau (τ) Sagittarii also form a shape known as the Milk Dipper, so named because it lies in a rich area of the Milky Way.

THE MAIN STARS IN SAGITTARIUS

M8 (THE LAGOON NEBULA) ◉♠⋊ A bright nebula, visible to the naked eye and a good target for binoculars. Elongated in shape, it is

336

M8 (THE LAGOON NEBULA)

almost three times the apparent width of the full Moon. A dark lane of dust bisects it – one half contains the cluster NGC 6530, with stars of 7th magnitude and fainter, while the most prominent object in the other half is the 6th-magnitude star 9 Sagittarii. The nebula, and the stars within it, are 5,200 light years away.

M17 (THE OMEGA NEBULA) 🌠🔭 A cloud of glowing gas of similar apparent size to the full Moon. It can be seen through binoculars, although a telescope is needed to see its true shape. A small telescope shows a star cluster, NGC 6618, within the cloud. The nebula and cluster both lie about 4,900 light years away.

M22 🌠🔭 The third brightest globular cluster in the sky, 10,000 light years away. It is visible to the naked eye under favourable conditions and easy to find with binoculars, which show it as a rounded patch about two-thirds the apparent size of the full Moon.

M17 (THE OMEGA NEBULA)

M23 🌠🔭 A rich open cluster, which is elongated in shape and is almost the same apparent width as the full Moon. It can be seen with binoculars, while a small telescope will resolve its stars. The cluster lies 2,100 light years away.

M24 👁🌠🔭 A large and bright field of stars lying in the Milky Way. It is visible to the naked eye and is an excellent sight through binoculars. Viewing it with a small telescope reveals a small open cluster – NGC 6603 – within it.

M20 (THE TRIFID NEBULA)

M25 🌠🔭 An open cluster, just visible to the naked eye, and a good object for observation with binoculars or a small telescope. Its stars, of 7th magnitude and fainter, are scattered over an area of sky the same apparent size as the full Moon. It lies 1,900 light years away.

M20 (THE TRIFID NEBULA) 🔭 A nebula with a faint double star at its centre, both of which are visible with a small telescope. Larger apertures show dust lanes trisecting the nebula.

BETA (β) SAGITTARII 👁🌠 A multiple star, although all the components lie at different distances and are unrelated. The naked eye sees it as a wide double with components of magnitudes 4.0 and 4.3. The brighter star, Beta-1 (β¹), has a 7th-magnitude companion that can be seen though a small telescope.

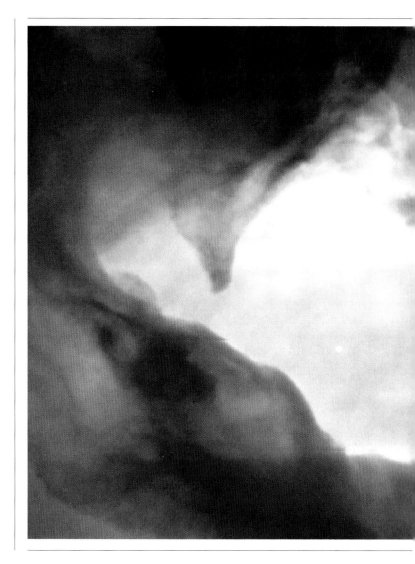

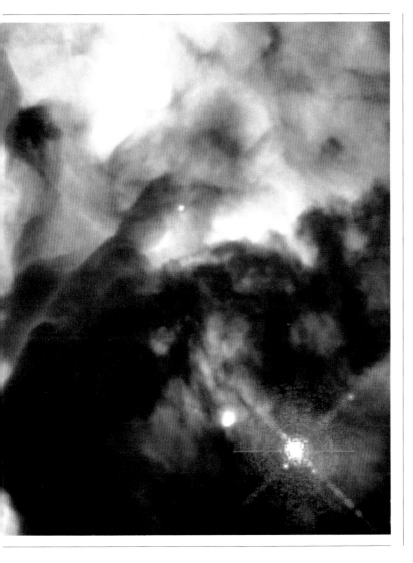

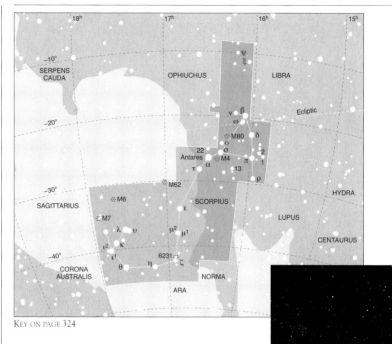

KEY ON PAGE 324

SCORPIUS

A CONSTELLATION OF THE ZODIAC,
Scorpius lies between Libra and

THE MAIN STARS IN SCORPIUS

Sagittarius. It depicts the scorpion that, in Greek
mythology, killed Orion with its sting – fittingly,
Orion sets as Scorpius rises. The constellation lies
in a rich region of the Milky Way, in the same
direction as the centre of our galaxy. The Sun
passes through it briefly, from 23 to 29 November.

NEBULOSITY AROUND ANTARES

those with good eyesight. Zeta-1 (ζ^1) is a blue-white supergiant of magnitude 4.7, the brightest star in the cluster NGC 6231. Zeta-2 (ζ^2), a red giant of magnitude 3.6, is much closer at 150 light years away.

ALPHA (α) SCORPII (ANTARES) A red supergiant star of variable brightness, ranging between magnitudes 0.9 and 1.2. It has a blue-white companion of 5th magnitude that can be seen with a telescope of moderate aperture.

BETA (β) SCORPII A double star, which has components of magnitudes 2.6 and 4.9 that are easy to separate with a small telescope. The two stars are unrelated, lying at distances of 530 and 1,100 light years.

NU (ν) SCORPII A multiple star. A small telescope, or even good binoculars, will reveal an optical double, with components of magnitudes 4.0 and 6.3. The fainter star of the pair has an 8th-magnitude companion that can be seen through a telescope with an aperture of 75mm (3in). Larger apertures show that the brighter star has an even closer companion of 5th magnitude – hence it appears to be a quadruple.

M4 One of the closest globular clusters, under 7,000 light years away. It can be seen with binoculars or a small telescope. A dark sky is needed as its stars are spread over a large area.

M6 An open cluster, 2,000 light years away. It is visible to the naked eye, and its individual stars can be seen with binoculars. Its brightest star is BM Scorpii, an orange giant that varies between 5th and 7th magnitudes.

M7 A large, glorious open cluster, visible with the naked eye and binoculars, and more than twice the apparent width of the full Moon. Its brightest stars, of 6th magnitude, are seen against a bright Milky Way background. The cluster is 780 light years away.

OMEGA (ω) SCORPII A naked-eye double star, with components of magnitudes 3.9 and 4.3, 420 and 260 light years away.

MU (μ) SCORPII A double star that can be divided with the naked eye. The brighter component is an eclipsing binary that varies between magnitudes 2.9 and 3.2 every 34 hours. Its companion is of magnitude 3.6.

NGC 6231 A prominent open cluster 5,900 light years away. Its individual stars are easy to see with binoculars or a small telescope. Zeta-1 (ζ^1) Scorpii is its brightest member.

ZETA (ζ) SCORPII A wide pair of unrelated stars, divisible with the naked eye by

M4

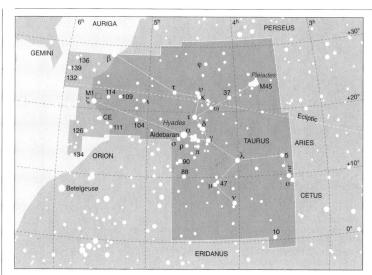

KEY ON PAGE 324

TAURUS

THIS IMPOSING ZODIAC CONSTELLATION, between Aries and Gemini, represents the bull into which the Greek god Zeus transformed himself. It contains two major star clusters – the Pleiades and Hyades. The Hyades cluster marks the bull's face, while the red giant star Aldebaran forms its bloodshot eye. The bull's horn-tips are marked by Beta (β) and Zeta (ζ).

M1 (THE CRAB NEBULA)

ALDEBARAN (ALPHA TAURI)

M45 (THE PLEIADES) ◐♨☌ A large, bright, open star cluster, easy to see with the naked eye and a superb sight through binoculars, appearing almost four times wider than the full Moon. Its brightest star is Eta (η) Tauri (Alcyone), a blue-white giant of magnitude 2.9. The naked eye can see about six stars, but dozens are visible with binoculars or a small telescope. The cluster is about 380 light years away. Long-exposure photographs show nebulosity around the stars, but a large telescope is needed to see this directly.

THE HYADES ◐♨☌ A large, loose, V-shaped star cluster, easily visible to the naked eye. It is best viewed with binoculars due to its considerable size, being scattered across the apparent width of 10 full Moons. The cluster lies about 150 light years away.

M1 (THE CRAB NEBULA) ♨☌ The remains of a supernova that was seen from Earth in 1054CE. Under good conditions it can be found with binoculars or a small telescope, but a moderate aperture is needed to see it well. It is elliptical in shape, appearing midway in size between the disc of a planet and the full Moon. It lies about 6,500 light years away.

THETA (θ) TAURI ◐♨ A wide double star in the Hyades cluster. Observers with good eyesight can divide the two stars with the naked eye. Theta-1 (θ¹) is a yellow giant, magnitude 3.8; Theta-2 (θ²) is a white giant of magnitude 3.4 – the brightest member of the Hyades.

ALPHA (α) TAURI (ALDEBARAN) ◐ A red giant star, which varies irregularly in brightness between magnitudes 0.75 and 0.95. Although it appears to be a member of the Hyades cluster, it is actually much closer to us, being 65 light years away.

LAMBDA (λ) TAURI ◐ An eclipsing binary star, which is of the same type as Algol. The magnitudes of this star range from 3.4 and 3.9 in a cycle lasting just under 4 days.

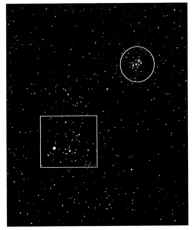

THE HYADES AND PLEIADES

URSA MAJOR

THE THIRD LARGEST CONSTELLATION, Ursa Major represents Callisto who, in Greek myth, was a hunting partner of Artemis. She was seduced by Zeus and then turned into a bear by the angry Artemis. Its brightest stars are Alpha (α) and Epsilon (ε), both with magnitude 1.8.

KEY ON PAGE 324

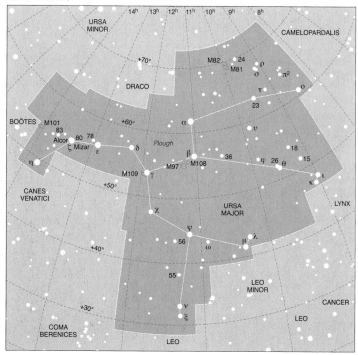

URSA MAJOR

THE PLOUGH (THE BIG DIPPER) ◉

One of the best-known patterns in the sky, consisting of the naked-eye stars Alpha (α), Beta (β), Gamma (γ), Delta (δ), Epsilon (ε), Zeta (ζ), and Eta (η) Ursae Majoris. The outline that they form is visualized in various cultures as that of a plough, a ladle, a saucepan, and even a wagon. All the stars in the Plough, with the exception of the outermost two (Alpha and Eta), are travelling in the same direction through space and form what is known as a moving cluster.

M81 AND M82 ♠≽

Two contrasting galaxies, about 10 million light years away. M81 is a beautiful spiral, visible with binoculars or a small telescope. One Moon diameter to the north is the smaller and fainter M82, a galaxy of peculiar appearance, which is now thought to be a spiral seen edge-on that is passing through a dust cloud.

ZETA (ζ) URSAE MAJORIS (MIZAR) ◉♠≽

A multiple star. Observers with good eyesight or using binoculars will see that this star, of magnitude 2.2, has a partner of magnitude 4.0, known as Alcor or 80 Ursae Majoris. Mizar and Alcor are 78 and 81 light years away, so they are not a true binary pair. However, a small telescope reveals that Mizar has a closer 4th-magnitude companion. This pair forms a true binary with a very long orbital period.

M101 ♠≽

A spiral galaxy, which appears face-on to us. It covers almost as much sky as the full Moon but it is quite faint, and good conditions are required if it is to be seen with binoculars or a small telescope.

XI (ξ) URSAE MAJORIS ≽

A binary star, with close components of magnitudes 4.3 and 4.8 that can be separated through a telescope of 75 mm (3 in) aperture. The yellowish stars, similar to the Sun, are 26 light years away and have an orbital period of 60 years.

M81

M101

POLAR STAR MAPS

THESE MAPS SHOW stars, clusters, and galaxies visible all year in both hemispheres. To see what is visible, face north in the northern hemisphere and south in the southern, turning the map so that the observing month is at the top. This will show the sky at 10 p.m. (11 p.m. in summer time). If it is earlier, for each hour before 10 p.m., turn the map 1 hour clockwise in the northern hemisphere and anticlockwise in the southern.

NORTH POLAR HIGHLIGHTS
The seven main stars of Ursa Major make an easily recognized pattern, called the Plough. The stars Merak and Dubhe point towards Polaris, the Pole Star, which is in almost exactly the same position every night. Opposite the Plough from Polaris is the W-shape of Cassiopeia.

PLOUGH

CIRCUMPOLAR STARS
Stars that never rise and set are called circumpolar. Though they are always visible, their position is constantly changing. The circumpolar area of sky varies as per distance from the equator. At the Poles, all stars are circumpolar; at the equator, they all rise and set.

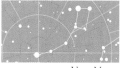

URSA MINOR

KEY TO THE STAR MAPS

Magnitudes								Open cluster
	−1	0	1	2	3	4	5 6	Globular cluster
Double stars								Bright nebula
Variable stars				Milky Way				Planetary nebula
								Supernova remnant
Constellation outline		Constellation boundary						Galaxy

CONSTELLATIONS
Originally, a constellation was a distinct pattern of stars, given a Latin name. In 1930, astronomers agreed to divide the sky into 88 areas, like countries on an Earth map, each containing a different constellation. The constellation name can now refer to this area of sky as well as the star pattern it contains.

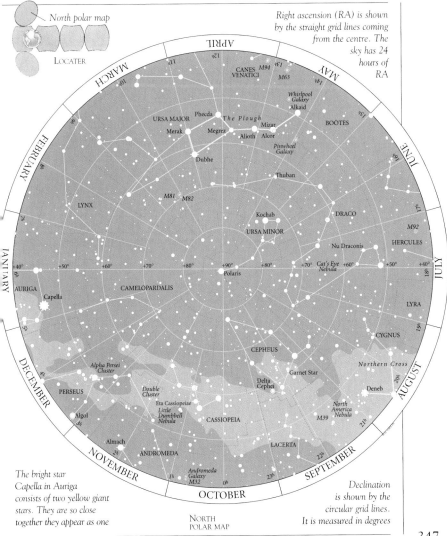

North polar map

LOCATER

Right ascension (RA) is shown by the straight grid lines coming from the centre. The sky has 24 hours of RA

APRIL

MARCH

MAY

CANES VENATICI — M94 — M63

Whirlpool Galaxy — Alkaid

URSA MAJOR — Phecda — The Plough

Merak — Megrez — Mizar — BOÖTES

Alioth — Alcor

Dubhe — Pinwheel Galaxy

FEBRUARY

Thuban

JUNE

M81 — M82

Kochab — DRACO — M92

URSA MINOR — HERCULES

LYNX

Nu Draconis

Cat's Eye Nebula

JANUARY

+40° +50° +60° +70° +80° +90° +80° +70° +60° +50° +40°

Polaris

AURIGA — Capella

CAMELOPARDALIS

LYRA

JULY

CYGNUS

CEPHEUS

Northern Cross

Alpha Persei Cluster

Garnet Star

DECEMBER

PERSEUS — Double Cluster

Delta Cephei

Deneb

AUGUST

Eta Cassiopeiae — Little Dumbbell Nebula

North America Nebula

Algol

CASSIOPEIA

M39

Almach

LACERTA

ANDROMEDA

SEPTEMBER

NOVEMBER

Andromeda Galaxy M32

The bright star Capella in Auriga consists of two yellow giant stars. They are so close together they appear as one

1ʰ 0ʰ 23ʰ

OCTOBER

NORTH POLAR MAP

Declination is shown by the circular grid lines. It is measured in degrees

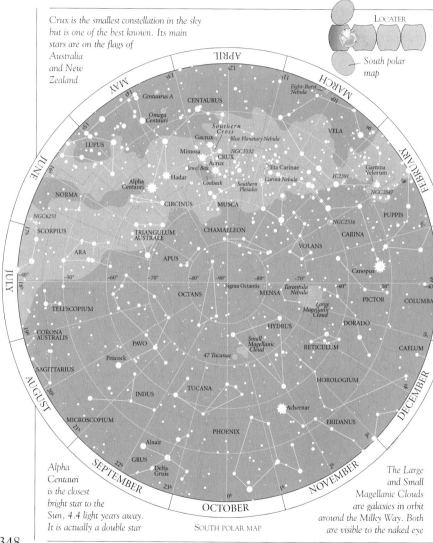

Crux is the smallest constellation in the sky but is one of the best known. Its main stars are on the flags of Australia and New Zealand

LOCATER

South polar map

APRIL

MAY

MARCH

JUNE

FEBRUARY

JULY

AUGUST

SEPTEMBER

OCTOBER

NOVEMBER

DECEMBER

Centaurus A

CENTAURUS

Eight-Burst Nebula

Omega Centauri

Southern Cross

Gacrux   Blue Planetary Nebula

VELA

LUPUS

Mimosa   NGC3532

CRUX

Acrux

Jewel Box   Eta Carinae

Hadar   Coalsack

Gamma Velorum

Alpha Centauri

Southern Pleiades   Carina Nebula

IC2391

NGC2547

NORMA

CIRCINUS   MUSCA

SCORPIUS   NGC6231

TRIANGULUM AUSTRALE

CHAMAELEON

NGC2516

PUPPIS

ARA   APUS

VOLANS   CARINA

Canopus

-40°   -50°   -60°   -70°   -80°   -90°   -80°   -70°   -60°   -50°   -40°

TELESCOPIUM

OCTANS   Sigma Octantis

MENSA   Tarantula Nebula

PICTOR

COLUMBA

CORONA AUSTRALIS

PAVO

HYDRUS

Large Magellanic Cloud

DORADO

SAGITTARIUS

Peacock

Small Magellanic Cloud

47 Tucanae

RETICULUM

CAELUM

HOROLOGIUM

MICROSCOPIUM

INDUS   TUCANA

Achernar

ERIDANUS

Alnair

PHOENIX

GRUS

Delta Gruis

SOUTH POLAR MAP

Alpha Centauri is the closest bright star to the Sun, 4.4 light years away. It is actually a double star

The Large and Small Magellanic Clouds are galaxies in orbit around the Milky Way. Both are visible to the naked eye

SOUTH POLAR HIGHLIGHTS

The best-known feature of the southern sky is the Southern Cross, which is made up of the five brightest stars of Crux. Follow a line from Gacrux through Acrux to locate the south celestial pole, which is at the centre of the map. Two bright stars, Alpha Centauri and Hadar, point towards the Southern Cross.

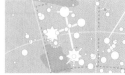

SOUTHERN CROSS

PHOENIX

SOUTHERN PLEIADES

This open star cluster, also known as IC 2602, is easily seen with the naked eye. It is called the Southern Pleiades because of its similarity to the Pleiades in Taurus. It contains about 30 stars, eight of which are brighter than magnitude 6.

USING A PLANISPHERE

A planisphere is a circular star map with a mask that rotates to show the area of sky visible over a specific latitude at any given date or time. Held upside down, it shows the stars visible at that point. Know your latitude before buying one.

PHOENIX

Phoenix lies near the southern end of Eridanus, close to the bright star Achernar. It is the largest of the 12 constellations invented at the end of the 16th century, and represents the mythical bird that was supposedly reborn from the dead body of its predecessor.

SCALE IN THE SKY

Hands can be used to measure distances in the sky. A full circle, with you at the centre, is 360°. A finger at arm's length covers about 1° – twice the size of the Moon. A closed hand is about 10°, the width of the Plough's bowl, while an open hand is 16° to 20°, the same width as the Square of Pegasus.

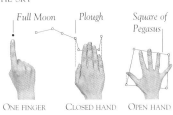

Full Moon *Plough* *Square of Pegasus*

ONE FINGER   CLOSED HAND   OPEN HAND

NORTHERN HEMISPHERE STAR MAPS JUNE TO NOVEMBER

The northern hemisphere maps show the stars with the observer facing south. Choose the map with the month in which you are observing. This will show the night sky as it appears at 10 p.m. (11 p.m. if summer time), with stars to the west visible earlier and those to the east visible later. The stars near the bottom of the map will be visible on the southern horizon, and those at the top will be almost overhead.

LOCATER

Nov, Oct, Sept

M15 GLOBULAR CLUSTER
This cluster can be seen about 20° to the right of the bottom of the Square of Pegasus. With binoculars M15 looks hazy, but a telescope shows it to be ball-shaped.

KEY ON PAGE 346

SEPTEMBER TO NOVEMBER HIGHLIGHTS
The Square of Pegasus is the key pattern to look for. Its four stars, although not very bright, are easy to find because there are few other stars around. Use the edges to point to Andromeda, which shares one star – Alpheratz – with the Square. Alpheratz is actually in Andromeda.

MAP DATA

• The maps are designed to overlap. Stars at the sides are repeated on the next map. Stars at the top also appear on the outer edge of the north polar map, and those along the bottom on the south polar map. If joined together, they would form one continuous map.

• Right Ascension, the equivalent of longitude on Earth, is labelled in hours along the top and bottom. Declination, the equivalent to latitude, is labelled in degrees on both edges.

• Andromeda Galaxy is the most distant object visible to the naked eye. Find it by moving northeast from Alpheratz.

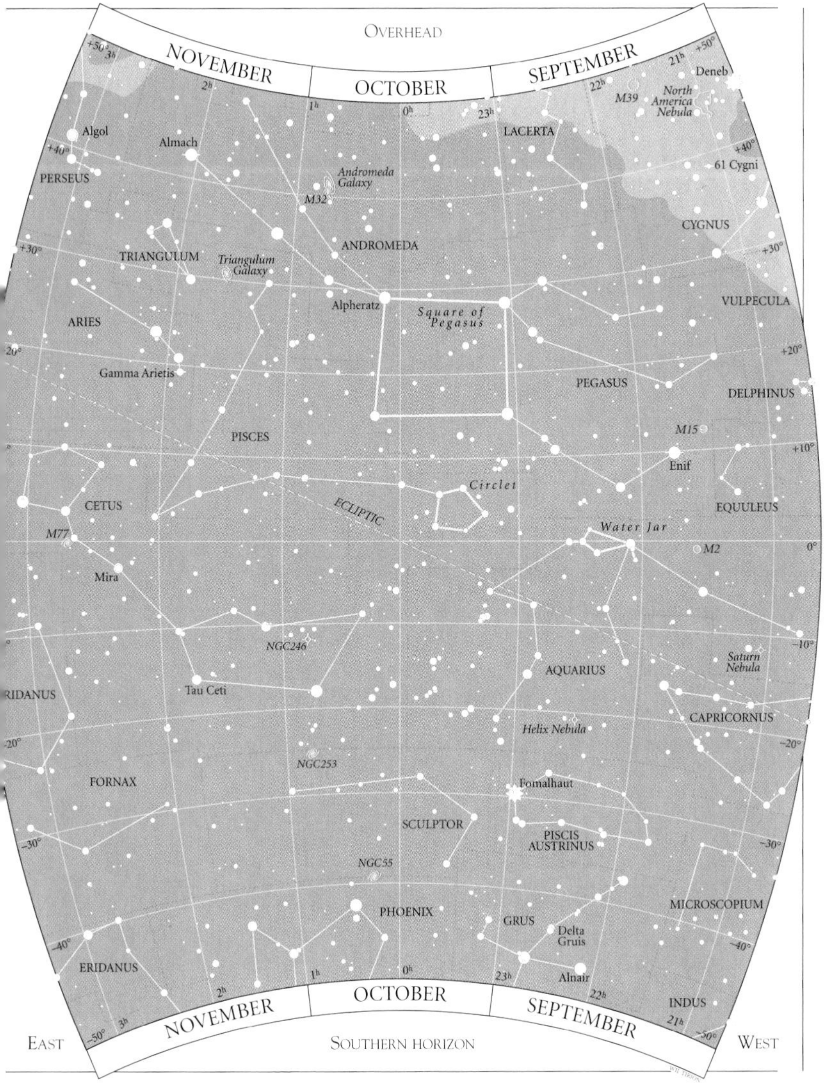

NOVEMBER OCTOBER SEPTEMBER

+50° 3ʰ
2ʰ 1ʰ 0ʰ 23ʰ 22ʰ 21ʰ +50°

Deneb

Algol
Almach
M39
North America Nebula

+40°
PERSEUS
Andromeda Galaxy
M32
LACERTA
61 Cygni +40°

TRIANGULUM
Triangulum Galaxy
ANDROMEDA
CYGNUS
+30°

ARIES
Alpheratz
Square of Pegasus
VULPECULA
+20°

20°
Gamma Arietis
PEGASUS
DELPHINUS
+20°

PISCES
M15
Enif
EQUULEUS
+10°

CETUS
ECLIPTIC
Circlet
Water Jar
+10°

M77
Mira
EQUULEUS
0°
M2

NGC246
AQUARIUS
Saturn Nebula
−10°

ERIDANUS
Tau Ceti
Helix Nebula
CAPRICORNUS
−20°

−20°
FORNAX
NGC253
Fomalhaut
−20°

SCULPTOR
PISCIS AUSTRINUS
−30°

NGC55
PHOENIX
GRUS
Delta Gruis
MICROSCOPIUM
−40°

ERIDANUS
Alnair
INDUS
−50°

3ʰ 2ʰ 1ʰ 0ʰ 23ʰ 22ʰ 21ʰ

EAST NOVEMBER OCTOBER SEPTEMBER WEST

SOUTHERN HORIZON

351

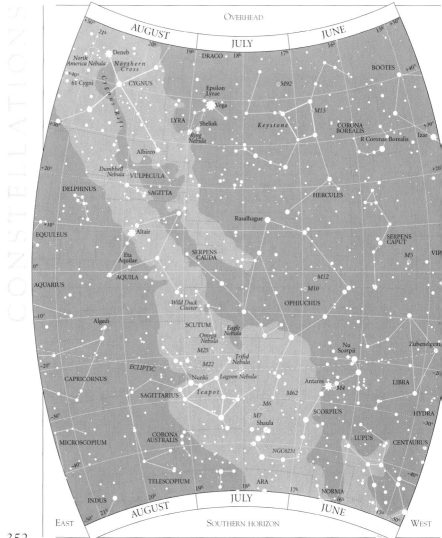

OVERHEAD

AUGUST
JULY
JUNE

+30° 21ʰ
20ʰ
19ʰ DRACO 18ʰ
17ʰ
16ʰ 15ʰ +50°

North
America Nebula   Deneb
Northern
Cross
+40°
61 Cygni
CYGNUS
Epsilon
Lyrae
Vega
M92
BOÖTES
+40°

Cygnus Rift
LYRA
Sheliak
Keystone
M13
CORONA
BOREALIS
Izar
+30°
Ring
Nebula
R Coronae Borealis

+20°
Albireo
Dumbbell
Nebula   VULPECULA
HERCULES
+20°

DELPHINUS
SAGITTA

+10°
Altair
Rasalhague
SERPENS
CAPUT
M5
VIR

EQUULEUS
SERPENS
CAUDA
0°
Eta
Aquilae

AQUARIUS
AQUILA
M12
M10
OPHIUCHUS
Zubenelgen

−10°
Wild Duck
Cluster
Eagle
Nebula

Algedi
SCUTUM
Omega
Nebula
Nu
Scorpii

M25
Trifid
Nebula
−20°
ECLIPTIC
M22
Nunki   Lagoon Nebula
Antares   M4
LIBRA

CAPRICORNUS
SAGITTARIUS
Teapot
M62
SCORPIUS
HYDRA

−30°
CORONA
AUSTRALIS
M6
M7
Shaula
−30°

MICROSCOPIUM
LUPUS
CENTAURUS

−40°
TELESCOPIUM
NGC6231
−40°

INDUS
21ʰ
20ʰ
19ʰ
ARA
NORMA
16ʰ 15ʰ −50°

AUGUST
18ʰ JULY 17ʰ
JUNE

EAST
SOUTHERN HORIZON
WEST

352

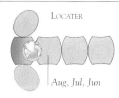
JUNE TO AUGUST HIGHLIGHTS

The Milky Way dominates the view, along with the Summer Triangle of Deneb, Vega, and Altair. Cygnus points along the Galaxy, while the dark band between Cygnus and Serpens – the Cygnus Rift – hides the stars beyond. Look for arrow-shaped Sagitta and Scutum – near to them is a bright patch of the Milky Way. To the south, the distinctive patterns of Scorpius and Sagittarius lie on either side of the Milky Way.

DUMBBELL NEBULA

Below Cygnus lies a small, faint planetary nebula. It is visible through binoculars, although its colours do not show up. It gets its name from its brightest parts that show up looking like a dumbell in small telescopes.

Dumbbell Nebula is the remains of a star that died thousands of years ago

WILD DUCK CLUSTER

This open star cluster, which is at the top of Scutum, is just visible with the naked eye. When viewed through a pair of binoculars its stars are in a V-shape that looks like a flight of ducks – hence its name.

KEY ON PAGE 346

MAP DATA

• Three bright stars from different constellations – Deneb in Cygnus, Vega in Lyra, and Altair in Aquila – make up the Summer Triangle.

• Albireo is a double star that marks the head of Cygnus, the swan. In high-powered binoculars, its two stars have contrasting yellow and blue colours.

• The Eagle Nebula, just below Serpens Cauda, is visible as a hazy spot of light in binoculars. A medium-sized telescope reveals a dark shape within the nebula, which in photographs looks like an eagle flapping its wings.

NORTHERN HEMISPHERE STAR MAPS DECEMBER TO MAY

In winter, constellations and stars – including the brightest constellation, Orion, and the brightest star, Sirius – are the main attractions because the Milky Way is faint. Most of the visible stars, as well as several star nurseries such as the Orion Nebula, are in the Local Arm of the galaxy. Star clusters are common too. By spring, the view shifts to looking sideways out of the Milky Way, and the Virgo cluster is visible.

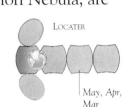

LOCATER

May, Apr, Mar

BLACK EYE GALAXY
A spiral galaxy just below Coma Berenices, the Black Eye Galaxy has a dark dust lane near its centre. Small telescopes just show a little hazy oval of light, but large telescopes make it look like an eye, hence the name.

KEY ON PAGE 346

MARCH TO MAY HIGHLIGHTS
The constellation Leo is easy to spot, with a curve of stars – called Sickle – marking its head. More difficult to see is Virgo and the Virgo Cluster of 2,000 galaxies, to the southeast of Leo. Below Virgo is a small constellation with four distinctive stars, Corvus. It is easy to find in the sky, though its stars are not very bright.

MAP DATA

• Arcturus, in Boötes, is a red giant and the fourth brightest star in the sky.

• The M65 and M66 galaxies in Leo are easy to find as they are quite bright and lie between two fairly bright stars. With a telescope, the galaxies look like tiny, hazy spindles.

• Porrima in Virgo is a double star. From 2005 to 2007, the stars will be so close to each other that even with a telescope they will look like a single star. The next time this occurs will be in 2174.

354

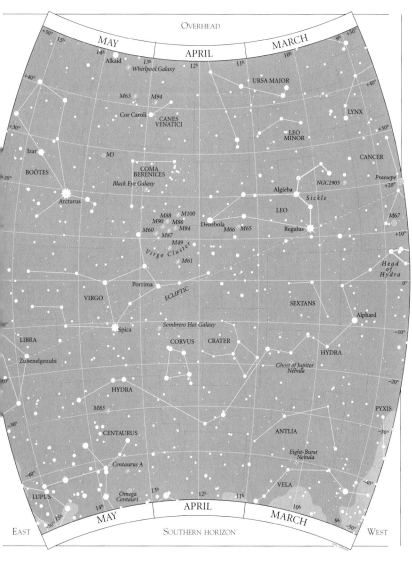

OVERHEAD

MAY
APRIL
MARCH

15ʰ
14ʰ Alkaid
13ʰ
Whirlpool Galaxy
12ʰ
11ʰ
10ʰ
9ʰ
+50°

+50°
+40°
URSA MAJOR
+40°

M63 M94
LYNX

Cor Caroli CANES
VENATICI
LEO
MINOR
+30°

+30°
CANCER

Izar
M3
BOÖTES
COMA
BERENICES
Black Eye Galaxy
Algieba Sickle NGC2903 Praesepe
+20°

+20°
Arcturus
LEO
M67

M88 M100
M90 M86
M60 M84
M87
M49
Denebola M66 M65
Regulus
+10°

Virgo Cluster
M61
Head
of
Hydra

VIRGO
Porrima
ECLIPTIC
SEXTANS
Alphard
0°

Spica
Sombrero Hat Galaxy
-10°

LIBRA
CORVUS CRATER
HYDRA

Zubenelgenubi
Ghost of Jupiter
Nebula
-20°

HYDRA

M83
PYXIS
-30°

CENTAURUS
ANTLIA

Eight-Burst
Nebula

Centaurus A
VELA
-40°

LUPUS
Omega
Centauri
13ʰ
12ʰ
11ʰ
10ʰ
9ʰ
-50°

14ʰ
15ʰ
MAY
APRIL
MARCH

EAST
SOUTHERN HORIZON
WEST

355

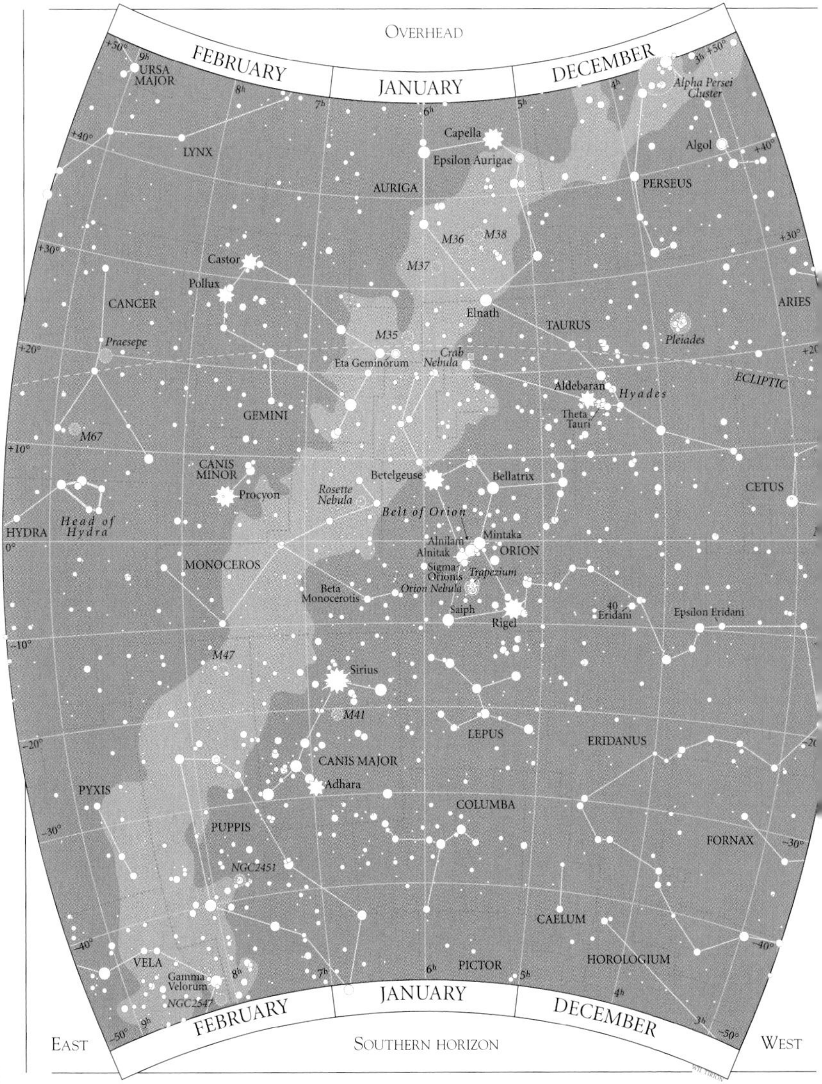

CONSTELLATIONS

FEBRUARY   JANUARY   DECEMBER

+50° 9ʰ
URSA MAJOR   8ʰ   7ʰ   6ʰ   5ʰ   4ʰ   3ʰ +50°
Alpha Persei Cluster

LYNX   Capella   Algol
Epsilon Aurigae   +40°
+40°
PERSEUS
AURIGA
+30°   M36 M38   +30°
Castor   M37   ARIES
Pollux   Elnath   TAURUS   Pleiades
CANCER   M35   Crab Nebula   +20°
+20°   Praesepe   Eta Geminorum   Aldebaran   Hyades   ECLIPTIC
Theta Tauri
GEMINI
+10°   M67   CETUS
CANIS MINOR   Betelgeuse   Bellatrix
Procyon   Rosette Nebula   Belt of Orion
0°   HYDRA   Head of Hydra   Alnilam Mintaka
MONOCEROS   Alnitak   ORION
Sigma Orionis   Trapezium
Beta Monocerotis   Orion Nebula
–10°   Saiph   Rigel   40 Eridani   Epsilon Eridani
M47
Sirius
–20°   M41   LEPUS   ERIDANUS
CANIS MAJOR
Adhara
PYXIS   COLUMBA
–30°   PUPPIS   FORNAX   –30°
NGC2451
CAELUM
–40°   HOROLOGIUM   –40°
VELA
Gamma Velorum   8ʰ   7ʰ   6ʰ   5ʰ   4ʰ   3ʰ   –50°
NGC2547   PICTOR

FEBRUARY   JANUARY   DECEMBER

EAST   SOUTHERN HORIZON   WEST

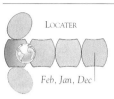

LOCATER

Feb, Jan, Dec

DECEMBER TO FEBRUARY HIGHLIGHTS

Orion is a signpost in the sky. Above it is Auriga, with the M36 and M38 starclusters. The three stars in Orion's Belt point down to Sirius in Canis Major, and up to Aldebaran in Taurus and the Pleiades beyond. Betelgeuse, Sirius, and Procyon (in Canis Minor) form the Winter Triangle. A diagonal through Rigel and Betelgeuse leads to Gemini.

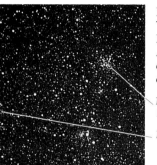

M36 AND M38 CLUSTERS

The brighter of the two open star clusters is M36. Both are visible with the naked eye. As M36 and M38 appear quite close, they can easily be mistaken for a comet at a casual glance.

M38 – a wide area with about 100 stars scattered across it

M36 is a compact cluster of about 60 stars

PRAESEPE

An open star cluster in Cancer, Praesepe – visible with the naked eye on clear and dark nights – is a splendid sight when viewed with binoculars.

M35 CLUSTER

An open star cluster of about 120 stars to the north of eta Geminorum, M35 is just visible with the naked eye. It is easy to spot with binoculars, which will show some of its brightest stars.

MAP DATA

• The Orion Nebula is the brightest nebula in the sky. It appears as a misty patch with the naked eye, but small telescopes show a group of four stars – the Trapezium – at its centre.

KEY ON PAGE 346

SOUTHERN HEMISPHERE STAR MAPS SEPTEMBER TO FEBRUARY

The southern hemisphere maps show the stars when viewed looking north. Choose the map with the month in which you are observing. This will show the night sky as it appears at 10 p.m. (11 p.m. if summer time), with stars to the west visible earlier and those farther to the east later. Stars near the bottom of the map will be visible on the northern horizon, and those at the top will be almost overhead.

Sept, Oct, Nov

LOCATER

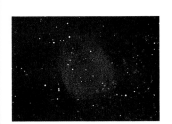

HELIX NEBULA
The largest, and closest, planetary nebula is the Helix Nebula in Aquarius. It can be seen in a very dark sky, using binoculars or a telescope. The red colour shows up only in photographs.

KEY ON PAGE 346

SEPTEMBER TO NOVEMBER HIGHLIGHTS
The brightest star in this part of the sky is Fomalhaut in Piscis Austrinus – the southern fish. The Square of Pegasus is in the northern sky. Use the edges and diagonals of the Square to locate Andromeda, Aquarius, Pisces, and Cetus. The stars in Pisces are all faint.

MAP DATA

• The maps have been designed to overlap. Stars at the edges are repeated on the next map. Stars at the top also appear on the outer edge of the south polar map, and those along the bottom on the north polar map. If joined together, they would form one continuous map.

• Right Ascension, the equivalent of longitude on Earth, is labelled in hours along the top and bottom. Declination, the equivalent of latitude, is labelled in degrees on both edges.

• Triangulum Galaxy, a misty patch the size of the full Moon, can be seen with binoculars in a dark night's sky.

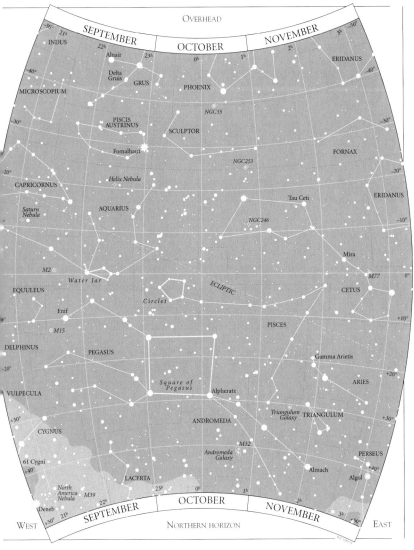

OVERHEAD

INDUS

Alnair

Delta
Gruis

GRUS

PHOENIX

ERIDANUS

MICROSCOPIUM

NGC 55

PISCIS
AUSTRINUS

SCULPTOR

FORNAX

Fomalhaut

NGC 253

Helix Nebula

ERIDANUS

CAPRICORNUS

Tau Ceti

Saturn
Nebula

AQUARIUS

NGC 246

Mira

M2

Water Jar

M77

EQUULEUS

ECLIPTIC

CETUS

Circlet

Enif

PISCES

M15

DELPHINUS

PEGASUS

Gamma Arietis

VULPECULA

ARIES

Square of
Pegasus

Alpheratz

CYGNUS

Triangulum
Galaxy

TRIANGULUM

61 Cygni

ANDROMEDA

PERSEUS

North
America
Nebula

M39

M32

Andromeda
Galaxy

Almach

Algol

Deneb

LACERTA

CONSTELLATIONS

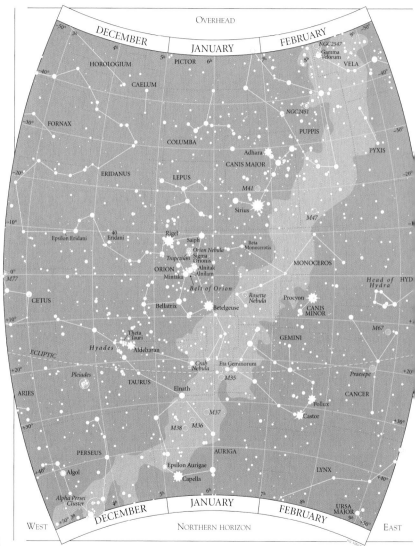

OVERHEAD

DECEMBER   JANUARY   FEBRUARY

-50° -30°
-40°

HOROLOGIUM
CAELUM

NGC2547
Gamma
Velorum   VELA

PICTOR

NGC2451

FORNAX

COLUMBA   PUPPIS   PYXIS

Adhara
CANIS MAJOR

ERIDANUS   LEPUS   M41

Sirius   M47

Epsilon Eridani   40
Eridani   Rigel   Saiph
Orion Nebula   Beta
Sigma   Monocerotis
Orionis
Trapezium   Alnitak   MONOCEROS
ORION   Alnilam
Mintaka   Head of
Hydra   HYD
Belt of Orion

Rosette
Nebula   Procyon

CETUS   Bellatrix   Betelgeuse   CANIS
MINOR

M77

Theta
Tauri   GEMINI   M67

Hyades   Aldebaran

ECLIPTIC   Crab   Eta Geminorum
Nebula

Pleiades   M35   Praesepe

ARIES   TAURUS   Elnath   CANCER

Pollux

M37   Castor

M38   M36

PERSEUS   AURIGA   LYNX

Algol   Epsilon Aurigae
Capella

Alpha Persei
Cluster   DECEMBER   JANUARY   FEBRUARY   URSA
MAJOR

WEST   NORTHERN HORIZON   EAST

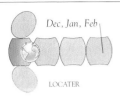

Dec, Jan, Feb

LOCATER

DECEMBER TO FEBRUARY HIGHLIGHTS

Orion acts as a signpost to many other constellations. The three stars of Orion's Belt point northeast to Sirius and Canis Major, and southwest towards Aldebaran in Taurus. Near Aldebaran is a V-shaped cluster of stars called the Hyades. The Pleiades, a little to the west, attract the eye because there are a few very bright stars nearby.

M41 is about 2,300 light years away, and contains about 100 stars

The Ancient Greeks observed M41, which is about the same size as the full Moon in the sky

MAP DATA

• Sirius is the brightest star in the sky and, at 8.6 light years away, one of the nearest. It is sometimes called the Dog Star because it is in the constellation of Canis Major, the great dog.

• Trapezium is a multiple star in the Orion Nebula, just south of Orion's Belt. The nebula is visible as a misty patch with the naked eye. A telescope shows four stars in the shape of a trapezium that were recently born and are now illuminating the nebula.

• Betelgeuse is a noticeable orange, while the other stars of Orion are mostly bluish. It is a red giant star, and varies slightly and unpredictably in brightness.

• The Crab Nebula in Taurus gets its name from its claw-like extensions. It is the remains of a brilliant supernova that appeared in 1054. Now all that can be seen with a telescope is a hazy blur.

• Capella, at a distance of 42 light years, is one of the sky's most famous double stars. Its two components are only about 95 million km (60 million miles) apart and travel around their respective orbits in just 104 days.

M41 CLUSTER

To the south of Sirius lies M41, an open star cluster in Canis Major, just visible with the naked eye. Binoculars show that many of the stars seem to form chains. This is probably because some stars lie almost along the same line of sight as more distant stars. Several of the stars in M41 are red giants, the most luminous of which is 700 times more luminous than the Sun. The cluster is about 26 light years across, and is estimated to be 190 million years old.

KEY ON PAGE 346

361

SOUTHERN HEMISPHERE STAR MAPS MARCH TO AUGUST

CONSTELLATIONS

SOUTHERN HEMISPHERE STAR MAPS MARCH TO AUGUST

In the early part of the year the sky is rich in galaxies. The great Virgo Cluster of galaxies lies at right angles to the line of the Milky Way, so there is no dust from our own galaxy to obscure the view. During May, the star clouds of the Milky Way start to appear low in the east, and then arch overhead in winter. Nebulas and star clusters are dotted along the Milky Way, many of them visible with binoculars.

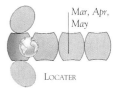

Mar, Apr, May

LOCATER

SOMBRERO HAT GALAXY
A spiral galaxy in Virgo, the Sombrero Hat Galaxy looks like a broad-brimmed Mexican hat in photographs. The dark line visible in a telescope is a dust lane, like the Cygnus Rift in the Milky Way.

KEY ON PAGE 346

MARCH TO MAY HIGHLIGHTS
There are three bright stars in this part of the sky – Arcturus in Boötes, Regulus in Leo, and Spica in Virgo. There are about 2,000 galaxies in Virgo, but only a few are visible in small telescopes. The stars are so sparse at this time of the year that Alphard in Hydra was named "the solitary one" by the Arabs.

MAP DATA
• The centre of the Sombrero Hat is stars concentrated in the middle of the galaxy, and the rim is its spiral arm.

• M83 in Hydra is a spiral galaxy, which appears in small telescopes as a round hazy blur. With large telescopes, the spiral arms become visible.

• M87, an elliptical galaxy, is near the centre of the Virgo Cluster. It is one of the largest galaxies known, but is not very spectacular in small telescopes as it lies 50 million light years away. It looks like a circular hazy spot, brighter in the middle.

362

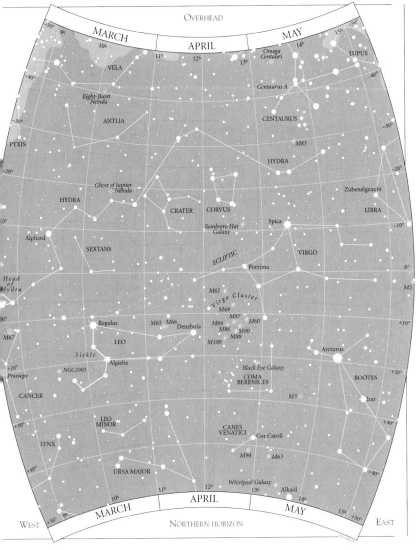

MARCH
APRIL
MAY

-50° 9ʰ 10ʰ 11ʰ 12ʰ 13ʰ 14ʰ 15ʰ -50°

Omega Centauri

LUPUS

VELA

-40° -40°

Centaurus A

Eight-Burst Nebula

ANTLIA

CENTAURUS

-30° -30°

PYXIS

M83

HYDRA

-20° -20°

Ghost of Jupiter Nebula

Zubenelgenubi

HYDRA

LIBRA

CRATER CORVUS

Sombrero Hat Galaxy

Spica

-10°

Alphard

SEXTANS

VIRGO

ECLIPTIC

Porrima

0° 0°

Head of Hydra

M5

M61

Virgo Cluster

M49

Regulus M65 M66 Denebola

M87 M60
M84
M86 M90
M100 M88

+10° +10°

M67

LEO

Algieba

Sickle

Arcturus

+20° NGC2903

Praesepe

Black Eye Galaxy

COMA BERENICES

BOOTES

+20°

CANCER

M3

Izar

LEO MINOR

CANES VENATICI Cor Caroli

+30° +30°

LYNX

M94 M63

URSA MAJOR

+40° +40°

Whirlpool Galaxy Alkaid

+50° 9ʰ 10ʰ 11ʰ 12ʰ 13ʰ 14ʰ 15ʰ +50°

MARCH APRIL MAY

CONSTELLATIONS

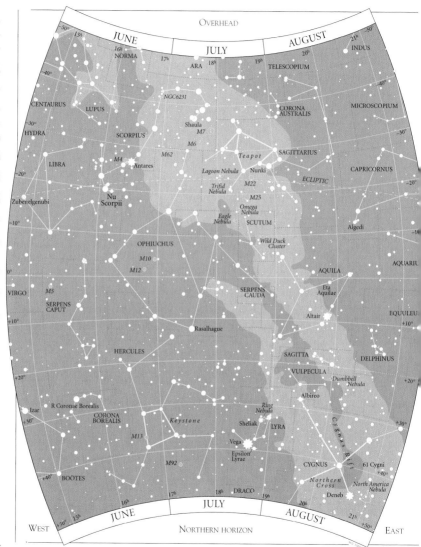

OVERHEAD

JUNE · JULY · AUGUST

NORMA · ARA · TELESCOPIUM · INDUS

NGC6231 · CENTAURUS · LUPUS · CORONA AUSTRALIS · MICROSCOPIUM

HYDRA · SCORPIUS · Shaula · M7 · M6 · SAGITTARIUS

LIBRA · M4 · Antares · M62 · Teapot · Nunki · CAPRICORNUS

Zubenelgenubi · Nu Scorpii · Lagoon Nebula · M22 · ECLIPTIC · Algedi

Trifid Nebula · M25 · Omega Nebula · SCUTUM

Eagle Nebula · AQUARIU

OPHIUCHUS · M10 · M12 · Wild Duck Cluster · AQUILA

VIRGO · M5 · SERPENS CAPUT · SERPENS CAUDA · Eta Aquilae · EQUULEU

Altair

Rasalhague · SAGITTA · DELPHINUS

HERCULES · VULPECULA · Dumbbell Nebula

Albireo · Cygnus Rift

Izar · R Coronae Borealis · Ring Nebula

CORONA BOREALIS · Keystone · Sheliak · LYRA · 61 Cygni

M13 · Vega

Epsilon Lyrae

M92 · CYGNUS · North America Nebula

BOÖTES · Northern Cross · Deneb

DRACO

JUNE · JULY · AUGUST

WEST · NORTHERN HORIZON · EAST

364

CONSTELLATIONS

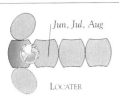

Jun, Jul, Aug

LOCATER

The centre of the Milky Way lies in the direction of Sagittarius, but huge dust clouds block our view of it. Some of the stars of Sagittarius make a teapot shape – a bright part of the Milky Way looks like a wisp of steam coming from its spout. To the west of Sagittarius is Scorpius, with red Antares at the scorpion's heart and a curve of stars marking its tail.

The Lagoon Nebula is one of only two star-forming nebulas faintly visible to the naked eye from mid-northern latitudes

The curving lane of dust, shaped like a lagoon, after which the nebula is named

MAP DATA

• To the naked eye, the M7 open star cluster looks like a bright part of the Milky Way, about twice the size of the full Moon. Binoculars or a small telescope show many stars in this and another nearby cluster, M6.

• Sagittarius is a rich viewing area. Not only does the centre of the Milky Way lie in this direction, but it contains more bright nebulas and star clusters than any other constellation.

• The dark band in the Milky Way – Cygnus Rift – is caused by dust clouds lying in front of the stars.

• Ring Nebula lies between the two stars at the top corners of Lyra, and looks like a tiny doughnut. This planetary nebula is quite bright, but is too small to be seen without a telescope.

LAGOON NEBULA

One of the brightest nebulas in the Milky Way, the Lagoon Nebula is visible to the naked eye. It gets its name because telescopes show a curved dark area within it that looks like a desert island lagoon. It is 50 light years across, and was discovered in 1747. It lies 5,200 light years away.

KEY ON PAGE 346

ASTRONOMY TIMELINE

3000BCE STONE ASTRONOMY

Stonehenge, built about this time in southern England, is a giant astronomical calendar with stones aligned to the Sun and possibly the Moon. Many other ancient sites are thought to have astronomical significance, such as the Egyptian pyramids (2600BCE) and, later, buildings in China and Central and South America (1st century CE).

750BCE LUNAR CYCLE

In Babylon, astronomers discover a 18.6 year cycle in the rising and setting of the Moon. From this they create the first almanacs – tables of movements of the Sun, Moon, and planets for use in astrology. In 6th century Greece, this knowledge is used to predict eclipses.

380BCE EARTH-CENTRED VIEW

Greek philosopher Plato founds a school of thought that will influence the next 2,000 years. It promotes the idea that everything in the Universe moves in harmony, and that the Sun, Moon, and planets move around Earth in perfect circles.

270BCE SUN-CENTRED VIEW

Aristarchus of Samos proposes an alternative to the geocentric (Earth-centred) Universe. His heliocentric model places the Sun at its centre, with Earth as just one planet orbiting around it. However, few people at the time take the theory seriously. They argue, if Earth is moving through space, then why do the stars not move through the sky?

164BCE HALLEY'S COMET

The earliest recorded sighting of Halley's Comet is made by Babylonian astronomers. Their records of the comet's movements allow 20th-century astronomers to predict accurately how the comet's orbit changes over the centuries.

150CE STAR CATALOGUE

Ptolemy publishes his star catalogue, listing 48 constellations, and endorses the Earth-centred view of the Universe. His views go unquestioned for nearly 1,500 years, and are passed down to Arabic and medieval European astronomers in his book *The Almagest*.

928 ASTROLABE

The earliest surviving astrolabe – an instrument to show the position of stars and planets – is made by Islamic craftsmen. Astrolabes are the most advanced instruments of their time. The precise measurement of the positions of stars and planets allows Arab astronomers to compile the most detailed almanacs and star atlases yet.

1054 SUPERNOVA

Chinese astronomers record the sudden appearance of a bright star. Native American rock carvings also show the brilliant star close to the Moon. This star is the Crab supernova exploding.

1543 COPERNICAN SYSTEM Nicolaus Copernicus publishes his theory that Earth goes around the Sun, in contradiction of the Church's teachings. However, he complicates his theory by retaining Plato's perfect circular orbits of the planets.

1577 TYCHO'S COMET A brilliant comet is observed by Tycho Brahe, who proves that it is travelling beyond Earth's atmosphere and, therefore, provides the first evidence that the heavens can change.

1608 FIRST TELESCOPE Dutch spectacle-maker Hans Lippershey (1570–1619) invents the refracting telescope. The invention spreads rapidly across Europe, as scientists make their own instruments. Their discoveries begin a revolution in astronomy.

1609 KEPLER'S LAWS Johannes Kepler publishes his *New Astronomy*. In this and later works, he announces his three laws of planetary motion, replacing the circular orbits of Plato with elliptical ones. Almanacs based on his laws prove to be highly accurate.

1610 OBSERVATIONS Galileo Galilei publishes the findings of his observations with the telescope he built. These include spots on the Sun, craters on the Moon, and four satellites orbiting Jupiter. Proving that not everything orbits the planet Earth, he promotes the Copernican view of a Sun-centred Universe.

1663 REFLECTOR Scottish astronomer James Gregory (1638–75) builds a reflecting telescope, using mirrors instead of lenses, to allow a larger aperture and reduce light loss. Within five years, Isaac Newton improves the design, creating the Newtonian telescope; other variations soon follow.

1687 THEORY OF GRAVITY Isaac Newton publishes his *Principia Mathematica*, establishing the theory of gravitation and laws of motion. The *Principia Mathematica* explains Kepler's laws of planetary motion and allows astronomers to understand the forces acting between the Sun, the planets, and their moons.

1705 HALLEY'S COMET Edmond Halley calculates that the comets recorded at 76-year intervals from 1456 to 1682 are one and the same. He predicts that the comet will return again in 1758. When it reappears as expected, the comet is named in his honour.

1750 SOUTHERN SKIES French astronomer Nicolas de Lacaille (1713–62) sails to southern oceans and begins work compiling a catalogue of more than 10,000 stars in the southern sky. Lacaille's star catalogue is the first comprehensive one of the southern sky.

ASTRONOMY TIMELINE

1781 URANUS Amateur astronomer William Herschel discovers the planet Uranus, although he at first mistakes it for a comet. Uranus is the first planet to be discovered beyond Saturn (the most distant of the planets known since ancient times).

1784 MESSIER CATALOGUE Charles Messier publishes his catalogue of star clusters and nebulas. Messier draws up the list to prevent these objects being identified as comets. However, it soon becomes a standard reference for the study of star clusters and nebulas, and is still in use today.

1800 INFRARED RADIATION William Herschel splits sunlight through a prism and, with a thermometer, measures the energy given out by different colours; this is the first study of a star's spectrum. He notices a sudden increase in energy beyond the red end of the spectrum, discovering invisible infrared (heat) radiation and laying the foundations for spectroscopy.

1801 ASTEROIDS Italian astronomer Giuseppe Piazzi (1746–1826) discovers what appears to be a new planet orbiting between Mars and Jupiter, and names it Ceres. William Herschel proves it is a very small object – only 320 km (199 miles) in diameter – and not a planet. He proposes the name asteroid, and soon other similar bodies are being found. We now know that Ceres is 932 km (579 miles) in diameter – but still too small to be a planet.

1814 FRAUNHOFER LINES Joseph von Fraunhofer builds the first accurate spectrometer and uses it to study the spectrum of the Sun's light. He discovers and maps hundreds of fine dark lines crossing the solar spectrum. In 1859, these lines are linked to chemical elements in the Sun's atmosphere. Spectroscopy becomes the method for studying what the stars are made of.

1838 STELLAR PARALLAX Friedrich Bessel successfully uses the method of stellar parallax (the effect of Earth's annual movement around the Sun) to calculate the distance to 61 Cygni: the first star other than the Sun to have its distance measured. Bessel has pioneered the truly accurate measurement of stellar positions, and the parallax technique establishes a framework for measuring the scale of the Universe.

1843 SUNSPOT CYCLE German amateur astronomer Heinrich Schwabe (1789–1875), who had studied the Sun for 17 years, observes a regular cycle in sunspot numbers – the first clue to the Sun's internal structure.

1845 LARGE TELESCOPES Irish astronomer the Earl of Rosse completes the first of the world's great telescopes, with a 180-cm (71-in) mirror. He uses it to study and draw the structure of nebulas, and within a few months discovers the spiral structure of the Whirlpool Galaxy.

1845 ASTROPHOTOGRAPHY French physicists Jean Foucault (1819–68) and Armand Fizeau (1819–96) take the first detailed photographs of the Sun's surface through a telescope – the birth of scientific astrophotography. Within five years, astronomers produce the first detailed photographs of the Moon. Early film is not sensitive enough to image stars.

1846 NEPTUNE A new planet, called Neptune, is identified by German astronomer Johann Gottfried Galle (1812–1910). He had been searching in the position suggested by Urbain Le Verrier. Le Verrier had calculated the position and size of the planet from the effects of its gravitational pull on the orbit of Uranus. An English mathematician, John Couch Adams (1819–92), also made a similar calculation a year earlier.

1868 SUN'S COMPOSITION Astronomers notice a new bright emission line in the spectrum of the Sun's atmosphere during an eclipse. The emission line is caused by an element giving out light, and British astronomer Norman Lockyer (1836–1920) concludes that it is an element unknown on Earth. He calls it helium, which is from the Greek word for the Sun. Nearly 30 years later, helium is found on Earth.

1872 SPECTRA OF STARS American astronomer Henry Draper (1837–82) takes the first photograph of the spectrum of a star (Vega), showing absorption lines that reveal its chemical make-up. Astronomers begin to see that spectroscopy is the key to understanding how stars evolve. William Huggins uses absorption lines to measure the red shifts of stars – the first indication of how fast stars move.

1901 SPECTRAL CATALOGUE A comprehensive survey of stars, the Henry Draper Catalogue, is published. In the catalogue, Annie Jump Cannon proposes a sequence of classifying stars by the absorption lines in their spectra, which is still in use today.

1906 STAR MAGNITUDE Ejnar Hertzsprung establishes the standard for measuring the true brightness of a star (its absolute magnitude). He shows that there is a relationship between colour and absolute magnitude for 90 per cent of the stars in the Milky Way Galaxy. In 1913, Henry Russell publishes a diagram that shows this relationship.

1916 BLACK HOLES German physicist Karl Schwarzschild (1873–1916) uses Albert Einstein's Theory of General Relativity to lay the groundwork for black hole theory. He suggests that if any star collapses below a certain size, its gravity will be so strong that no form of radiation will escape from it.

ASTRONOMY TIMELINE

1923 GALAXIES Edwin Hubble discovers a Cepheid variable star in the Andromeda Nebula and proves that Andromeda and other nebulas are galaxies far beyond our own. By 1925, he produces a classification system for galaxies.

1929 HUBBLE'S LAW Edwin Hubble discovers that the Universe is expanding and that the farther away a galaxy is, the faster it is moving away from us. Two years later, Georges Lemaître suggests that the expansion can be traced back to an initial "Big Bang".

1930 DWARF STARS By applying new ideas from subatomic physics, Subrahmanyan Chandrasekhar predicts that the atoms in a white dwarf star of more than 1.44 solar masses will disintegrate, causing the star to collapse violently. In 1933, Walter Baade and Fritz Zwicky describe the neutron star that results from this collapse, causing a supernova explosion.

1930 PLUTO Clyde Tombaugh discovers the planet Pluto at the Lowell Observatory in Flagstaffe, Arizona, USA. The planet is so faint and slow moving that he has to compare photos taken several nights apart.

1932 RADIO ASTRONOMY Karl Jansky detects the first radio waves coming from space. In 1942, radio waves from the Sun are detected. Seven years later radio astronomers identify the first distant sources – the Crab Nebula and the galaxies Centaurus A and M87.

1938 STELLAR ENERGY German physicist Hans Bethe explains how stars generate energy. He outlines a series of nuclear fusion reactions that turn hydrogen into helium and release enormous amounts of energy in a star's core. These reactions use the star's hydrogen very slowly, allowing it to burn for billions of years.

1944 V-2 ROCKET A team of German scientists, led by Wernher von Braun, develops the V-2, the first rocket-powered ballistic missile. Scientists and engineers from von Braun's team are captured at the end of World War II and are drafted into the American and Russian rocket programmes.

1948 HALE TELESCOPE The largest telescope in the world, with a 5.08-m (200-in) mirror, is completed at Palomar Mountain in California. At the time, the telescope pushes single-mirror telescope technology to its limits – larger mirrors tend to bend under their own weight.

1957 SPACECRAFT Russia launches the first satellite, Sputnik 1, into orbit, beginning the Space Age. The United States launches its first satellite, Explorer 1, four months later.

1923–1969

1959 MOON PROBES Russia and USA both launch space probes to the Moon, but NASA's Pioneer probes all fail. The Russian Luna programme is more successful. Luna 2 crash-lands on the Moon's surface in September, and Luna 3 returns the first pictures of the Moon's farside in October.

1961 HUMANS IN SPACE Russia again takes the lead in the space race as, in April, Yuri Gagarin becomes the first person to orbit Earth. Gagarin made one orbit in his Vostok 1 rocket, before successfully re-entering Earth's atmosphere. NASA astronaut Alan Shepard becomes the first American in space a month later, but does not go into orbit. John Glenn achieves this in early 1962.

1962 PLANETARY PROBE Mariner 2 becomes the first space probe to reach another planet, flying past Venus in December. NASA follows this with the successful Mariner 4 mission to Mars in 1965, and both USA and Russia send many more probes to planets through the rest of the 1960s and 1970s.

1963 QUASARS Dutch-American astronomer Maarten Schmidt measures the spectra of quasars, the mysterious star-like radio sources discovered in 1960. He establishes that quasars are active galaxies, and among the most distant objects in the Universe.

1965 BIG BANG Arno Penzias and Robert Wilson announce the discovery of a weak radio signal coming from all parts of the sky. Scientists work out that this must be emitted by an object at a temperature of –270°C (–454°F). Soon it is recognized as the remnant of the very hot radiation from the Big Bang that created the Universe 14 billion years ago.

1966 LUNAR LANDINGS The Russian Luna 9 probe makes the first successful soft landing on the Moon in January, while USA lands the far more complex Surveyor 1 in May. The Surveyor missions, which are follow-ups to NASA's Ranger series of crash landers, scout sites for possible manned landings.

1967 PULSARS Jocelyn Bell Burnell and Antony Hewish detect the first pulsar, an object emitting regular pulses of radio waves. Pulsars are eventually recognized as rapidly spinning neutron stars with intense magnetic fields – the remains of a supernova explosion.

1969 APOLLO 11 The United States wins the race for the Moon, as Neil Armstrong and Edwin (Buzz) Aldrin step onto the lunar surface on 21 July. The astronauts spent over 21 hours on the Moon, conducting scientific experiments and planting an American flag. Apollo 11 is followed by five further landing missions, three carrying a sophisticated Lunar Rover vehicle.

ASTRONOMY TIMELINE

1970 X-RAY ASTRONOMY The Uhuru satellite, designed to map the sky at X-ray wavelengths, is launched by NASA. The existence of X-rays from the Sun and a few other stars has already been found using rocket-launched experiments, but Uhuru charts more than 300 X-ray sources, including several possible black holes.

1971 SPACE STATIONS Russia launches its first space station, Salyut 1, into orbit. It is followed by a series of stations, culminating with Mir in 1986. A permanent platform in orbit allows cosmonauts to carry out serious research and to set a series of new duration records for spaceflight.

1975 PLANETARY VISIT The Russian probe Venera 9 lands on the surface of Venus and sends back the first pictures of its surface. The first probe to land on another planet, Venera 7 in 1970, had no camera. Both break down within an hour in the hostile atmosphere.

1977 VOYAGERS NASA launches the two Voyager space probes to the outer planets. The Voyagers return scientific data and pictures from Jupiter and Saturn and, before leaving the Solar System, Voyager 2 becomes the first probe to visit Uranus and Neptune.

1981 SPACE SHUTTLE Columbia, the first of NASA's reusable Space Shuttles, makes its maiden flight. The Shuttle carries large payloads to various orbits, provides crew rotation for the International Space Station, and conducts servicing missions to the Hubble Space Telescope.

1983 INFRARED ASTRONOMY The first infrared astronomy satellite, IRAS, is launched. It must be cooled to extremely low temperatures with liquid helium, and it operates for only 300 days before its supply of helium is exhausted. During this time it completes an infrared survey of 98 per cent of the sky.

1986 COMET PROBES The returning Halley's Comet is met by a fleet of five space probes from Russia, Japan, and Europe. The most ambitious is the European Space Agency's Giotto, which flies through the comet's coma and photographs the nucleus itself.

1990 MAGELLAN Launched by NASA, the Magellan probe arrives at Venus and spends three years mapping it with radar. Magellan is the first in a new wave of space probes including Galileo, which reaches Jupiter in 1995, and Cassini, which reaches Saturn in 2004.

1990 SPACE TELESCOPE The Hubble Space Telescope, the first large optical telescope in orbit, is launched using the Space Shuttle, but astronomers soon discover it is crippled by a problem with its mirror. A complex repair mission in 1993 allows the telescope to start producing spectacular images of distant stars, nebulas, and galaxies.

1992 COSMIC RIPPLES The Cosmic Background Explorer (COBE) satellite produces a detailed map of the background radiation remaining from the Big Bang. The map shows "ripples", caused by slight variations in the density of the early Universe – the seeds of galaxies and galaxy clusters.

1992 KECK TELESCOPE The 10-m (33-ft) Keck Telescope on Mauna Kea, Hawaii, is completed. The first of a revolutionary new wave of telescopes, the Keck's main mirror is made of 36 six-sided segments, with computers to control their alignment. New optical telescopes also make use of interferometry – improving resolution by combining images from separate telescopes.

1998 INTERNATIONAL SPACE STATION Construction work on a huge new space station begins. A joint venture between many countries, including Russia, Japan, and the USA, the space station can house up to seven astronauts in orbit at any one time and acts as a platform for microgravity research, astronomy, and further exploration of the Solar System. It is due to be completed in 2010.

2004 ORBITING MISSION Space probe Cassini arrives at Saturn. The probe was designed to make 74 orbits of Saturn and numerous fly-bys

of its moons. Cassini also carried a mini-probe called Huygens, which is exploring Titan, Saturn's largest moon. The Huygens probe has shown that Titan's surface is similar to Earth's, with evidence of lakes and rain clouds.

2004 MARS ROVERS The planetary rovers Spirit and Opportunity land on Mars and begin to explore the surface. As well as providing useful data on rocks and soil from the surface of the planet, the rovers send back evidence to NASA headquarters that water once flowed on Mars.

2004 ROSETTA COMET ORBIT Launched by the European Space Agency, Rosetta will be the first space probe to orbit a comet, one of the most difficult manoeuvres ever attempted. The probe will study Comet Churyumov-Gerasimenko for over three years and carries a separate craft that will land on the surface of the comet's nucleus. Rosetta is due to reach the comet in May 2014.

2005 MARS RECONNAISSANCE ORBITER (MRO) Launched from Cape Canaveral in August 2005, the MRO, at 2,100 kg (4,650 lb), is the most massive spacecraft to be sent to the red planet. It is a weather satellite designed to tell us if the global cooling that Mars suffered could happen to Earth. Observations by MRO will also support future Mars missions by examining potential landing sites.

BIOGRAPHIES

EDWIN (BUZZ) ALDRIN
born 1930

American astronaut who piloted the Lunar Module of Apollo 11 and, on 21 July 1969, became the second man to walk on the Moon. Aldrin is an engineer by training. In November 1966, he made a record 5-hour space walk during the Gemini 12 mission.

ARISTARCHUS OF SAMOS
about 320–250BCE

Greek astronomer who used geometry to measure the distance between the Sun and Moon. He calculated that the Sun was 20 times farther away than the Moon (it is actually 400 times farther), and suggested that Earth must travel around the Sun, as the Sun was seven times bigger than Earth (it is actually 109 times bigger). The idea gained ground over 18 centuries later.

NEIL ARMSTRONG
born 1930

American Air Force test pilot who, as commander of Apollo 11, was the first man to walk on the Moon on 21 July 1969. As he stepped onto the Moon, he said, "That's one small step for a man, one giant leap for mankind." After leaving NASA, he became a university professor.

WALTER BAADE
1893–1960

Emigrated to the United States from Germany in 1931. In 1943, he discovered that the Universe contained two types of stars – very old ones containing few metals, and newer ones rich in metals. This also applied to the Cepheid variable stars, whose properties are used to calculate the size of the Universe, which was then found to be twice as big as previously thought.

FRIEDRICH BESSEL
1784–1846

German astronomer who became the first director of the observatory in Königsberg in 1813. He concentrated on measuring the exact positions of stars. In 1838, he used parallax to measure the distance of the star 61 Cygni (10.3 light years). This was the first star to have its distance measured by parallax, and helped establish a scale for the Universe.

TYCHO BRAHE
1546–1601

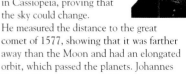

Danish astronomer who accurately measured the positions of stars and planets. Between 1572 and 1573, he recorded a supernova in Cassiopeia, proving that the sky could change. He measured the distance to the great comet of 1577, showing that it was farther away than the Moon and had an elongated orbit, which passed the planets. Johannes Kepler, his assistant, used his results to calculate the orbits of the planets.

WERNHER VON BRAUN
1912–77

German rocket engineer who developed the V-2 missile and the Saturn V Moon launcher. His work on rocket engines in the 1930s led to his appointment as technical director of a rocket establishment, where he developed the V-2 – a liquid-fuelled rocket weapon – during World War II. Between 1942 and 1945, more than 5,000 V-2s were built. After the war, he was selected for work in New Mexico. There he designed the Redstone rocket, which put Explorer 1 – America's first satellite – into orbit in 1958, and in 1961 launched Alan Shepard on the first Mercury suborbital mission. In 1960, von Braun was put in charge of the Marshall Space Flight Center in Alabama, where he developed the Saturn rockets that were used to send men to the Moon in the Apollo programme.

JOCELYN BELL BURNELL
born 1943

British astronomer who, as a research student at Cambridge, discovered pulsars. On 6 August 1967, while observing the rapid variations in signals from radio sources and looking for quasars, she discovered an unusual radio signal consisting of a rapid series of pulses that occurred precisely every 1.337 seconds. This turned out to be a pulsating neutron star (a pulsar).

ANNIE JUMP CANNON
1863–1941

American astronomer who classified the spectra of more than 300,000 stars into a temperature sequence. She joined the staff of Harvard College Observatory in 1896 and stayed there until she retired in 1940. Her work was the foundation stone of the Henry Draper Catalogue of stellar spectra.

GIOVANNI CASSINI
1625–1712

Italian astronomer who was the first to understand the nature of Saturn's rings. He suggested that they were not solid but made up of individual rocks. He discovered four of Saturn's satellites and a gap in its rings. He helped build and run the Paris Observatory, where he measured the distance between Earth and Mars and used this to calculate the Sun–Earth distance.

SUBRAHMANYAN CHANDRASEKHAR
1910–95

Indian-born astrophysicist who studied astronomy in Madras and England before moving to the United States in 1936. He received the 1983 Nobel Prize for Physics for his work on dying stars. Chandrasekhar realized that a white dwarf star with more than 1.4 times the Sun's mass could not stop shrinking, and would become a neutron star or a black hole.

ARTHUR C. CLARKE
born 1917

British science fiction writer who, in 1945, suggested that a satellite in geostationary orbit – 35,800 km (23,924 miles) above Earth – could be used to transmit TV and telephone signals between Europe and North America. Though the technology was unavailable at the time, geostationary satellites are now commonplace.

NICOLAUS COPERNICUS
1473–1543

Polish astronomer, doctor, and priest who suggested that the Sun and not Earth was at the centre of our planetary system. He studied mathematics and the classics in Poland, and law and astronomy in Italy. He returned to Poland in 1506 to become a Canon at Frauenberg Cathedral, a post he held until he died. His duties were light and he devoted most of his time to astronomy. By about 1513, he had realized that Earth was not at the centre of the Universe or even of the Solar System. Earth, which went around the Sun, was not special but was merely one of a collection of planets. He was aware that his idea went against the teachings of the church, and his book *De Revolutionibus Orbium Coelestrium* was not published until he was on his deathbed.

FRANK DRAKE
born 1930

American radio astronomer who, in 1960, pioneered the use of radio telescopes to listen for signals from extraterrestrial life. In 1974, using the Arecibo radio telescope in Puerto Rico, this project was continued.

ARTHUR EDDINGTON
1882–1944

English astronomer who showed how the physical characteristics inside a star could be calculated from its surface features. He devised a model of a star's interior, discovered the relationship between a star's mass and its luminosity, stressed that nuclear fusion produced stellar energy, and measured how much a ray of light is bent by a gravitational field.

ALBERT EINSTEIN
1879–1955

German-born American theoretical physicist whose theory of general relativity explains the evolution of the expanding Universe. He received the Nobel Prize for Physics in 1921 for explaining how light is radiated in packets of energy called quanta, but he is best remembered for his theories of relativity. Einstein found that mass (m) was equivalent to energy (E) according to his now famous equation $E = mc^2$.

ERATOSTHENES OF CYRENE
about 273–192BCE

Greek scholar who calculated the size of Earth. Born in north Africa, he was educated in Athens and then became the tutor to the son of King Ptolemy III of Egypt. A skilled geographer, he calculated the curvature of Earth by measuring the length of the shadow the Sun cast, at two places 950 km (590 miles) apart. From this he estimated Earth's circumference to be 46,500 km (28,895 miles). It is actually 40,075 km (24,903 miles) at the equator.

EUDOXUS OF CNIDUS
about 408–355BCE

Greek astronomer and mathematician who constructed a model of the Solar System, with Earth at its centre and the planets moving around Earth. The planets were in spheres, nested inside each other, with the axis of each sphere attached to the surrounding sphere. This model was replaced after a few centuries as it did not account for everyday changes in the distances between Earth and other planets.

JOHN FLAMSTEED
1646–1719

Britain's first Astronomer Royal, he was in charge of the Royal Observatory at Greenwich. Using a mural arc and a sextant with telescopic sights in conjunction with the new, accurate clocks that ran for a year, he produced a new catalogue of 3,000 stars, 15 times more accurate than earlier ones. He also made detailed studies of the shape of the orbits of both the Moon and Earth.

JOSEPH VON FRAUNHOFER
1787–1826

A Bavarian glass and lens maker, he noticed that the Sun's spectrum was crossed by numerous fine, dark lines. He measured the wavelengths of 324 of the 574 lines that he could see, which are now known as Fraunhofer lines.

YURI GAGARIN
1934–68

Russian cosmonaut who, on 12 April 1961, became the first person to fly in space. The flight on the Vostok 1 spaceship lasted one orbit of Earth. The spaceship reached a height of 344 km (214 miles) and Gagarin was airborne for 108 minutes. He died in a plane crash while training to return to space.

GALILEO GALILEI
1564–1642

Italian mathematician, physicist, and astronomer, who did much to disprove ancient Greek theories of physics. He discovered that the Sun spun around every 25 days, the Moon was mountainous, Jupiter had four satellites, and Venus showed Moon-like phases. The Venus observations helped prove that the Sun and not Earth was at the centre of the Solar System. His revolutionary ideas led to trouble with the Church, and late in life he was tried by the Inquisition in Rome and placed under house arrest.

GEORGE GAMOW
1904–68

Ukrainian physicist who defected to the USA in 1933. With Ralph Alpher and Hans Bethe, he showed how helium could be produced during the Big Bang, and could then combine with other nuclei to create elements. He predicted that the Universe would be filled with radiation left over from the intense temperature of the Big Bang.

JOHN GLENN
born 1921

 American astronaut who, in 1962, was the first American to orbit Earth. He made three orbits during a 5-hour flight. After retiring from the space programme in 1964, he took up politics, and, in 1974, was elected Senator in Ohio. In 1998, he became the world's oldest astronaut when he flew on a Space Shuttle mission.

ROBERT GODDARD
1882–1945

 American inventor and rocket engineer who made and launched the world's first liquid-fuelled rocket in 1926. In the 1930s, he launched his first stabilized rocket. This had a liquid-fuel motor that used petrol and liquid oxygen.

ALAN GUTH
born 1947

American particle physicist who devised the theory of inflation in 1979, in which he proposed that just after the Big Bang, the Universe expanded from the size of a proton to the size of a grapefruit in a tiny fraction of a second. This both smoothed out space-time and made a Universe that looks the same in all directions.

GEORGE HALE
1868–1938

American astronomer who invented the spectroheliograph that revealed details of the Sun's surface. He also discovered that sunspots had magnetic fields, and measured the strengths of these fields. He organized the building of several large telescopes, including Hale's Telescope on Palomar Mountain, California.

EDMOND HALLEY
1656–1742

English astronomer and mathematician who proved that some comets were periodic and predicted that Halley's Comet would return to the Sun every 76 years. He was a close friend of Isaac Newton and helped him to prepare his book *Principia Mathematica*. In 1698, he sailed over the Atlantic, measuring the deviation of the magnetic compass. He drew the first map of the southern sky, discovered that stars move, and realized that Earth was very old.

JOHN HARRISON
1693–1776

A British clockmaker who introduced a pendulum that did not change length as its temperature varied, and a ratchet that kept a clock going as it was being wound up. In the early 1730s, he was given money to build a clock that worked accurately when on board a ship at sea. His final precision clocks enabled a ship's longitude to be measured when out of port. Accurate clocks are important in astronomy for measuring the position of stars in the sky.

STEPHEN HAWKING
born 1942

British theoretical physicist who, even though he suffers from a neuromotor disease, has spent his life studying the behaviour of matter close to a black hole. Astronomers used to think that nothing could escape from a black hole, but Hawking showed that thermal radiation could be emitted. His book *A Brief History of Time* is one of the best-selling science books ever.

CAROLINE HERSCHEL
1750–1848

German astronomer who came to England in 1772 to collaborate with her brother William. She discovered eight comets between 1786 and 1797. In 1787, the British King granted her a salary to continue as assistant to her brother. She is remembered especially for her catalogue of 2,500 nebulas and star clusters.

WILLIAM HERSCHEL
1738–1822

German-born astronomer who moved to England in 1757. He made superb reflecting telescopes and discovered Uranus in 1781. He discovered hundreds of nebulas and found that the Sun was moving towards the constellation Hercules.

EJNAR HERTZSPRUNG
1873–1967

Danish astronomer who realized that the width of a stellar spectral line was a function of the light-emitting region's pressure, and that stars were of two basic types – dwarfs and giants. In 1906, he noticed that a star's luminosity was related to its surface temperature, which was independently discovered by Henry Russell in 1913. The Hertzsprung-Russell diagram, which plots standard brightness against temperature, is vital to the study of stellar evolution.

ANTONY HEWISH
born 1924

English radio astronomer who studied fluctuations in radio sources, and how the signals from two radio telescopes could be combined to mimic a dish as large as the distance between them. In 1967, he and his student Jocelyn Bell Burnell discovered pulsars. He was awarded the Nobel Prize for Physics in 1974.

HIPPARCHUS
about 190–120BCE

Greek astronomer, who is remembered for inventing an improved theodolite with which he measured the positions of 850 stars. He produced a catalogue of these, which was still in use 18 centuries later. He also classified the stars according to how bright they appeared in the sky. This system forms the basis of today's magnitude scale of stellar brightness. Earth's spin axis moves like a spinning top, and Hipparchus measured the rate at which the axis changed position, and the way in which the distance between Earth and the Sun varies throughout the year.

FRED HOYLE
1915–2001

English astrophysicist, who often visited the California Institute of Technology where he collaborated with William Fowler. In 1957, they showed how elements such as lithium, carbon, oxygen, and iron could be created inside stars. When large stars eventually explode as supernovas, these elements are distributed into space and are recycled in second-generation stars. In 1948, Hoyle, with Thomas Gold and Hermann Bondi, introduced the steady state theory of the Universe. This theory lost ground in 1965 after the discovery of the background radiation – the remnant of the Big Bang.

EDWIN HUBBLE
1889–1953

American astronomer who proved that the Universe contained a multitude of galaxies that were moving away from the Milky Way. At the Mount Wilson Observatory in California, he used the new 2.5-m (8.2-ft) telescope to study nebulas, and identified two types – those in our own galaxy and those beyond it. In 1924, he realized that the distant ones were separate galaxies. He also found that the fainter, more distant galaxies were moving away from ours more quickly. He classified the different types of galaxies but (incorrectly) suggested that one type evolved into another as they aged.

WILLIAM HUGGINS
1824–1910

English astronomer who sold his family drapery business to concentrate on observing the sky. In 1863, he showed that the Universe is made of the same elements as exist on Earth. In 1868, he became the first astronomer to use the spectroscope to measure the speed with which stars are moving away from Earth. He also discovered that some nebulas are made of gas.

CHRISTIAAN HUYGENS
1629–95

Dutch scientist who, in 1655, discovered a large satellite of Saturn – Titan. He realized that the bulges on either side of Saturn were a ring of particles in orbit around its equator. The telescope that he produced was the best telescope of his time. He also invented the pendulum clock, and proposed that light was a wave motion.

KARL JANSKY
1905–50

American radio engineer and the father of radio astronomy. He built a rotating radio aerial and receiver in 1932 in order to discover the source of interference in radio signals being used for ship-to-shore communications, and soon realized that the interference came from the constellation of Sagittarius. This is the densest part of the Milky Way, and the radiation was from electrons in its magnetic field.

JOHANNES KEPLER
1571–1630

German astronomer who formulated three laws of planetary orbits – Kepler's laws of motion – using data obtained by Tycho Brahe. He discovered that planets have elliptical orbits and orbit the Sun more slowly the farther away they are from it. His Rudolphine Tables allow astronomers to calculate the past, present, and future positions of planets.

SERGEI KOROLEV
1906–66

Russian engineer and founding member of the Moscow Group for the Study of Rocket Propulsion. He was responsible for the production of the first Russian inter-continental missile and for designing the Sputnik satellite, and the Vostok, Voskhod, and Soyuz crewed spacecraft.

PIERRE SIMON DE LAPLACE
1749–1827

French mathematician and astronomer who spent 13 years, starting in 1773, explaining how variations in the orbits of Jupiter and Saturn could be accounted for within Newton's laws of gravity. In 1796, he proposed that the Sun and Solar System were formed out of a gas cloud that rotated faster and faster as it shrank, and threw off rings of material as it got smaller. These rings then formed planets. This theory held till the end of the 19th century.

HENRIETTA LEAVITT
1868–1921

American astronomer who studied Cepheid variable stars and discovered that the cycle of variation was related to their luminosities – the longer the cycle, the more luminous the star. This led to the discovery that the Magellanic Clouds were about 100,000 light years away and were small galaxies beyond our own galaxy.

GEORGES LEMAÎTRE
1894–1966

Belgian physicist who was a priest that turned to cosmology. In 1931, Lemaître proposed that the Universe was once contained in a primeval atom about 30 times the size of the Sun. This exploded into space, scattering material that then condensed to form galaxies and stars. This later developed into the Big Bang theory.

BERNARD LOVELL
born 1913

Director of the Jodrell Bank radio observatory for more than 30 years. He developed airborne radar for non-visual bombing raids during World War II. After the war, he pioneered radar observations of meteors and instigated the funding for a 76-m (249-ft) radio telescope at Jodrell Bank in time to track the rocket of the first Russian satellite, Sputnik 1.

PERCIVAL LOWELL
1855–1916

American astronomer who set up an observatory in Flagstaff, Arizona. He concentrated on visual and photographic observations of Mars, and was convinced that a system of canals existed there. His prediction of the position of a Planet X in 1905 eventually led to the serendipitous discovery of Pluto in 1930 by Clyde Tombaugh, using Lowell's telescope.

CHARLES MESSIER
1730–1817

French astronomer who was the first to deliberately search for new comets, starting with Comet Halley in 1758–59. He discovered more than 15 new comets and was nicknamed the "comet ferret". He also compiled a list of 103 star clusters, nebulas, and galaxies. This list is still used today.

ISAAC NEWTON
1642–1727

English scientist who explained how gravity keeps the planets in orbit around the Sun, and also invented a reflecting telescope. He was professor of mathematics at the University of Cambridge at the age of 26. He revolutionized the concept of gravity, and his theory brought together Kepler's laws of planetary motion and Galileo's laws of falling bodies. He suggested that gravity applied throughout the Universe and not just near the surface of Earth. In the 1660s, he began to study the nature of light and found that white light is made up of a rainbow-like spectrum of colours, which is revealed when the light passes through a prism or a lens. He tried to make a telescope but, because of this effect, the images he saw had coloured edges. To overcome this, in 1668 he invented and built a reflecting telescope that used mirrors. His book *Principia Mathematica* was published in 1687.

HERMANN OBERTH
1894–1989

One of the founding fathers of astronautics and author of *The Rocket into Interplanetary Space* (1923) and *The Road to Space Travel* (1929). He worked on rocket motors in the 1930s and developed the German V-2 rocket during World War II. He also worked on satellite launchers in the United States.

JAN OORT
1900–92

Dutch astrophysicist who studied the Milky Way using radio waves, and proposed that its galactic centre was 30,000 light years away. He found that the Sun orbited the Milky Way every 200 million years, and that the galaxy's mass was 100 billion times that of the Sun. He also suggested that the Sun was surrounded by a huge reservoir of comets.

ERNST ÖPIK
1893–1985

Estonian astronomer who became director of the Armagh Observatory. In 1932, he proposed that the Solar System was surrounded by a cloud of comets – a cloud now named after Jan Oort. Öpik's work on how dust particles burn up as they enter Earth's atmosphere has been applied to the design of devices that protect spacecraft from heat as they re-enter the atmosphere.

CECILIA PAYNE-GAPOSCHKIN
1900–79

British-born astronomer who was the first to suggest that hydrogen and helium were the main constituents of the Universe. In 1923, she left England to work at Harvard College Observatory. She showed how the temperature of a star is related to its type or spectral class, and that the main sequence stars are made almost entirely of hydrogen and helium. She also identified variable stars while working with her husband, Sergei Gaposchkin. Her study of luminous stars is used today to measure distances to distant galaxies. Awarded the Harvard Chair in Astronomy in 1956, she was the first female professor at Harvard.

ARNO PENZIAS
born 1933

A German refugee who moved to the United States as a child and became a radio engineer in Bell Telephone Laboratories in 1961. In 1965, while trying to trace a source of radio interference, Penzias and Robert Wilson found radio waves that came towards Earth from all directions. The source had a temperature of –270°C (–454°F), and was what remained from the radiation made by the Big Bang. Penzias and Wilson received the 1978 Nobel Prize for Physics.

VALERI POLIAKOV
born 1942

Russian doctor and cosmonaut who holds two world records – the most time spent in space and the longest single stay in space. He travelled aboard Soyuz TM-6 to Mir on 29 August 1988, and stayed for 241 days. He returned to Mir on 8 January 1994, when he stayed for 438 days. As part of a medical experiment, he had some of his bone marrow removed before the mission so that it could be compared with another sample of bone marrow taken when he returned after months of weightlessness.

PTOLEMY
about 90–168CE

Egyptian astronomer whose works dominated scientific thought until the 17th century. He thought that Earth was a perfect sphere at the centre of the Universe, surrounded by seven transparent spheres each of which carried a moving object. In order of speed across the sky (and supposed distance from Earth), these were the Moon, Mercury, Venus, the Sun, Mars, Jupiter, and Saturn. An eighth sphere contained the stars. He compiled the astronomical ideas of the ancient Greeks in *The Almagest*, which built on the works of Hipparchus and others, added to his own observations. He also noted the latitude and longitude of many places on Earth and his maps were used by Christopher Columbus.

MARTIN REES
born 1942

England's 15th Astronomer Royal, based at the University of Cambridge. He has concentrated on the study of the centres of active galaxies, and the way in which jets of gas from these galaxies interact with the surrounding interstellar medium. Rees has also written extensively on cosmology and the dark matter in the Universe. He has enthusiastically promoted the communication of science to the general public.

HENRY RUSSELL
1877–1957

American astronomer who became the professor of astronomy at Princeton in 1905. Russell studied multiple stars and the relationship between their orbits and masses. From his work on stellar distances, he was able to show that there was a main sequence of stars by plotting stellar luminosity against surface temperature on a graph. This came to be known as the Hertzsprung-Russell diagram because Ejnar Hertzsprung had plotted a similar graph in 1906. Russell incorrectly predicted that stars evolved by moving either up or down this sequence. In 1929, he suggested, correctly, that stars consist mainly of hydrogen.

MARTIN RYLE
1918–84

British radio astronomer who produced a catalogue of 5,000 radio sources. He perfected a technique of combining signals from different movable radio telescopes to create a high-resolution  image of the object emitting radio waves. He mapped regions on the Sun, and distant galaxies that emit radio waves, and showed that galaxies were closer together in the early Universe – evidence for the Big Bang. In 1974, Ryle and Antony Hewish were awarded the Nobel Prize for Physics.

CARL SAGAN
1934–96

American astronomer who studied the atmospheres of planets. In the 1960s, he calculated that the surface of Venus was very hot due to a runaway greenhouse effect. He also researched the early atmosphere of Earth and ways in which life could be generated. His television series, *Cosmos*, was viewed around the world in 1980.

ALLAN SANDAGE
born 1926

American astronomer who started as Edwin Hubble's assistant. In 1960, with Tom Matthews, he was the first to optically identify a quasar. In 1965, he discovered the first "radio-quiet" quasars. In fact, only 1 in 200 quasars emits radio waves.

GIOVANNI SCHIAPARELLI
1835–1910

Italian astronomer who worked at the Brera Observatory in Milan from 1860 to 1900. In 1862, he realized that the Perseid meteor shower was produced by the decay of Comet Swift-Tuttle, and that they both had the same orbit. He made detailed observations of Mars and concluded it had channels (*canali*) on its surface, some of which he thought were splitting into two.

BERNHARD SCHMIDT
1879–1935

Estonian engineer who joined the staff of Hamburg Observatory in 1926. Large reflecting telescopes can cover only a very small field of view, so Schmidt devised a telescope for the observatory that used a spherical mirror behind a thin correcting lens to produce a very sharp image over a large field of view. Many Schmidt telescopes have been used for mapping the sky.

HARLOW SHAPLEY
1885–1972

American astronomer who started work as a journalist. While working at Mount Wilson Observatory in California, he used Cepheid variable stars to estimate the distance to globular star clusters, which he used to plot the shape and size of the Milky Way galaxy. He moved to Harvard in 1921 and became famous for his debate with Heber Curtis about whether the Universe consisted of one galaxy or a multitude. Shapley showed that galaxies are clustered into groups.

ALAN SHEPARD
1923–98

A United States Navy test pilot who was the first American in space. His suborbital hop on 5 May 1961 took him and his Mercury space capsule 180 km (112 miles) above Earth, before it landed in the Atlantic Ocean 485 km (301 miles) down range from the launchpad at Cape Canaveral, Florida. He returned to space in early 1971, when he commanded the Apollo 14 Moon mission.

JOSEF SHKLOVSKII
1916–85

Ukrainian astronomer who, in 1953, started the radio astronomy division of Russia's Astronomical Institute. He was among the first to suggest that spiralling electrons trapped in astronomical magnetic fields produced radio waves with a long wavelength called synchrotron radiation.

JILL TARTER
born 1944

American astrophysicist who was the first radio astronomer to start searching full-time for extraterrestrial intelligence in the early 1970s. As the chief scientist of Project Phoenix, she uses a multichannel analyser that takes the signal from large radio telescopes and then listens to many frequencies at the same time, searching for messages.

VALENTINA TERESHKOVA
born 1937

Russian cosmonaut, formerly a textile worker and amateur parachutist, who was the first woman in space. In June 1963, she made 48 orbits of Earth on the Vostok 6 spacecraft in a 71-hour flight. The next woman flew 19 years later. Tereshkova married Andrian Nikolayev, who was also a cosmonaut, in 1963 and, after having a child, continued to train as a cosmonaut until 1969. Tereshkova went on to become an important member of the Communist Party and a representative in the Soviet government.

CLYDE TOMBAUGH
1906–97

American astronomer who discovered Pluto. He was born in Illinois in the United States, and, in 1929, joined Lowell Observatory in Arizona as an assistant because he was too poor to attend university. In 1905, Percival Lowell had predicted the position of Planet X. To assist in the search, Tombaugh built a machine that looked at two photographic plates taken of the same area of sky, a few hours apart, to see if anything had moved against the fixed background of stars. On 18 February 1930, he discovered Pluto. Uncertain as to whether Pluto was big enough to disturb the orbit of Uranus, he continued his search for another planet for eight years, but without any success.

KONSTANTIN TSIOLKOVSKY
1857–1935

Russian pioneer of the theory of space flight. Sputnik I was launched to commemorate his birth centenary. By 1898, he had produced theories of rocketry but did not have the  resources to build a rocket. His book *Exploration of Cosmic Space by Means of Reaction Devices* (1903) contained designs of liquid hydrogen and liquid oxygen rockets, very similar to those in use today. He also showed that multistage rockets would be needed to leave Earth's gravitational field.

URBAIN LE VERRIER
1811–77

French astronomer who proved that the orbits of the planets were stable. He also studied how the orbits of the planets are pulled off course by the gravitational force exerted by adjacent planets, and predicted the position of undiscovered Neptune from its effects on Uranus's orbit. Johann Galle used his predictions to find Neptune.

FRED WHIPPLE
1906–2004

American astronomer who discovered six new comets and suggested, in 1951, that comets were made of snow and dust, the surface of which evaporated as it was heated in the inner Solar System. He also studied the orbits of meteors and spacecraft, and the effect of Earth's atmosphere on them.

ROBERT WILSON
born 1936

American physicist who joined Bell Telecommunication Laboratories, and, with Arno Penzias, received the Nobel Prize for Physics in 1978. He worked with Penzias on reducing the radio noise in a horn-shaped radio antenna. In 1965, he discovered radio waves coming in all directions from a source with a temperature of −270°C (−454°F). This was what remained of the hot radiation produced by the Big Bang.

JOHN YOUNG
born 1930

American astronaut who trained as a test pilot in the navy. In 1965, he flew in Gemini 3, the first United States two-man space mission. After flying in Gemini 10, he made 31 lunar orbits in Apollo 10 in 1969, the dress rehearsal for the first Moon landing. He was commander of the Apollo 16 mission in 1972, making three walks on the Moon. In April 1981, he commanded the first Space Shuttle flight.

FRITZ ZWICKY
1898–1974

Swiss astrophysicist who moved to the California Institute of Technology in the United States in 1927. He suggested that supernova explosions destroy most of a massive star, leaving only the central core as a neutron star. He calculated that only one supernova would appear every 400 years in a galaxy, and that, while the Universe was expanding, the clusters were not.

GLOSSARY

Words in *italics* have their own entries in the glossary.

Absolute zero The lowest possible temperature (−273°C).

Absorption line A dark line in a *spectrum*, caused by atoms absorbing *radiation* of a certain *wavelength*.

Accretion disc A disc of material that is spiralling into a *black hole*.

Active galaxy A *galaxy*, with a central *black hole*, generating huge amounts of energy.

Antimatter *Matter* made of *subatomic particles*, with equal and opposite properties to normal matter.

Aperture The diameter of a telescope's main mirror or lens.

Aphelion The point in an object's *orbit* at which it is farthest from the Sun.

Apogee The farthest point from Earth reached by the Moon or an orbiting artificial *satellite*.

Arc second A unit used to measure the size or separation of objects in the sky, equal to 1/3,600 degrees.

Astronomical unit (au) The average distance between the Sun and Earth – 149.6 million km (93 million miles).

Atom The smallest part of an element.

Aurora Green and red glow seen in the sky near the poles, caused by particles from the Sun colliding with gases in Earth's atmosphere.

Background radiation A faint radio signal emitted by the entire sky – the remnant of *radiation* from the Big Bang.

Barred spiral galaxy A *galaxy* with spiral arms linked to a central bulge by a straight bar of stars and gas.

Binary system A pair of stars in *orbit* around their centre of mass.

Black hole A collapsed object, with *gravity* so strong that nothing – not even *light* – can escape it.

Blazar An *active galaxy*, angled in such a way that we on Earth see *radiation* coming straight from its core.

Blue shift A shift in *spectral lines* towards the blue end of the *spectrum*.

Brown dwarf An object smaller than a star but larger than a planet, and which produces heat, but no *light*.

Celestial sphere An imaginary sphere of sky surrounding Earth, on which celestial objects appear to lie.

Cepheid variable A type of *variable star* that changes in *luminosity* and size, used to measure distances in space.

Circumpolar star Any star that does not appear to set, but instead appears to circle the celestial pole.

Conjunction The point in the *orbit* of a planet when it appears directly in line with the Sun when viewed from Earth.

Cosmic ray A tiny, fast-moving, electrically charged *particle* coming from space.

Dark matter Invisible matter thought to make up 97% of the Universe's *mass*.

Deep-sky object A collective term for *nebulas*, *star clusters*, and *galaxies*.

Doppler effect The change in *frequency* of waves (of sound or *radiation*) that reach an observer when the source is moving.

Dust Microscopic grains of "soot" from cool stars that absorb starlight in space.

Eclipse An effect caused by a celestial object casting its shadow on another.

Eclipsing binary A pair of stars in *orbit* around each other, where each passes in front of and behind the other as seen from Earth.

Ecliptic An imaginary line in the sky along which the Sun seems to move through the year.

Electromagnetic radiation Waves of energy, ranging from

gamma rays (shortest wavelength) to radio waves (longest wavelength) carried by photons that travels through space and matter at the speed of light.

Element Any of the basic substances of nature, each with unique properties, which cannot be broken down by chemical reactions.

Elliptical galaxy An oval or round galaxy with no spiral arms.

Elliptical orbit An orbit in the shape of an elongated circle.

Emission line A bright line in a spectrum caused by atoms giving out energy of a certain wavelength.

Escape velocity The speed at which one object must travel to escape another's gravity.

Extrasolar Beyond the Solar System.

Extraterrestrial Not belonging to Earth.

Filament A string of galaxy superclusters stretching across a huge expanse of space.

Fly-by An encounter between a space probe and a planet, comet, or asteroid, in which the probe does not stop to orbit or land.

Frequency The number of waves of electromagnetic radiation that pass a point every second.

Galaxy A body consisting of millions of stars, gas, and dust held together by gravity.

Galaxy cluster A group of galaxies held together by gravity.

Gamma rays Electromagnetic radiation of very short wavelength emitted by the most energetic objects in the Universe.

Gas giant A large planet, primarily made up of a very deep, dense gaseous atmosphere.

Geostationary orbit An orbit 36,000 km (22,320 miles) above the equator used by geostationary satellites.

Giant star A star in the last stages of its evolution, which has swollen in size, increased in brightness, and changed colour. Sun-like stars become red giants; stars with more than 10 times the mass of the Sun become supergiants, which are the most luminous stars in the Universe.

Gravitational well Distortion of space and time by the gravity of a massive object such as a star.

Gravity Force of attraction between any objects with mass.

Greenhouse effect The rise in temperature caused by gases – such as carbon dioxide and methane – trapping heat that a planet's surface should be reflecting back into space.

Hertzsprung-Russell diagram A diagram showing how a star's brightness and colour are related.

Inflation A period of rapid expansion occurring within less than a second of the Big Bang.

Infrared Heat radiation – a type of electromagnetic radiation, with wavelengths just longer than visible light.

Intergalactic Between galaxies.

Interstellar Between stars.

Interstellar medium Atoms and molecules in the space between the stars.

Ionosphere The electrically charged region of the Earth's atmosphere between 50 and 600 km (31 and 373 miles) above the surface.

Irregular galaxy A galaxy with no obvious shape.

Kuiper Belt An area of the Solar System, extending from Neptune's orbit to the Oort Cloud's inner edge, with millions of icy, comet-like objects.

Lava Molten rock released from the interior of a planet.

Light Electromagnetic radiation, with wavelengths visible to the human eye.

Light year A standard unit of astronomical measurement, based on the distance light travels in one year – roughly 9.5 million million km (5.9 million million miles).

Local Arm Also called the Orion Arm – the spiral arm of the Milky Way in which the Sun lies.

Local Group The cluster of about 30 galaxies to which the Milky Way belongs.

Low-Earth orbit An orbit about 250 km (155 miles) above Earth's surface, used by the Space Shuttle, space stations, and many *satellites*.

Luminosity The amount of energy given off by a star as *radiation* each second.

Magnetic field The magnetism generated by a planet, star, or *galaxy* that extends into space.

Magnetosphere The bubble around a planet where the *magnetic field* is strong enough to keep out the *solar wind*.

Magnitude The brightness of a celestial object, expressed on a scale of numbers. Apparent magnitude is a measure of brightness as seen from Earth; absolute magnitude is a measure of an object's *luminosity*.

Main sequence The region on the *Hertzsprung-Russell diagram* where most stars lie.

Mare (plural maria) A huge, lava-flooded depression on the Moon's surface.

Mass A measure of the amount of matter in an object.

Microgravity Very low *gravity*, as experienced in *orbit*.

Milky Way The name of the *galaxy* in which we live.

Molecular cloud An *interstellar* cloud made of molecules such as hydrogen and carbon monoxide.

Multiple star Three or more stars held in *orbit* around each other by *gravity*.

Nebula A cloud of gas and *dust* in space, visible when it reflects starlight or blocks out light coming from behind.

Neutrino A *subatomic particle*, of very small mass, produced by *nuclear fusion* in stars.

Neutron star A collapsed star composed mainly of neutrons.

Nova An explosion on the surface of a *white dwarf* star in a *binary system* that has pulled material off its companion star.

Nuclear fusion A combination of *nuclei* of atoms to form heavier ones at very high temperatures and pressures.

Nucleus (plural nuclei) The central part of an *atom*, made up of protons and neutrons, where nearly all its *mass* is contained.

Occultation One celestial object passing in front of another.

Oort Cloud A spherical cloud around the Sun and planets, containing billions of comets.

Orbit The path of one object around another, more massive, object in space.

Orbital period The time taken for one object to complete its *orbit* around another.

Parallax The shift in a nearby object's position against a more distant background, when seen from two separate points, used to measure distances of stars.

Parsec The distance at which a star or other object has a *parallax* of 1 *arc second*, equivalent to 3.26 *light years*.

Payload The cargo carried into space by a launch vehicle or on an artificial satellite.

Penumbra The outer, lighter part of a sunspot. Also, the lightest part of a lunar eclipse shadow, where the Moon lies only partially in Earth's shadow.

Phase The relative size of the illuminated portion of a planet or moon, as seen from Earth.

Photosphere A star's visible surface, at which the star becomes transparent, allowing the star's *light* to blaze into space.

Planetary nebula The shell of gas puffed off by a red giant star before it becomes a *white dwarf*.

Polar orbit A satellite *orbit* passing above or close to the Earth's poles.

Pole star The star Polaris, in the constellation Ursa Minor, around which the northern sky appears to rotate.

Protostar A young star that has not yet started *nuclear fusion* in its core.

Pulsar A spinning *neutron star* that beams *radiation* into space.

Quasar A distant *active galaxy* that releases huge amounts of energy from a small central area.

Radar The technique of bouncing *radio waves* off an object to measure its distance.

Radiation Energy released by an object in the form of *electromagnetic radiation*.

Radio galaxy An *active galaxy* that shines at *radio wavelengths*.

Radio waves *Electromagnetic radiation* of very long *wavelength*, produced by gas clouds and energetic objects.

Red shift A shift in *spectral lines* towards the red end of the *spectrum*.

Resolving power A measure of a telescope's ability to distinguish fine detail.

Satellite An object held in *orbit* around another by its *gravity*, such as moons or artificial satellites around a planet, or a small galaxy around a larger one.

Seyfert galaxy A *spiral galaxy* with an unusually bright centre – a type of *active galaxy*.

Solar flare A huge explosion above the surface of the Sun, caused as two loops of the Sun's *magnetic field* touch.

Solar System Everything trapped by the Sun's *gravity*, from planets to comets.

Solar wind A stream of high-speed particles blowing away from the Sun.

Spectral analysis The study of *spectral lines* to reveal the composition of a star or *galaxy*, or to find its *red shift*.

Spectral lines Bright or dark lines in the *spectrum* of a body emitting *radiation*.

Spectral type A method of classifying stars according to colour and surface temperature.

Spectroscope An instrument used for splitting starlight into a *spectrum* and revealing *spectral lines*.

Spectrum (plural spectra) A band of *radiation* split into different *wavelengths*.

Speed of light A measure of how far a ray of *light* travels in one second – nearly 300,000 km (186,420 miles). Nothing can travel faster than this speed.

Spiral galaxy A galaxy with spiral arms emerging from a smooth central hub.

Star cluster A group of stars held together by *gravity*. Open clusters are loose groups of a few hundred young stars; globular clusters are dense balls with many thousands of old stars.

Starburst galaxy A *galaxy* that has undergone a sudden period of star formation.

Subatomic particle Any particle smaller than an *atom*, primarily, protons, neutrons, and electrons.

Supercluster A group of *galaxy clusters* held together by *gravity*.

Supernova An enormous stellar explosion that happens when a *supergiant* star runs out of fuel, or when a *white dwarf* explodes.

Tidal force A force on the surface of one object caused by a nearby object's *gravity*.

Ultraviolet *Electromagnetic radiation* with a *wavelength* just shorter than visible *light*.

Umbra The inner, darker region of a sunspot. Also, the darkest part of a lunar *eclipse* shadow, where the Moon is completely eclipsed.

Van Allen belts Regions of *radiation* around Earth, where Earth's *magnetic field* traps particles from the *solar wind*.

Variable star A star that changes in brightness. Many variable stars also regularly change size.

Wavelength The distance between the peaks or troughs of electromagnetic waves.

White dwarf The collapsed core of a Sun-like star that has stopped generating energy.

X-rays Radiation with a very short *wavelength*.

Key to Greek Alphabet Symbols

α alpha	ν nu
β beta	ξ xi
γ gamma	o omicron
∂ delta	π pi
ε epsilon	ρ rho
ζ zeta	σ sigma
η eta	τ tau
θ theta	υ upsilon
ι iota	φ phi
κ kappa	χ chi
λ lambda	ψ psi
μ mu	ω omega

INDEX

ACKNOWLEDGMENTS

Dorling Kindersley would like to thank Julie Ferris for editorial support; Merle Read for proof-reading; Lynn Bresler for the index; Christine Heilman for Americanization; and Hoa Luc for editorial assistance.

Picture credits

The publisher would like to thank the following for their kind permission to reproduce their photographs:

Abbreviations key: t-top, b-bottom, r-right, l-left, c-centre, a-above, f-far

Anglo Australian Observatory: 19 (crb), 144-145, 154 (bl), 161 (bl), 166-167, 189 (tr), 191 (tl), 203 (tc), 205 (tr), 261 (tr) David Malin 17 (crb), 183 (cla), 202 (bl), Malin/Pasachoff 193 (tl), Royal Observatory Edinburgh 167 (cra), 188-189, 204-205; akg-images: 376 (br), 377 (br), 378 (cl), Erich Lessing 376 (cl), 384 (c); Bryan And Cherry Alexander Photography: 123 (cbl); Associated press: 253 (tr); www.bridgeman.co.uk: 381 (bl); Cambridge University Library: 219 (c); Central Press Photos Ltd: 382 (cl); Ciel et Espace: 218 (bl), 218-219, 219 (tr), Serge Brunier 6 (bc); Colorific!: 116 (bl); Corbis: 5 (br), 50-51 (b), 68-69 (b), 102 (tr), 263 (crb), 267 (bl), 272 (bl), Bettmann 286 (cr), European Southern Observatory 223 (tl), Hulton-Deutsch Collection 287 (cl), Kipa 309 (crb), Roger Ressmeyer 46 (br), 219 (br), 307 (tl), William Taufic 143 (br); Dr. Thomas Dame: Centre for Astrophysics/Smithsonian Institution 187 (tr); Empics Ltd: Fiona Hanson 376 (tc); European Space Agency: 245 (c, bl), 296 (clb), 302 (cr), 303 (bl, cr), B. Paris 256 (cb), CNES 257 (tl, c), CNES/CSG 257 (r), D. Ducros 102 (b), 253 (tl), ESTEC 270-271 (c), 271 (tc), NES/CSG 256 (tr); European Southern Observatory: 133 (tr), 146 (cl), 158-159, Meylan 5, 228 (tr), 277 (tl); Mary Evans Picture Library: 375 (cr), 378 (br), 379 (tr); Vivian Fifield,: 378 (bl); Galaxy Picture Library: 62 (b), 64 (br), 81 (cr), 85 (cl), 87 (tr), 91 (cr), 117 (crb), 135 (ca, cl, cr), 140 (cr), 147 (cr), 154 (br), 159 (bc), 189 (br), 191 (cr), 209 (br), 211 (tl, tc), 254 (cl), 325 (crb), 347 (c), 348 (c), 349 (c, clb, cla), 353 (cl, cr), 354 (cl), 357 (cb, cla, clb), 358 (cl), 361 (cra), 362 (clb), 365 (c), Eric Hutton 335 (tc), Gordon Garradd 79 (tl), 326 (br), 327 (tl), 332 (cra), 334 (cl), 341 (br); M. Stecker 2 (bl), 191 (crb), 324 (tr), 327 (br), 331 (tr) 335 (br, tl), 337 (bl, tl, cr), 341 (tl), Nick Szyanex & Ian King 331 (bl) 342 (br) 345 (br), R. Scagell 126 (crb), 329 (tl), 330 (cl), 336 (br), 340 (crb), 343 (br), 345 (tl), Terry Platt 345 (tc), Trevor Searle & Phil Hodgins 345 (bl); 2005 Garmin Ltd. or its subsidiaries: Photo courtesy of Garmin: 267 (tr); Gemini Observatory/Association of Universities for Research in Astronomy: 214 (bl); Genesis Space Photo Library: 229 (tr), 251 (cr); Getty Images: 383 (cl), 385 (tc), Evening Standard Collection 379 (br), Hulton Archive 375 (tl), 376 (cr), 382 (cr); Harvard University Art Museums: 383 (tr); Hencoup Enterprises: 43 (c), 240 (tr), 384 (tr), 386 (cr), Royer 199 (br); Hughes Space & Communications: 251 (tr); FLPA - Images of Nature: 212 (tr); Ernest Orlando Lawrence: Berkeley National Laboratory 41 (tr); Courtesy of Lockheed Martin Aeronautics Company, Palmdale: 250 (cra, cr); Lunar and Planetary Institute: 82 (c); Lund Observatory: 185 (tl); Mullard Radio Astronomy Observatory: University of Cambridge 148 (bl); NASA: 5 (clb), 13 (tr), 14 (c), 45 (tr), 48 (cr, bl), 62 (c), 63 (crb), 64 (c), 79 (cl), 90-91, 95 (cb), 103 (clb, cbl), 107 (tr), 108-109, 117 (cb), 122 (bl), 125 (cr), 126 (cl), 167 (tc), 184 (tr), 223 (br), 227 (cr), 228 (b), 237 (cr), 244 (tr, c), 245 (t), 273 (tr, cr), 276 (b), 286 (cra), 287 (cr), 290 (cl, br, tl), 292 (bl, br), 293 (cla, clb), 296 (br), 297 (br), 299 (br, tr), 300 (cr, tr), 301 (br, cl, tr), 303 (tl), 305 (clb, cr, tl), 306 (cr) 307 (br), Brad Whitmore/STScI 178-179, Egret 183 (bl), Ford/Ferraresa 170 (bl), GSFC 237 (br, fbr), JPL 22 (bl), 38 (tr), 69 (tl), 82 (cb), 98 (bc), 130 (tr), 176 (tr), 177 (tl), 229 (br), 247 (cl), 274 (tr), 276 (tr), KSC 249 (br), 252 (clb), Palomar Observatory 227 (cla), W.M. Keck Observatory 227 (tr); NOAA:

269 (cb); NSSDC/GSFC/NASA: 65 (tc, c, b), 74 (bl), 76 (c), 77 (bc), 83 (cr); Orbital Sciences Corporation: 250 (bl); Patrick Air Force Base: 251 (ca, bl); Max Planck Institute of Radioastronomy: 234 (cl), 239 (cl, br), 241 (tc), ROSAT 204 (bl); planetary.org: 99 (cr); popperfoto.com: 273 (bl); Royal Astronomical Society: 281 (tr), 381 (br); Royal Greenwich Observatory: 224-225, 235 (cl), Dr. Seth Shostak 235 (tl), Simon Tulloch 224 (clb); Royal Observatory Edinburgh: 233 (tl), David Malin/Anglo-Australian Observatory 154-155, 191 (tr), 193 (cr) 374 (br); Satellite Visualisation Software, created by Geometry Center, University of Minnesota: 265 (cr). Science & Society Picture Library: 380 (br). Science Photo Library: 29 (tr), 41 (c), 42 (br), 43 (tr), 44 (c), 55 (c), 60, 79 (br), 262 (b), 380 (tr), 387 (tc), A. Barrington Brown 380, Alex Bartel 216 (tr), Celestial Image Co. 205 (br), Chris Butler 71 (tr), CNES 1987 Distribution Spot Image 271 (bc), D. Golimowski, S. Durrance & M. Clampin 71 (br), D.L. DePoy & N.A. Sharp/NOAO 197 (br), Damien Lovegrove 263 (tr), David A. Hardy 112 (br), 220-221, David Ducros 298 (cb), David Nunuk 5 (tc), 44-45, 47 (br), David P.Anderson SMU/NASA 83 (cb), David Parker 126 (br), Dennis Milon 120 (bl), Dr Leon Golub 45 (cb), Dr Michael J. Ledlow 74-75 (t), Dr. John C. Good 179 (bl), Dr. Luke Dodd 198 (bl), Dr. Seth Shostak 272-273, Earth Satellite Corporation 271(cr), ESA/CE/Eurocontrol 266 (bl), 266-267, European Space Agency 115 (cl), F. Yusef-Zadeh/NRAO/AUI/NSF 197 (cla), Francois Gohier 234 (tr), Fred Espenak 77 (tr), 187 (bl), 209 (t), Hank Morgan 383 (br), Hasler & Pierce NASA GSFC 269 (tl), Joe Tucciarone 124 (bc), John Chumack 233 (cr), 343 (tl), John Sanford 63 (tr), 150 (tr), Julian Baum 280 (bl), 282 (cr), 309 (tl), Luke Dodd 148-149, McDonnell Douglas Aerospace 304 (tr), NASA 2 (cla), 44 (tr), 61 (bl), 78 (tl, crb, bc), 81 (tl), 83 (tr), 90 (tr), 92 (cb, bl), 94 (cr), 94-95 (x2), 95 (tl, tr), 99 (tl), 102-103, 103 (br), 106 (bc), 229 (cl), 237 (tr), 248 (c), 268 (cr), 268-269, 269 (br), 270 (cl), 280-281, 281(br), 282-283, 283 (tr), 287 (bl, tr), 291(tl, b), 297 (bl), 299 (cra), 374 (tl), NASA/ESA/STScI 5 (br), 93 (br), 162-163, 189 (c), NASA/JPL 233 (fcr), NOAO 114 (tr), 199 (tl), Novosti 0 (bl), 286 (cb), NRAO/AUI/NSF 179 (cr), 193 (bl), 197 (tr, clb),

Pekka Parviainen 116-117, 213 (tl), Phillippe Plailly/Eurelios 267 (cr), Royal Observatory Edinburgh 195 (bl), Royal Observatory Edinburgh/AATB 152 (tr), 198-199, Starlight 208 (tr), STARSEM 246 (tr), Tony Hallas 202 (tr, cl), US Geological Survey 84 (bl), 86 (bl), 87 (cr); SETI Institute/Seth Shostak: 386 (bl); spaceimage.com: 270 (bc); Carole Stott: 121 (tr); Stsci/aura/nasa: 26 (br), 97 (tl), 159 (tr), 168 (br), 178 (bl), 183 (tl, clb), 261 (br), Association of Universities for Research in Astronomy Inc. 25 (tr), Hubble Space Telescope 134 (b), J. Hester & P. Scowen (Arizona State University) 27 (bl), W.N. Colley and E. Turner (Princeton University)/J.A. Tyson (Bell Laboratories, Lucent Technologies) 26 (t); Institute for Cosmic Ray Research, University of Tokyo: 221 (tr); University of California: HCO/Lick Observatory 144 (cl, fcl).

All other images © Dorling Kindersley.
For further information see: www.dkimages.com